COMMUNITY IS POSSIBLE

Also by the Author
The Backyard Revolution

Community
Is Possible

REPAIRING AMERICA'S ROOTS

HARRY C. BOYTE

HARPER & ROW, PUBLISHERS, New York
Cambridge, Philadelphia, San Francisco, London
1817 *Mexico City, São Paulo, Singapore, Sydney*

FIRST EDITION

Designer: Sidney Feinberg

Library of Congress Cataloging in Publication Data

Boyte, Harry Chatten, 1945–
   Community is possible.

   Includes index.
   1. Community organizations—United States.   2. United States—Social conditions—1980–   3. Populism—United States. I. Title.
HN90.C6B69 1984   306'.0973   84–47558
ISBN 0–06–015335–0   84 85 86 87 88 10 9 8 7 6 5 4 3 2 1
ISBN 0–06–091157–3 (pbk.)   84 85 86 87 88 10 9 8 7 6 5 4 3 2 1

To the Pioneers

He that outlives this day, and comes safe home
Will stand a tip-toe when this day is named, . . .
And Crispin Crispian shall ne'er go by,
From this day to the ending of the world,
But we in it shall be remembered;
We few, we happy few, we band of brothers.

William Shakespeare, *Henry V*

Contents

Acknowledgments

Community Is Possible grows out of a number of years of work around the themes of community revitalization, populism, and democratic participation, over the course of which I have received an amount of help which is somehow simultaneously daunting and heartening. Much of the activity of the Citizen Heritage Center, an educational institution in Minneapolis which I directed for a year and a half, contributed to the book project. Jim Scheibel, associate director, deserves much credit, as do Si Kahn and Elizabeth Minnich, who greatly helped Citizen Heritage along. The support Citizen Heritage received for various programs also facilitated the development of many of the themes which appear here. Of course, I bear sole responsibility for their mode of presentation, along with the flaws which will undoubtedly be apparent. I want to express gratitude especially to the Field Foundation, for its support of Citizen Heritage throughout its existence, and to Richard Boone, Field's executive director, for his variously encouraging, prodding, provoking, and challenging feedback; to the New World Foundation, the Minnesota Humanities Commission, Macalaster College, the Hubert H. Humphrey Institute and other supporters of the "Democracy in America" conference on the 150th anniversary of the travels of de Tocqueville—a conference whose impact on this work will be evident to those from around the nation who braved the record-setting Minnesota winter to attend; to the Northwest Area Foundation for its help in Citizen Heritage's history project of citizen activists in Minnesota—and Karen Starr and Renae Hanson for their probing interviews, which gave me many ideas. Finally, I want to express my great appreciation to the Youth Project, to Louis Alemayehu, Jon Pratt, and Dawn Stockmo in the Midwestern Office, and to its national director, Karen Paget. The Youth Project was the initial sponsor of Citizen Heritage, a generous aid in its programs, and an enthusiastic supporter of this book in particular. Youth Project staff also kindly tolerated my rummagings in Project files.

Many people's thoughts and readings of various portions of this work have been valuable, at different stages. Kathy Robbins and my editor at Harper & Row, Hugh Van Dusen (who, along with Janet Goldstein, helped in many other ways as well) had much to do with the work's story-telling form. I want to express many thanks to Tom Dewar, Craig Calhoun, Lawrence Goodwyn, Colin Greer, Deborah Meier, Christopher Lasch, and Manning Marable for discussions and feedback on the meaning of democratic populism. Dewar, Greer, and Lasch also made apt suggestions about framing the argument. Barbara and Allen Isaacman, from another perspective, have been invaluable critics—I treasure our exchanges over Friday evening pizza, and various debates, expositions, exhortations, and other forms of dialogue with Allen on morning runs through the woods. Dick Johnson was a most helpful source of ideas about theological underpinnings of "populist organizing." John de Graaf pointed out the connections between themes in the writings of Jurgen Habermas and this work and helped me understand the "culture of silence" which pervades our society. Sheldon Wolin's comments on my work for *Democracy* magazine—and our discussions in the first stages of this project—proved a great aid as well.

In conclusion, I want to thank members of my family. Janet Boyte Ferguson's careful proofreading of *Community Is Possible* along with her suggestions were valuable, indeed. Once again, my children, Craig and Rachel Lee, contributed much to this project, through their tolerance and their completely irresistible insertions of reality into my musings, alike. And with this work, as with my last, my continuing intellectual and personal partnership with Sara Evans proved most important. For her thoughts, and her presence, I am deeply grateful.

COMMUNITY IS POSSIBLE

Prelude

Oneida, Wisconsin, is a study in contradictions. On the face of it, the community seems much like any other blue-collar suburb one might find around Green Bay, several miles to the east, or around most cities of the Midwest. A sign along Highway 54 tells the visitor that he has reached the headquarters of the Oneida Indian Nation, in the midst of the tribal reservation. Yet the scene looks familiar enough. Suburban tract-style homes sit across the road from the clubhouse of VFW Post 7784—tribal members have fought in every one of America's wars, including the American Revolution. Nearby is a baseball diamond. Down the road a nightly bingo game, the tribe's major source of revenue along with sales of cigarettes, is held in a large, cinder-block building named the Irene Moore Activity Center. Buses line up in the parking lot outside, after bringing the crowds from as far away as Milwaukee. Inside, the atmosphere reminds me of bingo nights in ethnic parishes from Chicago to Pittsburgh. There is a constant, low buzz of conversation. Blue clouds of cigarette smoke overhang the rows of tables. Now and then shouts of the winners punctuate the conviviality.

Only the artwork hints at anything unusual. One wall of the Activity Center is adorned with an enormous portrait of the building's namesake—Irene Moore, first woman tribal council president, wearing traditional Indian dress. The sign of the Oneida Nation bears the emblems of the tribe's three ancient clans—wolf, turtle, and bear. These are visible manifestations. Deeper changes have also been at work.

Chas Wheelock, who showed me around Oneida, somehow

embodies the community's complexity. His father was in the army, so he traveled a good deal growing up, but he graduated from a local high school in 1968. School officials in those years divided the Oneida reservation into five districts. As an Indian, Chas had felt different from almost everyone else in his white American classes.

Yet in his case, difference meant advantages—a badge of distinction—as well as loneliness. Chas was a star athlete on both wrestling and football teams. "I was called 'chief,' but it was meant in a good way in athletics," he explains. He was also bright. His academic successes meant that he bore his family's hopes in another sense. "They told me that the way to get away from the system was to beat it," Chas remembers. " 'Go away, get a good education in college, make something of yourself.' " College was seen as a passport into the American dream and, perhaps, beyond in some vaguely understood sense.

These days, Chas Wheelock is a leader in a group of young Oneida women and men who have spearheaded reconnection with the tribe's heritage. Many are trying to learn the Oneida language, which had almost disappeared from the reservation. They have built a traditional Indian meeting place, called a "longhouse," out of pine and poplar logs. When knowledge of some construction technique was missing, they would simply "wing it," as they put it. Rick Hill, vice-chair of the tribal council, told me that a decade before few in the tribe would go to traditional Indian ceremonies and dances, and those who went could almost never be drawn into participating. Now, dances and festivities are held in the longhouse. The crowds overflow. "It's a complete turnaround," he says.

The tribe has started an Indian school, which perhaps a third of the reservation's children below high-school age now attend. Artley Skenandore, Jr., a friend of Chas's, teaches culture classes there, acquainting students with traditional Iroquois and Oneida ways, trying to communicate the heritage as a whole way of thinking and living. Women like Vicki Cornelius have begun holding classes in home birthing techniques, recalling the old practices, and raised money to send one woman to a course in midwifery. The young "traditionalists," as those like

Wheelock, Cornelius, and Skenandore call themselves, have also begun to relearn farming skills that were almost forgotten. For a time they staffed a farming cooperative that combined organic methods and appropriate technology like solar energy. Chas's appearance makes it vivid. He wears his hair long, in traditional fashion, flowing down his back. To his surprise, all these changes began for him in college.

"When I went to college, after the first year I worked out west," Chas recalls. "That was my first real experience with Indians who talked about the land, about farming, about traditions. They were Hopis." The next year in school, he was further encouraged by a college professor who described to him the fabled Iroquois Confederacy of which the Oneida is a member tribe. The following summer, Chas returned to the Oneida's original homeland in upstate New York, taking a bus to the Onondaga region of upstate New York. There, the "council fire" of the Iroquois Confederacy had burned almost continuously for nearly five centuries. Representatives of the different tribes met at Onondaga, in the longhouse, to make decisions. "I didn't know who was out there," Chas says. "But I found that Oneidas were still there. I went to ceremonies, and began to learn about my culture."

Chas's experiences paralleled many other young adults in his tribe during the late 1960s and early 1970s. Ron Hill, another friend, pointed out that Indian youth, like blacks, began questioning "the American dream" as normally defined. "We began to become disillusioned with the rat race and working for IBM, living for material wealth. A lot of us had made it to the top education-wise and discovered that surviving isn't all that difficult. But there was something we lost. We realized that just more clothes or toys wouldn't make our kids happy. We began to get the idea of going back to our community and our heritage. Blacks went back to Africa. We didn't have to go as far," he points out. America was where they came from.

A strange linkage has bound Indians and those who called themselves "Americans" together since the beginning of European settlement. If Oneida people came to be more and more tempted by the ways of the white men's world, white immigrants, at certain moments, also imagined becoming more like the Indians.

According to legend, the Iroquois Confederacy was established in the mid–fifteenth century by Hiawatha. Hiawatha's vision of Dekanawidah in the forest led him to call five tribes to make peace with each other, form an intricate system of participatory government, share land and other goods in common, and spread their hopes for a peaceful and pluralist continent to others.

The Confederacy never functioned according to its noblest ideals. Tribes outside the alliance, for instance, were sometimes victims of attack by fierce Iroquois warriors. Periodic squabbling would break out within the Confederacy itself. Yet it endured with remarkable resilience, nonetheless. And to some making comparisons, the values that the Iroquois prized—sharing of goods, participation and free expression, respect for ancestors, kinship with nature, and love of the land—seemed remarkably like the values Europeans periodically claimed to be establishing in the New World, with very mixed results. "The chiefs are generally the poorest among them," said one Dutch missionary in the seventeenth century, "for instead of their receiving from the common people as among Christians, they are obliged to give." Or as a French Jesuit put it in 1657: "A whole village must be without corn before any individual can be obliged to endure privation. Their kindness, humanity and courtesy not only make them liberal with what they have, but cause them to possess hardly anything except in common."

In his work *Forgotten Founders,* historian Bruce Johansen documents the impact of the Iroquois on the colonists during the seventeenth and eighteenth centuries, especially detailing their effects on the thinking of architects of American government like Benjamin Franklin and Thomas Jefferson. Franklin, for instance, throughout his career, was fascinated and inspired by the Iroquois, often taking their side in controversies concerning regulation of trade and settlement. "Savages we call them," he wrote, "because their manners differ from ours." But Indians, he pointed out, welcomed the traveler and gave him free lodging. "If I go to a white man's house in Albany and ask for Victuals and Drink, they say 'where is your money?' And if I have none, they say, 'Get out, you Indian dog!' " Franklin's concept of "property" as "the creature of Society . . . subject to the calls of that Society" drew directly from the example of the Iroquois. "All property . . . except the savage's temporary cabin, his bow, his matchcoat and other little acquisitions absolutely necessary for his subsistence, seems to me to be the Creature of Public Convention."

For Thomas Jefferson, the Iroquois primary reliance not on law but on the moral force of community opinion to control crime and other social maladies furnished the model for the appropriate foundation of democratic self-government—the moral vitality and spirit of the people themselves. "What country can preserve its liberties if their rulers are not warned from time to time that their people preserve the spirit of resistance?" he wrote in his *Notes on Virginia.* He held up the Iroquois in striking contrast to Europeans, whom he claimed "have divided their nations into two classes, wolves and sheep." For the Indians, "controls are their manners and the moral sense of right and wrong." The Iroquois, in his view, "enjoy . . . an infinitely greater degree of happiness than those who live under European governments."[1]

Such sentiments, influential as they might have been in the formation of the new nation, were not dominant. In the mainstream view, Western civilization meant "progress." The point for Indians was to assimilate—or get out of the way. Stephen Riggs, a missionary, put what became increasingly the official policy of the American government through the nineteenth century quite simply: "As tribes and nations, the Indians must perish and live only as men."[2] More than 100 years later, in the 1950s, Artley Skenandore, as a young child, heard much the same thing from an official of the Bureau of Indian Affairs. "He said there will be some day when you won't even be able to distinguish Indians from the rest of Americans, the blood will be so diluted," remembers Skenandore. "It burned in my brain."

Looking for bridges between the world of whites and Indian culture, I asked an elder of the tribe, Melinda Doxtator, who now teaches in the language program at the tribal school, if she knew of the biblical concept of the commonwealth. In Leviticus, God tells the Hebrew people that every fiftieth year shall be the year of Jubilee, when all land shall return to the common pool and liberty shall be proclaimed. "The land shall not be sold in perpetuity, for the land is mine," reads the passage. "For you are strangers and sojourners with me." The commonwealth idea, threaded through English history, arriving on American shores with the first Puritans, still finds echoes in official names: the Commonwealth of Massachusetts, for example, or the Commonwealth of Virginia.

Mrs. Doxtator indeed knew of the idea. But the question brought out an ineffable sadness, mixed with bitter memory. "Until the white man came," she said, "we didn't know any other way. There wasn't any idea of 'this land belongs to me and you can't step on it.' The water and the land were for everybody. People would share what they had. That was the way it was, even in my grandfather's day. What you had you shared."

Mrs. Doxtator compressed the story but told it accurately. Her grandparents came to Wisconsin from New York, part of a group migrating from the original homeland in the 1820s and 1830s. They moved in part because of pressure from land-hungry timber interests. And many came out of their own wish to forestall further acculturation by encroaching white society. The area where the Oneida settled in Wisconsin resembled the land they had left behind. "The people who live among the standing rocks," as the name Oneida means in native language, found large standing rock formations near Green Bay. Deep forests sheltered deer. Fish and berries furnished staples for their diet. And the land proved suitable for farming maize and other traditional crops.

The Oneida of Wisconsin reproduced divisions that had developed in New York. Distinct neighborhoods formed in the new reservation, as well as broader factions. The First Christian party, for instance, had been the first to convert to Episcopalianism, preached by a missionary, Eleazar Williams, who had arrived in 1816. Members of the party settled in the northern area of the reservation. To the south were members of the

Orchard party, descended from a political faction once known as the Pagan party. They were largely Methodists.

But intermingling across family and neighborhood lines eased the divisions, as did a range of cooperative activities and a political structure representing the tribe on the reservation as a whole. For fifty years or more, through the times of Mrs. Doxtator's grandparents, the tribe retained a markedly communal cast. They held the land in common. They worked it together. And, through their tribal council, they dealt as best they could with missionaries, local timber interests, land speculators and other entrepreneurs in Green Bay, and the Indian agents often in collusion with such interests. Their position after the Civil War—still holding 65,426 acres of land (reduced by treaty from an initial 650,000)—was vulnerable. "All efforts to civilize the Oneidas have failed," wrote one agent, M. L. Martin, in 1868. "The Oneidas are a nuisance and an obstacle to progress. . . . The Government of the U.S. ought to accede to the wishes of the people of Green Bay and remove the Oneidas to some place where they may be no longer such a hindrance. . . ."

Forcible removal was blocked in Congress. Religious leaders helped; despite Christian paternalism, missionaries also championed Indian interests against the federal government and land-grabbing speculators. But the General Allotment Act, which Congress passed in 1887, provided more indirect but scarcely less effective tools of what was known as "progress." Hitting directly at Indian conceptions of common wealth, the act directed Indian tribes to hand over title of reservation lands to individuals. It authorized sales of land not so allotted. And it provided incentives to Indians who would take individual land allotments.

With land thus atomized, the power of tribal governments across the country was shattered for half a century. Only in the 1930s did federal policies, under the Indian Reorganization Act, again begin to allow a measure of self-determination—and until the 1970s, government policy allowed such self-determination only within very narrow limits. Directly to the point, moreover, land titles became prey to speculators, tax collectors, and others who took advantage of the law with zeal. By the 1920s on Wisconsin's Oneida reservation, Indians had lost all but 2,000-odd acres. The tribal council itself held only a few hundred directly.[3]

Though the council has acquired bits and pieces in subsequent years, the holdings remain a crazy quilt, scattered widely among private farms, state-owned facilities like a reformatory for boys, the airport, and other uses. Moreover, along with the dispersal of land came a concerned assault upon the culture. "The first generation, the Oneida language was beaten out of children," Rick Hill of the tribal council describes. "The next weren't taught it at all. To my generation, the language is very distant," Mrs. Doxtator tells of the Bureau of Indian Affairs boarding schools to which most Indian children in her parents' generation were sent, often as young as six or seven. They were forbidden to speak Oneida. When they violated the rules, their mouths were washed out with soap. "By the time they came back after high school," she explains, "they only spoke English."

Younger traditionalists like Chas, Skenandore, Cornelius, and Ron Hill express a good deal of anger at the injustices done to their elders, but the bitter sadness is not there. Instead, they express confidence that they will be able to "rebuild our community and our people," as Skenandore puts it. He talks with great enthusiasm about the culture class he teaches at the tribal school, comparing the lessons to the biblical concept of the commonwealth. "It requires a new kind of thinking, a new kind of mind again. The exterior economy has come into our culture—acquisitiveness, drugs, alcohol. In order to challenge people to think of themselves as a community—giving, sharing, cooperating—we have to have demonstrations. So the kids make things like herbal medicines. This fall we will have a family day when we give them all out, like in Jubilee. We have a Thanksgiving meal for grandmothers and grandfathers. We teach recognition of all the things around us—how the plants have powers that can be utilized, how the animals are our relatives." One cannot help but be impressed and moved by such a spirit. And wonder where it will take the community of Oneida.

Bingo profits go into a fund to acquire more land. The tribe is connected for the first time in decades with other Oneida settlements, in upstate New York and in Canada. (A favorite sport of the young traditionalists is setting records for travel to and from New York. "For a long time, they had the record," Artley Skenandore laughs. "Now, we've found a way to make our car invisible to the cops. We have it for a while.") More and more Oneidas have moved back to the reservation, and the population of about 3,000 is an all-time high. The tribe has an extensive plan for future economic development, especially emphasizing small businesses and other enterprises that will contribute to local control and community self-reliance. Chas Wheelock is now a staff member of the Wisconsin Community Development Finance Authority, a state agency that provides technical assistance and early funding aid to communities seeking to develop their own resources and local economies.

But Oneida still sits on the outskirts of Green Bay. Almost everyone has forgotten how to farm—the cooperative, called the Iroquois Farm Project, failed under a burden of debt. The tribe places considerable hopes—and focuses considerable anxiety—on the outcome of a large Iroquois land claim in New York, to be decided in the next several years. But such hopes suggest a reliance on the judicial system, which also grates. ("There is a basic conflict," Chas tells me, "between the legal world view and the natural world view of Indians.") The tribe is similarly, uncomfortably, dependent upon the marketplace, whose invasions it simultaneously seeks to resist. Tribal members eagerly solicit corporate relocations to an industrial park they have prepared, despite their preference for smaller, locally controlled businesses. They plan a large hotel near the airport to generate more revenue.

On balance, it is clear that the tribe has set out with doughty determination to seek ways of gaining more control over its destiny. The new journey will undoubtedly lead to some destination other than conventional notions of "progress." But where that might turn out to be remains, still, an entirely unanswered question.

It is this sort of story which *Community Is Possible* explores. In the most immediate sense, the work grows from earlier writings that sought to describe and survey a ground swell of citizen activism which emerged in the 1970s, often from the most unexpected of places. But as I have worked with, spoken to, written about, and sought to understand a great many community efforts in recent years, I have increasingly come to realize that explaining *what* the new grass roots ferment represents is no simple or easy process.

In the 1980s, discouragement has spread widely through America. The growth of giant institutions, the "media hype" and consumerism, economic shifts, environmental crises, the deadly perils of the arms race—such things seem, to many, more and more out of control. They threaten to make living human beings obsolete. And they erode the ground of community life itself, our sense of the "public," as Parker Palmer has recently described: "We live in a culture of brokenness and fragmentation. Images of individualism and autonomy are far more compelling to us than visions of unity, and the fabric of relatedness seems dangerously threadbare and frayed. . . . We have all but lost the vision of the public [understood as] our oneness, our unity, our interdependence upon one another."

In turn, such a loss of public vision mars our very ways of speaking. Though the search for democratic, vital community animates the efforts of enormous numbers of people, there is simultaneously a kind of conspiracy of silence about such a search. The stark dynamic—in this ironically most self-professedly "open" of societies—is that the subjects about which we care most deeply are often taboo. In the mass media, the "sentimentalization" of language which social historian Ann Douglass traced to 19th-century separations between home and the worlds of work and politics has reached its apogee, feeding great cynicism and the corruption of language itself. On television, "God" appears as the voice overhead in commercials for toilet cleaners; "family" is displaced to distant mountainsides in the 1930s; and "local control" is invoked by politicians who front for great concentrations of wealth and power. The values which are *truly* taken seriously are those expressed in the titles on paperback book shelves and embodied in the "heroes" our children are told to admire: "Look Out for Number One"; "Winning Through Intimidation"; "Go For It!"

The silence which pervades the public world reappears as well within community efforts. Again and again people have told me, "You know, we have never talked before about why we are doing all of this"; or "what speakers normally tell us is to become more business-like and not worry about values and principles." In these terms, the problem identified by C. Wright Mills becomes the basic dilemma of our times: people "in a mass society are gripped by personal troubles which they are not able to turn into social issues. They do not understand the interplay of these personal troubles of their milieu with problems of social structure."[4]

To move beyond a *defensive* reaction against the things which threaten us to any sort of positive initiative, then, requires the most elemental of steps. It means relearning how to talk to each other. It means discovering how to share spaces. It involves recovering memories, in this most forgetful of societies. It requires the repair of our capacity to solve common problems and to discern the common values in different heritages and traditions.

Conventional approaches do not address the dilemma. In normal political campaigns, for instance, the candidate is the focus, and the electoral process turns the candidates themselves into commodities to be "packaged." The language of politics stresses what government or the candidate will do *for* the people, not what people can do for themselves. In this sort of politics, the values and competencies of actual communities become largely irrelevant. People are appealed to as various interest groups and "issue constituencies," with a presumption of narrow selfishness part of the equation. Even when a rare candidate articulates a more visionary idiom, scant connection normally exists between their ideas and actual processes through which people learn the skills, procedures and values of democratic action.

Moreover, normal political ideologies of left and right alike make serious treatment of democratic communal values largely impossible. From the typical conservative point of view, themes such as family, neighborhood, community, religion and the American heritage are honored too often largely in the breach. They become rhetorical buzzwords, defined in the narrowest and most static of terms, easily discarded whenever such values conflict with the "real world" concerns of the marketplace and private property. In contrast, in the main currents of liberal and left-wing thought, communal values are seen as the preserve of the private conscience at best. At worst they are viewed, simplistically, as obstacles to an authentically "cosmopolitan," sophisticated and enlightened perspective.

Community Is Possible can be seen as an effort to "listen in" on places where people begin to have serious discussions about those things that matter the most, an alternative to "politics as usual," and fashion in the process the tools of public life with which to act upon such discussion. In the 1960s, I had the great privilege of working for Dr. Martin Luther King, Jr., as a teenager on the staff of the Southern Christian Leadership Conference. Through those years, I saw his "Dream" come alive in countless small towns across the south. As communities began to believe that they might in fact control their futures, they also achieved for a time at least a remarkable transformation of spirit—what King called the "new sense of somebodyness" which he believed was the civil rights movement's greatest achievement. This spirit is manifestly present in the communities described in this book as well.

King's dream might be termed democratic and populist. It held forth the hope that ordinary people could take their lives in their own hands. It affirmed the dignity of a great pluralism of heritages and communities—even those of southern segregationists, faith in whose redemption, and positive features, King never abandoned. And it grounded a vision of change in our nation's finest traditions and values, the strands he believed offered an alternative possibility to bigotry, unbridled individualism, greed and violence.

Martin Luther King's call to "make democracy real in America" embodied, in sum, the best insight of American populism: the understanding that we are joined by our common wealth, those public purposes and values which express the common threads of our history and our common aspirations for the future, alike. Indeed, in America's democratic movements, from the Revolution through the great struggles of blacks, women, farmers and workers for dignity and justice, the vocabulary of the commonwealth has reappeared again and again. It symbolizes a public sphere which simultaneously reflects and reinforces the virtues of individual citizens, joined in communities conscious of their moral interdependence.

Far from disappearing after his death, moreover, King's retrieval of the sensibility of the commonwealth has spread, despite the difficulties. It has acquired new and enduring bases. And its basic values, drawn from the myriad of peoples who have settled here, have begun to acquire new relevance and power in the process. Thus, the final two chapters are meant to indicate ways in which the language and spirit of democratic populism have once again begun to surface. They stress the fashion in which the renewal of our public life, informed by deepened appreciation for our common bonds and values, in turn depends upon the repair of our roots as a society, our living communities.

That America suffers from a deep and dangerous crisis—indeed, a multiplicity of crises—has now become a commonplace. What is rarely noted is that alongside the drift, other possibilities begin to appear as well. *Community Is Possible* is meant to aid in their discovery. It is dedicated, moreover, to their promise.

1

A Tradition Without a Name

On a cold, wet day in February 1963, a small group of women and men gathered to watch the wrecking crane smash apart Neighborhood House, the community settlement on the West Side of St. Paul. "It is quite possible to feel something akin to love even about a building," recalled Bill Hoffman, there that afternoon. "Even more about a structure that was a second home. It is not easy to stand by and watch the very stuff of your childhood and young adulthood irreverently battered to oblivion."

Harry Gaston was there, too. He had lived on Eaton Street, had coached the football team, taught boys to box, and worked at a dozen other jobs in Neighborhood House for more than twenty years. Gaston's father was the first black policeman in St. Paul. He had had "the West Side beat" as far back as anyone could remember. Ben Stoddard, the boys' director, was there. Theresa Beardsley, secretary to Constance Currie, the settlement's director. Red Cooper. John Hernandez. Jack Farley, the coroner. And Helen Gransberg Turner.

People talked about Helen and Neighborhood House together, like motherhood and apple pie. She had, of course, been there the day the "new building" first opened, back in 1923. Her father had learned to read there, along with the other Jewish immigrants who flooded into the West Side from Russia and Eastern Europe, escaping wars and pogroms in the 1880s, 1890s, and early 1900s. Helen had spent most of every day at Neighborhood House. She had gone to the dances every week, skated on the playground in the winter, starred on the girls' basketball teams. She had learned to cook and sew in the classes, and had taken her showers there because her home (like most in the Flats area, the low-lying land off the Mississippi on the West Side) had no running water. And Helen was the only one who would ever argue with Miss Currie, the redoubtable woman who knew every person on the Flats (and once told a friend she knew the color of the wallpaper in each room of each house), who oversaw the area like a kindly monarch, and who even to this day—a quarter century after her death—is spoken of in reverential tones.

Helen is a storyteller, a fighter, a poet. I have never met anyone more identified with a place and the history of that place. In her backyard now, twenty years after she was forced to leave the area, is a street sign that explains: "Texas and State," crossroads of the Flats. Helen dug it up as she left.

When Helen tells stories of the Flats, she sometimes points— "Down there," "Over that way"—and then she remembers. "It's like I'm still there," she explains. Helen stretches her arms, drops her voice, sometimes sighs, talks with great animation. "It always stays with you." She somehow recalls the spirit of the old West Side and of Neighborhood House itself.

"There was prejudice. How could there not be? We were all there together.

"People would say, 'Oh, you Irish pig. Oh, you dirty sheeny. Oh, you bohunk.' But Miss Currie would reprimand them right then and there. She'd say, 'If you want to come to Neighborhood House, there won't be such talk.' She set such an example.

"One time, one of my best friends told me, 'You can't belong to our club because you're a dirty Jew.' She had set up an Irish club. Miss Currie saw me crying and asked why. I told her, 'Mary says I can't belong to the club because I'm a dirty Jew.' Miss Currie wouldn't let that club exist. She said anybody in this Neighborhood House can't have a club that discriminates. You can have your club if you want to *be* a Catholic. But not if you're going to call people dirty Jew or whatever it is. Those things you never forget."

But memory can be a private and elusive thing. Though the group that gathered to watch Neighborhood House torn down

reminisced about Miss Currie, recalled the teams and the showers and the dances, thought about the Christmas and Hanukkah
parties and the citizenship classes and other things, the sign-
posts of their recollections were rapidly disappearing. People
were leaving Fairfield, Robertson, McCarthy, Water, Kentucky, Eva, Texas, Filmore, Fenton, Dakota, and a dozen other
streets. The synagogues had been vacated years before—a half-
dozen of them, one for each nationality of Jewish immigrant.
The Catholic Irish, German, and Syrian parishes had all moved
elsewhere. Peddlers, dairy farmers, stonemasons, carpenters,
tailors and seamstresses, Mexican workers in the sugar-beet
fields and the packinghouses down south, the Rosenbergs, the
Yavitches, the San Petros, the Stonkers, Widow Schwartz, and
hundreds more had already left.

"Progress" was coming to the West Side. An extensive urban-
renewal program—Helen had organized a group from Neighborhood House to battle it to the end, unsuccessfully—was
demolishing the residential areas of the Flats. A large industrial
park was to replace the homes. Factories were already under
construction, banks rising. Dikes had finally been built—promised for years, to keep out the floodwaters of the Mississippi.
And although people talked about remembering, doubts
gnawed away. Hoffman, seeking to chronicle the old West Side
stories in a series of local books, argued bravely that "all that was
good still remains in the strivings of those who once lived there
—toward dignity, compassion and respect for their fellowman
and his community." But Bill Kuehn, Hoffman's and Helen's
friend, made a more realistic assessment. "What do you do
when all the checkpoints and landmarks are missing?" he asked,
drawing on his long years of surveying checkpoints and landmarks. "Any competent surveyor will tell you that an accurate
'backsight' is necessary to obtain a reliable 'foresight.' How do
we tell our kids (and how will they tell their kids) where we've
been or how we lived? The Old West Side Flats and Upper
Levee areas (just across the river) have been so completely
changed during the past 50 years that almost no evidence remains of their history."[1]

Unbridled individual ambition justified in the name of "progress" and "community": America has always held them in tension at the very center of our cultural dynamic. On the one hand, John Winthrop's famous sermon to the Puritans in 1633 articulated a communal vision that would sustain wave after wave of immigrants crossing the oceans in crowded boats, hoping for a new life on a strange continent: "We must be knit together in this work as one. . . .We must delight in each other, make others' conditions our own, rejoice together, mourn together, labor together and suffer together; always having before our eyes our commission and community in the work, our community as members of the same body."

Recent scholarship in immigration history suggests that new arrivals, into the twentieth century, most commonly came from village backgrounds. Often they left their homes because land enclosures, land speculation, inflation, and other impersonal forces were intruding on settled traditional communal patterns. As the English social historian Peter Laslett put it, in *The World We Have Lost,* New England communities were modeled on villages in Stuart England, "where no gentlemanly household was to be found and where the yeoman and the husbandman ran things themselves."

Each townsman received a plot as a freehold and, at least initially, planting was done in groups on adjoining strips. Land not given out in plots was common land used for haying, timbering, grazing, and hunting. At the center of the New England town was the meetinghouse. The house was a symbol of the community, center of the farmers' market and the local militia, the gathering place for political discussion. Each town was seen as a community "with no great differences of holdings," as Richard Lingeman has described; "each man was his brother's keeper, obliged to watch his conduct." The colonies were imagined as *commonwealths,* networks of communities organized around wealth shared, joined together by mutual concern for the common good.[2]

English settlers fled the corruption and individualism they believed was growing, uncontrollably, in the Old World. But for Irish, Scotch, German, and, later, Italian, Polish, Chinese, and Mexicans as well, their very understanding of America was inextricably bound to communal values. For black slaves, communal traditions like extended family patterns and a pervasive spirituality furnished the essential ingredients for cultures of survival and resistance. America was the land of mutual aid societies, of fraternal societies and sororal associations, of quilting bees and barn raisings and voluntary fire departments and religious groups of every kind. The French observer Alexis de Tocqueville, crossing the continent in the 1830s, marveled at Americans' unparalleled talents for forming associations of every variety, upon every occasion.

Yet on the other hand—Tocqueville himself, among many others, made this argument—Americans had to *work* so hard at building community because other forces in our society constantly eroded it. America was the land of "individualists" escaping parochial and constricting relations for freedom of worship, for new opportunity, for experimentation of all sorts. And America was above all described as the "land of progress."

"We live in an age of improvement," wrote Edward Everett, editor of the *North American Review,* in the mid–nineteenth century. "What changes have not been already wrought in the condition of society! What addition has not been made to the wealth of nations and the means of private comfort by the inventions, discoveries and improvements of the last hundred years!" Progress was synonymous with America. To be opposed to one made alienation from the other. "There can be no pause," Everett expounded, in the spirit of the age, "for art and science are, in themselves, progressive and infinite. . . . Nothing can arrest them which does not plunge the entire order of society into barbarism."

To a society still remembering, uneasily, Puritan jeremiads against avarice, progress justified individual ambition and drive. "Is not the hope of one day being able to purchase and enjoy Luxuries a great Spur to Labor and Industry?" Benjamin Franklin asked his countrymen and -women in 1784, contemplating the future. However defined, individual ambition threatened community; in most explicit form, the threat was overt: "Forget your past, your customs and your ideals. Run, work, do and keep your own good in mind. That's the way to get ahead in America!" counseled one advice manual for immigrants in New York in the 1890s.[3]

These dual images—of progress and community, of individual advancement and mutual support—still have a contemporaneity as fresh as the morning paper. They lace Fourth of July celebrations and our commencement addresses, Ronald Reagan's speeches and our most popular television shows. "Miller time" is the moment for friends to gather in the advertisements; the shows that follow feature football heroes and oilmen, high tech and high-powered success.

Beyond the apparent tensions between unbridled individualism and community has existed an equation holding sway over our imaginations regardless of other differences about politics, religion, or other matters. Technological change, urbanization, the growth of "modern" and enormous institutions, the uprootedness of older forms of community—all of these have been seen as inevitable. Depending upon one's viewpoint, the issue has been posed: how to adjust, preserve what can be salvaged, build new forms of relationships when necessary and desirable.

In *The Concept of Community*, Scott Greer and David Minar put the conventional wisdom simply. Older, close communities give way with the onslaught of the modern world: "Modern life has raised havoc with men's ability to identify themselves with the locality, to create a community in it." Instead of intimate involvement with smaller-scale, face-to-face relations, people turn elsewhere: "The technology and life style of the modern urban man pulls much of his attention and activity into broader spheres, into the larger world of the corporation, the profession, the labor union and the like." Certain things might be lost through such a process. But, they argue, a new freedom, and the possibilities for new relations, more than compensate: "Local boundaries . . . no longer confine his occupational life and often not his leisure, his shopping or his friendships," they suggest. "Must community . . . be place oriented? This is a way of asking if urban life is workable."[4]

Minar and Greer expressed what has been, until recently, a well-nigh universal consensus—indeed, to question it was all but unthinkable. Yet in recent years, forms of resistance began to emerge to the confident heralds of progress. They grew most commonly out of direct and disillusioning experience.

I interviewed Rita and Jean Pinard in their small kitchen in a second-story apartment on the outskirts of Lowell, Massachusetts. I had heard about their recent move from a neighborhood next to a hazardous-waste dump site, named Silresim.

Events that week seemed to highlight this story. The Environmental Protection Agency, plagued with scandal and rumors about its handling of toxic wastes, announced that two officials had resigned. Six congressional committees were investigating reports of wrongdoing. EPA administrator Anne Gorsuch Burford called a press conference in Times Beach, Missouri, a community poisoned with the deadly waste dioxin, to announce that the government was prepared to buy out the town.

It all began to have political impact, in the view of worried Reagan administration officials. It was proving to be "a motherhood issue in this country," one senior aide told *Newsweek*. "Our environmental policies are not politically profitable."

Rita is a slender woman with curly brown hair who models upon occasion. She moves with unselfconscious grace. Her husband, Jean, is dark-haired, bearded. The Pinards are devout Catholics whose religion has led them to varied work with children and adolescents. Jean helps teen-agers who have had drug problems, his muscular build, conditioned through many years of weight lifting, lending authority. Rita, shy, apologetic about the apartment's slightly unkempt appearance, worked with a group devoted to natural childbirth. She took in preschoolers, too, at their old house.

Jean had grown up in the Ayer City neighborhood of Lowell, an older working-class community that he described as a "United Nations" of French, Irish, Portuguese, Greek, and black families. Despite the different ethnicities, they both remembered a neighborhood spirit. "You'd have a typical old man who'd yell at you if you parked your car in front of his house." recalled Rita, "but everybody knew everybody. People would talk as they cut their bushes or stood in their yards." A baseball diamond was in constant use during the spring and summer. In the winter, an old open field had, at one time, regularly turned into a skating rink.

Jean came out of the service in 1973, and shortly afterward they got married. In 1977 they moved back to his childhood neighborhood with their six-month-old daughter, Rachel, a couple of blocks away from the field.

At that time Lowell was beginning a major renewal and "reindustrialization" process, connecting high-technology industry with a historic revival project around the theme "Lowell: Birthplace of the American Revolution." Jean believes that the public-relations-conscious city did not want any scandal as it sought new industry and a $40-million grant for historic preservation and the creation of a park. Whatever the reasons, the Pinards fell victim to calamities that they did not understand.

"We started getting sick a month after we moved there," described Rita. "Jean developed these allergies, his eyes would burn. He had bronchial problems for the first time in his life.

"Rachel was only six months old. She began to get strep throats and infections all the time. I took her for blood work and they found a high amount of lead. I was shocked. They said she must have chewed paint, but I knew she couldn't have chewed paint. Then I got a license to have a day care, and the kids that were coming started getting sick with bronchitis, croup, and pneumonia."

In 1971 the Silresim Chemical Corporation operated a chemical-waste-dump facility in the old field near the Pinards, in the Ayer City neighborhood of Lowell. The dump handled a variety of chemicals, from acids to alkalies, hydrocarbons, ketone, and other agents. According to a state-commissioned study released in October 1979 (though not made known to residents according to the several families interviewed), from 1973 to 1977 Silresim had been repeatedly cited by the Massachusetts Division of Water Pollution Control for violations. They included "unsatisfactory chemical handling procedures leading to soil contamination and surface runoff"; an excessive "inventory of stored chemicals, at one time numbering nearly 30,000 drums," many deteriorating, unmarked, holding more than 1 million gallons of waste; illegal discharge into the municipal sewer system; and acceptance of a number of chemicals forbidden by law.

On July 13, 1978, the Massachusetts State Legislature passed an act "providing for the Emergency of Certain Hazardous Wastes in the City of Lowell," and declaring that the act was "an emergency law, necessary for the immediate preservation of public health, safety and the environment." City officials gave no notice of the law to the Pinards, or any of their neighbors.[5]

Rita described their confusion. "We thought something was fishy. Sometimes at midnight you'd hear trucks outside. And in the summer there would be a plume of stuff so thick you could cut it with a knife." When I later visited the site—after the toxins had been removed—my eyes watered and I smelled an acrid odor.

"We would go outside and the smell was so bad you could throw up breakfast." Neighbors reported that plants and trees near the field became deformed; vegetables in nearby gardens grew into grotesque shapes. Jean and Rita regularly called the city to ask about the smell. "They would tell us we were smelling raw sewage that was leaking from a broken sewer line. They said they didn't have the funds to clean it up yet, but it was on the agenda to do something about it and they would do it when they could." The Pinards made no connection between their health and the toxic smells. "Who were we to think otherwise or to even suspect?"

In 1979 the Pinards said, workers near the site were overcome and had to be taken to the hospital. The Pinards knew by that time something was wrong and that it was somehow connected to the barrels on the dump. Their suspicions grew when a fire caused a number of barrels to blow up and it seemed to them that the fire department did not have facilities to put out the fire. Yet they still saw no link between their health problems and the dump, believing themselves to be victims somehow of bad luck.

It got worse and worse. "Rachel had constant strep throats," remembered Rita. "She would have convulsions with a temperature of 105. I was bleeding a lot, and finally they took me to the hospital, I had such a bad infection. We couldn't understand. We didn't smoke or drink. I am very nutrition-conscious in what I feed my family." When they had another child that year, the new baby also was constantly ill. Jean steadily lost strength. "He used to be strong as an ox," said Rita. "But finally they took him to the hospital. He couldn't even feed himself; they had to lift his head up."

According to the Pollution Control Agency study, "there was evidence of runoff onto adjacent property or into site drains which led to the Lowell sewer system. The soil was permeated and the surface was characterized by colored pools, stains, evaporated residues and elastic gels. . . . Air quality at and near the site was poor due to the presence of volatile substances, requiring visitors to use organic vapor respirators."

When the legislature passed the emergency legislation in 1978, they neglected to provide sufficient funds to clean up the contamination. A start was made, then terminated. State and federal bureaucracies moved slowly on other fronts. The Pollution Control Agency revoked Silresim's operating license in late 1977, though a local bank, Union National, which received the corporation in receivership, continued for a time to use the site for chemical storage. "Although the stored chemicals represented an emergency situation, the DWPC [the pollution agency] in conjunction with the Region I EPA . . . chose to take a cautious approach in determining the methods of removal and disposal," concluded the state report. In 1981, the agency still had not determined a final procedure for dealing with the wastes.[6]

By this time, Jean and Rita were frantic. When a consumer group, Massachusetts Fair Share, came by their house and suggested that their health problems might be connected to the hazardous-waste dump, they jumped at the chance to become involved. "We went down to the health department. They might have thought they had us over a barrel because we were just regular citizens," Rita recounted. "They showed us these reports and told us, 'Don't worry about it, the chemicals are right here and it's all contained.' But Fair Share had told us how to get information about the chemicals. And we did research, and got more information from a sympathetic doctor." Rita Pinard is an encyclopedia of knowledge about chemical wastes and their effects on health.

Armed with such information, they also enlisted their neighbors. "We'd go door to door with advice, telling people who they could go to see and who they could call. People would say, 'My God, so that's it,' and the puzzle pieces would fall into place. Almost everybody seemed to have had severe health problems. There were stillbirths, babies born whose navels didn't stop bleeding." A health study commissioned by Massachusetts Fair Share and conducted by sympathetic scientists found high incidences of bronchitis and other respiratory illnesses and also a number of cases of cancer and bladder disorder in a group of 163 households near the site.

The Fair Share chapter used imaginative tactics. They picketed the home of the bank president ("My knees were shaking when we went out there, but after that, it was a piece of cake," said Rita). During the 1982 elections, they pressured both candidates, partly drawing on other Fair Share chapters around the state, and won promises of action. Finally, health officials cleaned up most of the materials remaining, though Fair Share continued to press for removal of earth they believed was contaminated.

A major part of their campaign was aimed at Lowell's image. For instance, Fair Share members made up bumper slogans like "See the real Lowell: the Silresim chemical waste dump!" "It scared the pants off them," Jean believes. *The Lowell Sun* has, over the past several years, written several editorials highly critical of Fair Share's "disruptive" behavior (at one point the organization picketed the newspaper for what they considered biased coverage); and the managing editor, Kendell Wallace, denies there was ever a cover-up. But he admits that Fair Share forced action on the issue. "There is no doubt. They waked people up."

Yet doubts remain. And the Pinards feel their lives have been permanently altered. "We left when Dr. Gilchrist said we should," recounted Rita. (Michael Gilchrist, a local pediatrician familiar with some of the literature on hazardous waste, had warned them in a letter in the spring of 1982 that "continued and chronic exposure to many of these inhaled contaminants can lead to increased numbers of upper respiratory infections and perhaps even crippling pulmonary disease" and had recommended that "you and your family look into the possibility of changing your residence for the benefit of your children's health.")[7] "Our health got better right away."

But Rita's voice lowered. "It still seems like a bad dream. Who knows what things will show up someday? Will we get cancer? What about our children?" She began to cry softly. Jean reflected with bitterness, "It gets to the point where you're not shocked anymore. Where do people who work for this country come in? The country is supposed to be ours. What does America stand for?"

Jean Pinard's question "What does America stand for?" was asked with increasing frequency in the 1980s. Pollster Louis Harris charted a sharp rise in the "alienation index" over the period 1966 to 1983, from 29 percent to 62 percent. The number of people believing that "the rich get richer and the poor get poorer" had grown from 45 percent of the population in the earlier year to 79 percent. The portion subscribing to the idea that "what I think doesn't count very much" had mushroomed, from 37 percent in 1966 to 62 percent. And the part of the survey reporting that "the people running the country don't really care what happens to you" stood at an unprecedented 57 percent, up from 50 percent the year before, more than twice the 26-percent figure of seventeen years earlier.

Such indexes of alienation had a more positive side. The growth of citizen activism around issues such as nuclear arms represented, in a sense, the expression of trends that had been building over a decade. Trend monitor John Naisbitt suggested that "for the first time in the nation's history there is more decentralization than centralization taking place in America," pointing mainly to signs of public mood and opinion. The failure of large-scale approaches to problem-solving, the impersonality and corruption of big institutions, the changing economic base of society, all fed a growing impulse: "We saw that those macro, top-down solutions didn't work," argued Naisbitt. "The only thing that really works is local initiative."[8]

Growing citizen activism took a variety of forms. Larger groups like Massachusetts Fair Share had grown up in more than half the states. They formed into coalitions such as the Association of Community Organizations for Reform Now (ACORN), the National People's Action (NPA), the Citizen Lab or Energy Coalition, and Citizen Action, a network of over a dozen groups with which Fair Share is affiliated. By 1983, the major media were reporting the growth of these larger groups all around the country, what John Herbers of the *New York Times* called "a new wave of citizen initiatives." *Los Angeles Times* reporters Larry Green and Joanna Brown surveyed the Citizen Action network itself and reported that on a given night, door-to-door workers canvassed up to 60,000 homes (12 million households in 1982), asking for support on consumer issues and financial contributions.[9]

Heather Booth, who helped to create the alliance of citizen groups in Citizen Action, directs the Midwest Academy training center, a resource formed in the early 1970s to provide organizers and leaders of local groups with new skills in organizing. In the 1960s, Booth was a student activist who went south during the civil-rights struggle. Her time working with "freedom schools" in Mississippi—formed to teach black history, voter registration knowledge, and other things—changed her life goals. "Mississippi was a life-shaping experience," she recounted. "When I came back, I decided that I was a teacher." Booth founded the Midwest Academy as an heir to that "freedom school" tradition, in the belief that "without pretention, we needed to have a way to pass on the skills and insights of organizing to new generations." In the last several years, Heather Booth has seen a tremendous growth in the groups she works with. "We see it everywhere, with environmental, church, community groups—people are becoming more active."

The Citizen Action coalition of organizations sees itself as a

"new voice" for low- and moderate-income citizens. As Ira Arlook, director of the coalition, put it, "We want to make it
possible for the concerns of an overwhelming majority of
Americans to be felt in economic and political decision-making."[10] In sum, it represented a visible—and national—expression of local ferment. But the activism out of which such coalitions emerged was more widespread and varied yet.

According to pollsters, almost one-half of all adult Americans
now volunteer an average of seventeen hours a week. The
number of Americans volunteering to work on issues and community problems seven hours or more a week increased from
24 million in the mid-sixties to 46.4 million in 1981—more than
93 percent.

Activity in specific communities is the most prevalent form.
The *Christian Science Monitor,* describing what it termed "the
invisible story of the 1970s," found that one-third of all adults
in large cities claimed to have been active in recent years in
some form of community group. In New York City alone, more
than 3,000 block clubs developed from 1975 to 1978, working
on issues ranging from health care and urban gardening to
crime control. More than 1 million people a year joined cooperatives of different kinds—food, health care, housing, and so
forth. The presidentially appointed National Commission on
Neighborhoods listed more than 8,000 community organizations, almost all formed since 1970.

Citizen activism had also increased dramatically around specific issues. For instance, the FBI in 1982 reported the first
major decrease in serious-crime rates for many years, and at-
tributed such a decrease to citizen-involvement efforts,
through block-watch programs and other means. In New York,
where the number of crimes reported decreased from 725,844
in 1981 to 688,567 in 1982, the police department gave as the
cause "152,000 volunteers taking part in 13 types of programs."
Perhaps most striking of all has been the growing protest
against the nuclear arms race, reaching from the smallest villages in New England to the Catholic bishops.[11]

On May 25, 1982, 3,409 citizens in Manhattan went to town
meetings to talk about the nuclear freeze. "This is Jeffersonian

democracy in action," said one participant, Dr. Robert Lifton, professor of psychiatry at Yale. "We should take advantage of it—and we will." Meetings throughout the borough that night, in the spirit of meetings that had spread through the New England states earlier in the spring, had distinctive styles that reflected their communities. In Harlem, participants meeting in the Canaan Baptist Church sang "I want to Be a Follower of Christ" and heard the Reverend Carolyn Knight ask for God's help in achieving the nuclear freeze and in fighting poverty. A meeting on the Upper East Side included performing artists such as Andre Gregory and Estelle Parsons, who gave dramatic readings. The final vote in meetings that evening in favor of freezing the testing, production, and deployment of nuclear weapons and transferring funds "from the military to human needs" was an overwhelming demonstration against the arms race: 3,316 for the resolution; 42 against; 51 abstaining.

Again and again the notion of the right and responsibility of local citizens to take action emerged clearly. "I want to make a statement that nuclear war is not unthinkable," explained one woman in Murray Hill. "We dream about it, we have nightmares about it. This is a town meeting and this is my town."

The movement to end the nuclear arms race, like other forms of citizen action, represented this kind of assertion of citizen self-confidence, a statement that ordinary people can become knowledgeable about the most complex of issues and can bring their values to bear on such issues in the hope of influencing events. Harold Willens, the Los Angeles businessman who began the campaign to put a freeze initiative on the California ballot in the fall of 1984, put it clearly. Grass-roots citizen action, he said, breaks the monopoly of the "nuclear metaphysicians" and adds the "citizen common sense that had been the missing ingredient."[12]

America's "poet of the tape recorder," Studs Terkel, has described such new ferment as an invisible and unreported countertrend to the "new privatism" and the "me decade." "There is a flowing of life juices that has not been covered on the Six O'Clock News," said Terkel, writing in *Parade*'s Sunday magazine. "The heralds are from all sorts of precincts: a family farmer, a blue collar housewife, a whistleblowing executive—noncelebrated people who bespeak the dreams of their fellows."

Terkel went on to sketch the astonishing variety of citizen protests, which, he argued, represented people reaching out *toward* each other rather than drawing inward. In Fort Myers, Florida, citizens sought to stop the building of a bridge that would destroy the community. In San Francisco, the disabled demonstrated to force action by the Department of Health and Human Services. In Northfield, Minnesota, students protested the draft-registration requirement.

A nine-city campaign against porn parlors showing young children involved in sexual activities was launched in Highland Park, Michigan. "In a society and time with changes so stunning and landscapes so suddenly estranged," Terkel concluded, "a long buried American tradition may be springing back to life."[13]

Terkel's poetic imagery suggested the breadth of ferment at work in heretofore invisible recesses of the society. Yet it also pointed to the complexity of the growing citizen activism. That *something* was beginning to stir into existence once again seemed, as the Eighties progressed, unmistakable. What it represented was far more uncertain.

Groups like the Citizen Action network had begun supporting candidates—overwhelmingly Democrats—for office partly in reaction to the success of Reaganite Republicans. Their rationale was a defense of the values of community. "America, born of hope, now is becoming a society overwhelmed by fear: of crime, of losing our jobs, our social security payments, our homes and neighborhoods," read the Fair Share program approved in the summer of 1982. The organization pointed to what it called "a crisis of values" in America. It declared that "the ethics of respect, decency, cooperation, quality and hard work" had been weakened, and that the country was prey to a new selfishness and cynicism. It pledged its support for principles of "democracy, the family, work, neighborhoods and community, fairness, initiative and self-reliance, respect and tolerance and security."

But to an outside observer, there seemed no small irony in such a listing. These themes had, after all, formed the rhetorical centerpiece of the Republican party platform in the 1980 election, and Ronald Reagan continued to make them the centerpiece of his rhetorical arsenal, with considerable effectiveness. In 1980, Republicans had lauded neighborhoods as "arenas for civic action and creative self-help," places where cooperation could be nourished. They called for "a rebirth of citizen activity in neighborhoods and cities across the land." And into his presidency, the new president continued to call for "a renaissance of the American community . . . this is the heart and soul of rebuilding America." Indeed, the sorts of citizen efforts charted by reporters or chronicled by Terkel ran the political gamut from rock-ribbed Republican farmers to youthful gay communities in the midst of urban areas.[14]

Heather Booth pointed to the difficulties in even describing the citizen action groups. "We really don't have a vocabulary yet for saying who we are, or what we represent." Karen Paget, a political scientist who formerly served as deputy director of the federal agency ACTION and now directs a consortium, the Youth Project, furnishing technical assistance and support to local citizen efforts, argued further that the lack of definition meant a great difficulty in translating particular citizen campaigns into broader cultural symbols and terms. "With the collapse of consensus in the body politic and the manifestations of change everywhere—mobility, the changing economic base— all actors are increasingly conscious of a struggle to define reality itself. You can't have a neutral debate about policy X versus Y. The background is that the way the data is shaped, organized, and selected involves fundamental notions of value that are almost never articulated."

In such an environment, those with the most power are at a tremendous advantage in terms of mobilizing resources and manipulating public opinion. And citizen groups, without clarity about what they represent in any broader terms, can do little more than say "Stop." Said Paget: "The citizen movement is hopeful in the sense that it may be the only thing that creates some resistance to an increasingly centralized, technological society. But it is a mitigating force. It stops excesses here and there. It's not at all clear what positive thing it represents, or what other moral options it brings to the fore."

As I interviewed activists in a variety of citizen groups, a phrase often occurred to me from *The Book of Laughter and Forgetting,* the great novel by Czech writer Milan Kundera. "The struggle of man against power is the struggle of memory against forgetting," said one character, raging against officials' distortions of history in Communist bloc countries. Yet what does it mean to be a citizen of America, when memory disappears through more subtle processes?[15]

Memory is handed down formally, through history books and public lectures. But it takes on life in day-to-day relations. In *Number Our Days,* Barbara Myerhoff described the life of a community of elderly Jews in California, distanced from relatives and from their home countries. The formal traditions of Judaism retained importance for them. But what was most central to their "Jewishness," what they missed the most and tried to re-create, with courage and with difficulty, was the rich life of the folk communities from which they had originally come in Europe. It was in such communities that an intricate Jewish folk culture (the *Yiddishkeit*) had been sustained for centuries, along with a distinctive language, Yiddish, separate from formal Hebrew.[16]

Almost all Americans in the 1980s have experienced forms of wrenching detachment from the communal settings that might nourish a deep and continuous sense of what it *means* to be an American. America, after all, is the most mobile society in the world. Though signs of resistance to mobility began to appear in the late 1970s, according to the Census Bureau—about 94 million out of 210 million people five years of age and older moved from 1975 to 1980. Western states had the largest percentages of those moving. In Alaska, more than 65 percent of the population changed residences; in Nevada, 62.5 percent; in Oregon, 56.9. But the figures were nonetheless huge even in those states with the smallest portion uprooted: 34.2 percent in Pennsylvania; 35.8 percent in New York; 37.2 percent in Massachusetts.[17]

Such rapid flux necessarily disrupts and weakens close ties to neighbors, friends, and relatives. It makes any community tied to place, and to the face-to-face relations and institutions associated with place, infinitely more difficult. "Home is the expectancy of familiar things, the places, people and the movements of time that in their way are ours," Baker Brownell wrote more than thirty years ago. But in the modern world, "homelessness has become a kind of lethal normalcy of western culture. Millions of men and women of the so-called labor force, millions among the 'white collar' workers and in the business and professional groups, and more millions of children live in no accustomed place. The have no stable milieu of friends, families and familiar routines. They have no homes; there is no rooting place."[18]

In cross-cultural studies of human groupings, John Pfeiffer found that people tend to congregate in basic, "primal" units of about twenty-five, across variations in culture. The next natural grouping occurred at about 500—people with whom one has frequent, though not necessarily day-to-day, contact. In smaller groups, intimate bonds form. Closeness "involves not only the same language and dialect but the same familiar intonations, expressions, and gestures, and a common store of idioms, jokes, myths and allusions." Other studies have suggested that when such primary groupings are weakened or shrink significantly, the incidence of suicide and psychological breakdown increases dramatically.[19]

Other forces as well as mobility undermine intimate communal ties in America. The disappearance of local merchants and other small businesses, for instance, can change the texture of life in a neighborhood. Small businesses advertise in ways different from larger economic enterprises. The local grocer may give out samples of candy to children. The milkman stops by to inquire about the family's needs that week. "We independents have to depend much on personal relationships and know our customers," explained a small southern merchant. "Once we forget a man's name or neglect to inquire about the health of his family, the condition of his crops, or about his hobby, we are in a way to lose his business."[20]

As early as the *Federalist Papers,* James Madison argued that American government must be structured to control and regulate different factional interests because the communal bonds generating values of cooperation among citizens were much weaker than the divisions that separated them. In the last hundred years, however, the problem has become far more acute.

The growth of large-scale institutions has been accompanied by legitimizing ideologies that consciously seek to erode the authority of communal relations. Urban sociology, shaping urban planning and design, furnishes a case study. According to Robert Park, for instance, a Gothic figure in the field, the great value of the city was the aggregation of people by common interests, replacing what he calls "sentiment," community ties. For Park, neighborhood life produced irrational prejudice, "elementary forms of conservatism." In analogous fashion, the emergence of the modern welfare state has meant the rise of professions that reduce laymen to incompetence and to dependence on experts. "The medical and psychiatric assault on the family as a technologically backward sector went hand in hand with the advertising industry's drive to convince people that store-bought goods are superior to home made goods," as Christopher Lasch has described.[21]

In sum, "progress" in different guises has undermined community. And through such a process, it makes even the terminology of "community organizing" or "community action" problematic. What does it mean to "organize" a community that has little sense of itself? I found this sort of question posed with increasing frequency, in a variety of settings.

"Many of us have been calling for citizen action to a whole range of issues, but gradually some of us have come to realize we were making a huge assumption," explained Loren Halvorson, for many years an executive with the Lutheran Division of Higher Education. "[We assumed] people were ready and able to act."

Halvorson concluded, indeed, that the church approach to educating people about problems such as racial injustice, world hunger, and international affairs reflected assumptions that themselves tended to undermine people's capacities for action. "I too had been beguiled by the planning process, the engineering of human community by the use of the latest methods and devices of communication—all with the highest intentions, of course, to 'raise the consciousness' of the masses."

Halvorson began to see things differently. Before it made much sense to talk about changing the world, one had to look concretely at where one lived: "Too few have had a healthy primary community experience to draw on. Therefore for some of us, rebuilding base communities . . . has become the first priority." Halvorson remains active in church education work, but his major effort now goes into a retreat center, called the ARC, that helps people grapple with change in their lives and in the world in the context of rebuilding the substance and sense of community. "To change the way we live with each other in an arena over which we do have some control is already to begin a vast revolution."[22]

In recent years, many in the fields of community organization and community development have developed such a sensibility, concluding that to do more than call a halt to further erosion of community and of community values requires attentiveness to the *renewal* of deep values and relations. Traditionally, community organization gave little explicit attention to questions of value. "The mistake of our first thirty years of community organizing was that we never reflected much on what organizing means," explained Ed Chambers, director of the Industrial Areas Foundation network of community groups established by the "dean" of modern community organizing, Saul Alinsky. "We were very good at action, clever and imaginative. But we didn't make a commitment to the growth process of the people." Chambers contrasted such an approach with the more recent IAF emphasis on building organizations around communal values. "In organizations based on values, social change is not some kind of abstraction that happens out there. It happens to people. It involves your whole life."

In terms of impact, the IAF network includes the largest and most powerful community efforts in the country—organizations like Communities Organized for Public Service, for instance, which has revived an enormous area of Mexican-American parishes in San Antonio, Texas. But such groups contrast their approach with more-typical "political" action, or groups defined mainly in terms of specific issues. "Contrary to common opinion, we are not a grass-roots organization" was the way the Reverend Johnnie Ray Youngblood, pastor of St. Paul's Community Baptist Church in Brooklyn and president of a strong community coalition called East Brooklyn Churches, put it. The East Brooklyn group, affiliated with IAF, began with extensive programs of parish training in organizing skills and reflection on the values of community: religious principles of justice, love of neighbor, preference for the poor; democratic values of citizen participation, including the challenging to unresponsive structures. "Grass roots grow in smooth soil," continued Youngblood. "Grass roots are shallow roots. Grass roots are tender roots. Grass roots are fragile roots." Youngblood contrasts the spiritual and community values that EBC has brought to life "in the shattered glass of East New York, in the blasted brick and rubble of Brownsville," with more-transient forms of community activism. "Our roots are deep roots. Our roots are tough roots. Our roots are determined roots." And indeed, the organization in its brief life has achieved remarkable results. For instance, to the surprise of a jaded city political establishment, it has made a significant beginning on its plan to build 5,000 homes for low- and moderate-income residents, in the midst of devastated city blocks. The plan is named Nehemiah, for the biblical leader who returned to Jerusalem to lead the rebuilding of the temple.[23]

I became convinced that exploring the broader implications of citizen activism would require attention to the efforts to revitalize community life undertaken by groups like East Brooklyn and the ARC, in different terms. Where is it in America that people begin to move beyond protest to the rebuilding of relations that have been weakened or lost? How are memories of older values and traditions revived through such a process and made relevant to the present world? And how might community renewal efforts weave together to suggest directions for the country in a time of great uncertainty about our very purposes as a society?

These were the sorts of questions that came to guide my travels. They are questions arising from my explorations of places such as St. Paul's West End and Lowell's Ayer City, which will be examined in more depth in the following chapters. Ultimately my discoveries led to a new appreciation for the vitality and creativity that still flourish in America, for all our present difficulties—in part, in response to them.

2

Those Were the Days

Trang Le remembers Vietnam with soft melancholy. "In 1975, there was a war going on in my country," she explains. "We had to leave." The armies of North Vietnam gathered on the outskirts of Saigon for the final assault. Just hours before bombs started to rain down on the city, Trang Le and her family—her father, a civil engineer; her mother, an employee of an American firm—boarded a small fishing boat with several others and took to sea. "I was eight years old," Trang recalls. "It was stormy and we had to sleep on the deck." The boat went first to the Philippines; then it set sail for America, across the Pacific. In midvoyage the vessel sprang a leak and began to sink. Trang, her parents, brothers and sisters, and the others on board were rescued at the last moment by the Coast Guard. After several months, they ended up on the West Side of St. Paul.

Trang's story is unique. So, in their own distinct ways, were the stories of earlier immigrants to the West Side. "You marvel at what it was like, the streetcars, the food. All those peddlers on the streets selling fruits and vegetables." Trang describes the interviews she has been doing as part of the Humboldt High School oral history project directed by Stephen Sandell, a teacher long interested in the old West Side Flats. Since arriving in America, Trang had always enjoyed history. But "history," she explains, had been taught as "significant things, great big events. On the West Side, it's the little things that make a big difference."

Trang's family settled in the West Side "Hills," a large residential community still remaining after the Flats were destroyed. Many from the Flats had relocated there, with vivid stories.

I interviewed Trang and another student, Naomi Glessing, shortly after they participated in a panel about labor unions and working conditions on the Flats. Like other workshops and plenaries that weekend, their session drew a large and enthusiastic audience. The occasion was entitled "A Flood of History: West Side Conference on Local History."

"Without a profound sense of history, we are victims of caprice," argued Clarke Chambers, a University of Minnesota historian who keynoted the event. Chambers went on to link the sort of neighborhood historical revival evident that weekend with the flowering of social histories of many powerless groups in the last two decades—blacks, women, laboring people, and others. "If we are going to gain control over the forces which shape our lives," he concluded, "we have to gain a sense of who we are in a communal sense." Through many media, West Siders that weekend were building such a sense of historical identity.

Bill Hoffman gave anecdotes from his childhood in the Flats. "Texas Street had running water. It ran all the time down the street." "In our house I was always proud to say we had two colors of toilet paper. Orange wrappers and apple wrappers." Helen Turner and other old-time residents greeted each other and told stories. Around the walls of the new Humboldt High School where the conference was being held were dozens of pictures: an old photo of Wabasha Bridge from the nineteenth century; scenes of the legendary flooding in 1881; a picture of the horse attached to "Horse Car #41," which ran from downtown St. Paul to the West Side from 1883 to 1889; a scene from Jobst Horseshoeing and General Blacksmithing. Neighborhood House, which along with many residents had moved in the 1960s, resettling in the Concord Terrace area where many Mexican families lived, had its own extensive displays: pictures of ethnic dances; a group of Lebanese families; photos of different athletic teams and scenes from camps; a brochure listing holiday festivities for the 1930–31 season—Hanukkah program, Mexican piñata, a candlelight party and a religious pageant, the distribution of baskets, the Mexican Boys' Club party. And Bill Kuehn's masterful creation always drew crowds. Kuehn, who had designed models for many years for the State Department of Transportation, was working with high-school students and others to construct an enormous model of the Flats in 1930. Scheduled for completion a year later, to be accompanied by "a large computer that will list information about every building," the model itself was to be amazingly detailed, including "every home, church, synagogue, commercial and industrial building, the old Neighborhood House and the old schools, along with the old playgrounds, movie houses, railroads, streetcars—you name it," as Kuehn wrote in the description.[1]

Sponsoring the weekend was the West Side Citizens Organization (WESCO), formed about ten years before. Leaders in WESCO had become convinced over the years that learning about the community's history was an invaluable resource for helping to create a spirit of community in the present and gaining a voice in the city as a whole. Indeed, the signs of such a voice were visible. Jim Scheibel, a founder of WESCO and an ardent booster of the community history, was there representing the St. Paul City Council. Scheibel, first city-council member to come from the West Side, read the official city resolution declaring the weekend of May 6–8 "West Side History Days."

On the last day of the conference, WESCO planned a concert, tour of the area, a play, and finally the official creation of a West Side Historical Society to carry on the community history efforts. They knew from the attendance it would prove successful. People were excited by the weekend.

Trang Le recounted stories she had heard about classes in Neighborhood House, the zoo on Harriet Island, how people never had to lock their doors. "During the depression," she said, "nobody had much, but one family would help another." She looked up. "I'd like to be back there, to see how it was."

The story of how it was on the West Side, explained an account from the 1880s, "has been a somewhat checkered one; its career has been attended by many vicissitudes of fortune."[2]

From the air, one sees a striking bend in the Mississippi as it curves northward through St. Paul and then sharply back south, like the outline of one of the Indian burial mounds, perhaps, rising in the Dayton's Bluff area on the northern banks of the river, or a squirrel's tail, arched and wary. Down from Dayton's Bluffs on the southern shore, the land between the water and the white cliffs still further south forms a crescent, carved out by nature.

Some 17,000 years ago, a cataract twice as high and wide as Niagara Falls dug through the sand and limestone. An enormous lake had formed out of the melting waters of the Ice Age, Lake Agassiz in western Minnesota. The river Warren carried the runoff northeasterly, hollowing out what is now the Minnesota River Valley, joining with the Mississippi around the area that would someday be Fort Snelling at the southern and easternmost tip of Minneapolis.

The combined rivers ran along the level of the bluffs northward. At the northernmost point, they plunged hundreds of feet into an old riverbed and headed straight south, toward the distant waters of the Gulf of Mexico. When the waters receded, the falls moved upriver, becoming St. Anthony's Falls in Minneapolis, a modest remnant of their glory. South of the river—on its "western side" as described by cartographers—lowlands remained, covered with forests of elm and maple, dotted with marshes.

The view was stunning. "There is no doubt that at some future period mighty kingdoms will emerge from these wildernesses," wrote Jonathan Carver, an explorer who ventured to the area in 1767 after the French and Indian War. "Stately temples with gilded spires [will someday] supplant the Indian huts." True to prophecy, Indian huts were first to experience the march of progress.

The bluffs and the West Side lowlands formed an Indian crossroads, part of an old trail of the Dakota up to the wild rice areas in Mille Lacs to the north. On both sides of the river, sacred mounds marked the burial places of ancestors. By 1838, remaining Sioux tribes had been moved entirely across the river to the western bank. A permanent Indian village appeared at Kaposia, a bit to the south, and the West Side proper may have been the site of a temporary village at times.

These regions, however, proved to be a lucrative pathway for farmers and traders, bringing up furs and crops from the south. A market for such goods was growing across the river. Before public-relations-conscious settlers christened the area St. Paul, for a Catholic mission, the European community bore the name of a legendary and notorious character, Pierre ("Pig's Eye") Parrant, a whiskey peddler who set up a drinking establishment with the "Pig's Eye" address. (Pig's Eye, reputed to be the first white settler in St. Paul after the area was opened by treaty in 1838, was so called because of his "swinish" false eye: "Blind, marble-hued, crooked, with a sinister white ring glaring around the pupil, giving a kind of piggish expression to his sodden low features.")[3]

Demand for European settlement along the trade route increased. By 1850, regular ferry service crossed the river daily; in 1858, 600 carts crossed. That year the Wabasha toll bridge across the river opened, followed some years later by Robert Street Bridge and the High Bridge, a long expanse linking St. Paul to the hills on the West Side.

On July 23, 1851, the Sioux finally ceded rights of settlement on the West Side, in the Traverse de Sioux. But even before the treaty, a few Europeans had established illegal homesteads, including one George Bell, soon to become the first mayor. In the 1850s, several hundred people moved to the lowlands, though periodic flooding made farming difficult. The first school opened in 1855 in a log house. And in 1858, with enthusiastic oratory, George Bell and other local notables received a charter from the legislature to establish a town. Ten thousand copies of Bell's inaugural address were printed. Evidently, the Flats were polyglot from the beginning: 5,000 were in English, 2,500 in German and another 2,500 in French.

Unfortunately, zeal and ambition raised little revenue, and Bell and other city officials, voting themselves large salaries, rapidly drove the village into bankruptcy. In 1862 the territo-

rial legislature unceremoniously stripped the town of its charter, ordering the county auditor to hand over all books, accounts, records, and the town seal.[4]

From the bustling vantage point of downtown St. Paul across
the river, the West Side, it seems clear, always looked rather
seamy. Surviving pictures of the area in the Minnesota Historical Society archives convey this aura. There are scenes of the
huge flood of 1881, covering almost the entire Flats. A group
of unkempt characters lounge around the door of Bircher's Last
Chance Saloon, at the end of Wabasha Bridge, in a photo dated
1875. Through these years, the area was evidently considered
useful mainly as a commercial setting, close to downtown yet
also separated by a comfortable stretch of water. Yoerg's Brewery opened on Commercial and Ohio Streets on the West Side
in 1871, using the caves in the limestone cliffs at the back of the
Flats for cooling. Brueggerman's Brewery soon followed. A rock
quarry dug the native limestone. Drake Marble and Tile Company, importing marble from southern Minnesota, brought in
marble and tile workers from Canada to polish and cut stone for
the more elegant businesses, houses of worship, and mansions
rising in Minneapolis and St. Paul. Villaume's Box and Lumber
Company, one of the West Side's largest employers for more
than 100 years now, started in December 1882.

The different views from both riverbanks were suggested by
the arguments used when a proposal was made in 1873 to annex
the West Side (originally part of Dakota County, tying it ad-
ministratively to the south) to the city. West Siders demanded
an end to tolls on Wabasha Bridge as the price of their support
for annexation. By way of contrast, "In St. Paul," wrote the
Reverend Edward Neill in his *History of Ramsey County*, pub-
lished in 1881, "the chief reason for such a step was to be found
in the fact that it was desirable to extend the jurisdiction of the
city, for the purpose of repressing crime, as it often happened
that criminals eluded the grasp of justice by flying across the
river."[5]

Businesses brought in their wake a more skilled population
than the popular imagery of the times would have it, however.
The school log of first-graders attending the River School, soon

to be renamed Lafayette, in 1883 indicates a high proportion of artisanal trades: Butcher, plasterer, car repairer, policeman, carpenter, shoemaker, stonecutter, foreman, stone contractor, confectioner, seamstress, grocer, bricklayer, tailor, machinist, basket maker, and so on are common occupations. Out of 140 students, all of whom came from the Flats area, 37 listed their fathers' occupations as carpentry or stonecutting.

The immigrant flavor of the population is also notable. First settlers were often French fur traders, retiring from a diminishing trade. A scattering of Sioux people remained as well, including the descendants of Petit Corbeau (Little Raven), a famed Dakota chieftain. Women of the family would one day teach Helen Turner to string beads in Indian fashion.

Germans, Irish, Scandinavians, and the first few Jewish families followed. Names like Bourgeau, Terrieau, Lunde, Peterson, Eckman, Lindblad, Hanson, Lipker, and Pouleau fill the River School ledger. Twenty-six first-graders had been born in Canada, of French-Canadian parentage. The total foreign-born student population among the first-graders was sixty-one, including thirteen from Germany, eight from Sweden, seven from Norway, three from Ireland, and one from Russia.[6]

"Come along with me to the Old Union Depot and the long wood sidewalk that some of you, and most of your parents, trod when you first stepped off the train in St. Paul," wrote Bill Hoffman in his first collection of stories and reminiscences of Jewish life in the Flats, *Those Were the Days*. "This was not the noisy, boisterous, frightening city of New York. Your 'landsleit' (countrymen) were waiting to greet you—or was it your husband?"[7]

In the middle 1880s, a major transformation began to take place in the Flats population. It was connected, by invisible threads, to terrible events many thousands of miles away. Ferocious violence, known as the pogroms, broke out against Jewish communities in Eastern Europe and Russia. Tens of thousands came to America. And over a period of two decades or so, several thousand settled on the West Side. The West Side was the area of choice for poorer immigrants; land was cheap or free, partly because of the periodic flooding and the community's reputation, and relatives or friends from one's village had often prepared the way. But despite such ties, the move was a wrenching break with communal roots.

In her description of a Jewish retirement community, Barbara Myerhoff tells the history of the villages, called *shtetls,* that the elderly Jews had left behind in Europe many decades before during the same exodus that brought many to the Flats. "When times worsened," she observes, "it often seemed that Eastern Europe social life intensified proportionately. Internal ties deepened and the people drew sustenance and courage from each other, their religion and their community."

Shmuel, a wise, elderly tailor, served as Myerhoff's guide into and interpreter of the retirement center's culture. To make her understand, he regaled Myerhoff with images of the *shtetl.* Biblical characters and stories were the stuff of *shtetl* children's games and fantasies, becoming central to their views of the world. "Until the present day I can feel the greatness of those stories working in me, giving color, giving itself into my own way of thinking," Shmuel observed. Itinerant Hasidic rabbis, visiting the *shtetl,* would leave unforgettable reflections, "full of wisdom, full of humor. These rabbis could speak to you in such a way that it stays with you all your life." From the outside, such communities might look stagnant or parochial. From the inside, the fusion of tradition, religion, and communal ties gave the smallest details of life vibrancy. "We could turn everything around," explained Shmuel, "like a spoon in a cup, and give it extra life. It's very small when you look at it from above, standing upon those hills. But when you walk down into it, you see it become life size, larger than life."

The daily rounds of life, the buildings and houses on the street, the ways holy days patterned the calendar, the corner merchant, the places for play and the stories associated with each place, the curses and blessings in Yiddish (language of everyday life, which "had words in it that could be used differently for the inside sweet world and the hard world outside," as he put it)—all these were the ground of community and identity. "Culture," Shmuel concluded, "is not a thing of nations ... is not about Goethe and yeshivas. It is children playing. It is like a mother who would pick up her child and kiss it." And it was this rich, complex, fertile ground of common life that people sought to re-create in the new country, in the little universe bounded by the white cliffs and the river.[8]

The Lafayette School ledger in 1901 marked the shift. Of 217 first-graders, 57 were born in Russia. Names like Rosenberg, Stohosky, Shapiro, Shalit, Schaefer, Kedansky, Stonker, and Shumanson now dominated. Bill Hoffman estimates that of the 650 or so families in the Flats by 1916, perhaps 70 percent were Jewish.[9]

"Texas Street was the street. Like Basil Street in New Orleans? Texas Street." Helen Turner recalls the scene. "You couldn't take a step down the street without saying 'Hi.' Everybody knew what was cooking in everybody's pot. People had a sense of community." Texas Street was called, with a mixture of affection and disgust, "the Texas bullyards." Mudholes would be left after rain. Cows and horses walking down the road made matters worse. They were common in the area.

The Mississippi shaped the calendar and the rhythms of life. Every spring, around Passover, people would prepare for the "high water," when melting waters from northern tributaries often poured the river over its banks and onto the Flats. In Helen's house, all the furniture was made to be disassembled. "Every spring, we'd have to move all our stuff upstairs." Beds, tables, even the stove, which could be attached to a chimney on the second story made for such a purpose. "We'd live there for two or three weeks during high water."

Boards passed from one second-story window to another, like temporary sidewalks across the waters. People went out in boats. Helen remembers going to the store down on State Street by boat, and sometimes landing behind the Lafayette School, which was on a little hill and rarely was reached by the water. When she was a child, her mother would not let her go out on a boat alone. But one time she went with her mother to help a woman catch her drowning chickens. "They were flopping around in the water. I almost fell in." In the years it came, high water would last as long as two or three weeks. "It was horrible," says Helen, screwing up her face. "It was a mess. Fish this big"—she stretches her arms.

Down from Helen's house was the corner with State Street, "crossroads of the Flats" in the years between 1900 and 1940 when the Jewish population gave the distinctive style and character to the community. On one corner lived Burstein, a Jewish butcher. On another was Betty Agranoff, who later taught at Roosevelt Junior High School. Next door to her was a synagogue, and kitty-corner across the street was Makarofsky's fish store. Helen would often stop off at Mr. Makarofsky's to get fish for her mother on the way home from school. Whitefish, carp, and other sorts; he kept them cool in a house in the back. Makarofsky was "very old and venerable," a deeply religious and observant Jew much beloved by his neighbors.

A block away was Gershon Abramovitz's hardware store. It served as an informal town hall. "All the men used to sit around or stand around and settle the woes of the West Side and the world in Gershon's," remembers Helen.

Abramovitz's was a two-story brick building on the corner of Fairfield and State, a block and a half away from Helen's, a block away from Neighborhood House. Upstairs was a rented apartment. The large door in front was set at an angle to both Fairfield and State. Two windows flooded the area with light. On the right of the store were reins, collars, and other gear for horses; on the left, barrels of nails and other housewares. Straight ahead through the entrance was the long counter behind which Gershon Abramovitz sat or stood. A short man with a moustache and, normally, a vest, Gershon had "a full head of hair" and "a beautiful smile," says Helen. "Anything to be settled, people would go to see him. I call him the 'burgermeister' of the West Side."

Gershon Abramovitz spoke and wrote fluently in seven languages. Because of his proficiency, he was the main link between the Flats and Europe. Syrians, German Catholics, Irish as well as Jews would come to him to have letters read or letters written. Gershon's was where one could find out about the latest rumors of political intrigue or war in Europe. Gershon was the man who arranged passage for one's family.

Helen's father had come to the Flats because he knew some-one there, escaping in 1905 from the Russian army, which at that point was conscripting Jewish males. A glazier, or glass cutter, by trade, he found scant work of this sort in St. Paul. But like many Jewish immigrants, he was determined to remain independent. A loan association formed in the community ad-vanced him $25 for a horse, and he became a peddler. He saved his money. When he had enough, he took it to Gershon, who bought a ticket for his wife and her brother. Helen was born three years later. She remembers the grazing land down the street, later Minnetonka playground, where people would take their cows to pasture during the day and come and get them in the evening for milking. And Mr. Goldstein, who would pass each day at 4:30 when she was three. "I used to wait at the window so I could wave."

The area was peopled with peddlers. More than a third of Lafayette first-graders in 1901 listed peddling or similar occu-pations, like "peddler supplier," as their fathers' occupation. Fruit, vegetables, scrap iron, junk, clothes, fish—almost any-thing that could be sold from carts or collected and taken some-where else to be sold became the basis of a new industry. Those who didn't peddle often bought from peddlers; other listings included feed stores, secondhand dealers, grocery stores, and the like.

Like other immigrants, Jews sometimes built their houses from scratch. "Whenever you got yourself a piece of land, you didn't survey. You built yourself a shack," described Ralph Stacker, whose father owned the first kosher delicatessen, "Ce-dars Temple of Lebanon," which sold kosher sausage and "Jew-ish newspapers every day from New York." Stacker continued: "First it was a regular lean-to house with an outhouse, and then later you'd improve the house."[10] Others, like Bill Kuehn, re-member the Jewish houses as always neat, with flowers often growing outside. Plumbing didn't come until the teens, and sometimes it was problematic. "When the toilet was frozen and didn't work," Sylvetsky the plumber would come. "He'd bring the blowtorch. You had no water till he came over and thawed out the pipes." As a boy, Stacker helped his father peddle. Every day after school, he would hitch up the wagon and deliver to the grocery stores. The Stackers would get deliveries in return. "We used to have a loaf of bread delivered to the house fresh from the baker wagon in the neighborhood, horse and wagon. We would get twenty-five tickets for one-pound loaves." Twenty-five tickets cost one dollar.

People speak of the poverty often. Hoffman frequently tells the story of a doctor, "now prominent in the Twin cities," who was so poor he had two left shoes, so his right foot got calluses, which remained all his life. Bill swears that seven doctors called him up to thank him for writing the story of their childhood. Not one was the man he originally had in mind.

The Boonstein family, described by Stacker, lived down near the river. Socialists and left-wing Zionists were common in the Jewish community, and the Workmen's Circle, a Jewish labor and political group, became a major institution in the Flats, often meeting and holding events in Neighborhood House. Apparently Mr. Boonstein was especially radical, so radical, he did not believe in working. His wife, however, of a more practical bent, supported the family with a cow, selling sour cream, cottage cheese, and fresh milk. One especially cold winter, they had to keep the cow inside the house since they didn't have enough money for a barn. Otherwise, it might have frozen. Hoffman, too, has a tale in this vein, of another "prominent doctor" whose boyhood home also housed the family goat.

Alongside poverty and the spirit of independence manifested in peddling and other trades was a strong sense of communal solidarity and mutual aid. "Everybody helped each other out" is a virtually universal memory of the Flats fifty or sixty or seventy years ago. Streets were full of people congregating, talking late into the night. "Charity was done by neighbors themselves," Stacker remembered. "They'd go out and collect; they would bring food into the house or take care of the children because the mother was sick and couldn't do it."[11]

This spirit flowed partly from the Jewish religion. Religion was integral to the life of the Flats. It had peculiarities. Six synagogues existed in the Twenties, one each for the Lithuanians, Latvians, Polish, and Germans, and two for Russians. Traveling between, mediating, collecting modest subsistence from each, was Rabbi Simon, "the head rabbi of the Northwest."

Sometimes Rabbi Simon was on the road, attending to small communities in North or South Dakota or Iowa that needed a religious leader for weddings, bar mitzvahs, and other special events. But he was a fixture on the West Side as well. Several people told me of his "secret talent," piano playing. The "secret" evidently was not carefully guarded. Helen Turner recalls walking up Filmore. "He'd be playing the piano. It was beautiful."

Rabbi Simon evoked great respect. "He was a true scholar, a delightful man, a quiet man of many varied talents," says Bill Hoffman. Apparently he was also a terrible speaker. "You had to sit practically on his lap to hear him" was a common theme. The rabbi was, moreover, quite orthodox. "I'll never forget when he married me he kept looking at my husband," Helen describes. "He wasn't supposed to look at another woman. He could talk to them but not look in close proximity." When the service called for him to speak to Helen, it created problems. "He didn't know where I was, so his wife would be next to him and tell him to move more to the left or right."

I asked Helen why Rabbi Simon was not supposed to look at another woman.

"You know, it was meant to prevent those kinds of feelings."

"Which?"

"You know, lust." She smiled.

On Friday evenings along Texas Street, each house would burn candles in the windows at the beginning of the sabbath. Men would come home from synagogue, dropping off one by one. "It was beautiful to see," Helen says with a sigh. "I could have had a hectic day or whatever, but Friday night it just seemed to subdue you. You knew that the Jewish people lived there. It made you feel so secure."

Jews were the majority in the Flats. But the area remained polyglot. "Across the tracks" to the east of Helen's house was a small Polish community that she called "Polackpatch." Each Sunday as far back as she could remember, a family procession would make their way down St. Lawrence, a block from Texas, and then down State, on their way to mass at St. Michel's. Along State Street, many Syrians had settled. Syrians also tended to be peddlers. Toward the eastern end of Texas Street were remaining French-Canadian families. On the western side of State and farther up into the "hills" were Germans, Irish, a few black families, and, beginning in the teens, growing numbers of Mexicans. Mexican families, sometimes illegally, left the migrant stream that came up each year to work in the sugar-beet fields, hoping to put down roots and become United States citizens.

Along the waterfront lived an assortment of odd and colorful characters: Shine Meyers was there, for instance. In one particularly active year, he was arrested 250 times for making moonshine. (This was a common pastime on the Flats in the twenties. People would hide the illicit liquids under trapdoors in their floors. One major distributor was disguised as a barrel factory. Bill Kuehn, picking up grain along the tracks behind the establishment, could not understand why his chicken wobbled around the room and fell over after eating it. His father explained.) Meyers lived out on McBole Island, a bit of land eventually dredged out that was home for squatters, who built small shacks out of piano crates and other odds and ends from the city dump. A row of houseboaters stretched between Wabasha Bridge and Harriet Island. Fisherman John lived in the area. And across the water was "Little Italy," the dense community of Italians who lived on a slender strip of land below the downtown bluffs of St. Paul. "If we went over to visit our friends on the Lower Levee, in Little Italy, we'd use the High Bridge to get over there," explained Bill Kuehn. "But we never walked back. Every one of them had boats."

The West Side was a poor, tough community. Friction and conflict were parts of life. Helen Turner remembers that every year around Christmas she would be called "Christ killer." Once, she was beaten up. Kuehn's introduction to the West Side came the day after he arrived, at the age of ten. "I was walking back from Zaire's store down on Wabasha, carrying a dollar's groceries for my mother." Bill obviously relishes this story, which he inevitably tells when asked what the Flats were like.

His eyes twinkle and he balls up his fist. "About three blocks from my home, a big guy came up and said, 'What's your name, kid? Put up your dukes!' " Bill, whose father's business troubles had brought them to the West Side after a number of years in a middle-class St. Paul neighborhood, "didn't know what dukes were." He received a quick lesson. "I got a couple of dukes in my face in a hurry. The groceries were all over the sidewalk."

A passerby gave the older boy "a kick in the butt" and then told Kuehn he would need to go down to Neighborhood House "to learn how to fight." When he arrived, he came into a little hall. Miss Currie, the director, was sitting there behind a registry. She looked up. "Well, hello, young man. Where did you get those beautiful shiners?"

Bill replied tearfully, "A kid hit me."

Miss Currie wanted to know the name of the assailant, but Bill "was smart enough even then to know if I told I would get creamed." At any rate, when she found out where Bill lived, she knew who the boy must be. She sent Bill down to the gym with a note for the coaches, Ben Stoddard or Leroy Jesme, that said simply, "This boy needs instruction in self-defense."

By the end of the first week, after his fifth fight, Bill had begun to hit back. "Stoddard told me, 'You're probably going to have to fight with every kid in the neighborhood.' One by one it was true." Boxing, indeed, was a major sport. Golden Gloves and Diamond Belt League contenders were local heroes. One fight at Neighborhood House is reported to have attracted 1,200 fans. "It was like a United Nations meeting," Kuehn remembers.

What was remarkable about the community was not the prejudice and violence—common enough, after all, in communities with far less heterogeneity—but the bonds that formed and endured across them. Helen's "best friend" turned out to be the girl who had beaten her up after calling her "Christ killer." Bill, of German background, found his strongest lifelong friends among Jews, Irish Catholics, Lebanese, and Mexican Americans. Rabbi Simon and Father John, the priest at St. Michel's, could be seen every Sunday afternoon walking together; and at one point of financial crisis, Simon made a highly successful plea in every synagogue for help to "our friend Father John and his church." "I consider myself so doggone lucky," says Bill. "I had friends in every nationality. You'd go over to a Lebanese home and you'd have kivi. You'd go to a Mexican home and have enchiladas. I had Italian friends. One's father was the popcorn man. We got to know different ethnic ways of communicating."

Thus the question remains: How did such diverse peoples find common ties, across their differences?

Common values had to be given places for articulation and discovery, for they were not immediately identifiable either from the language of other ethnic groups or from the dominant values of the broader society. Indeed, in many ways common American themes of individual success, competition, material acquisition and consumption tended to divide and isolate. As early as 1633 John Winthrop had warned that avarice would destroy community, turning neighborliness into bombast: "If our hearts shall turn away so that we will not obey, but shall be seduced and worship the gods of pleasure and profits and serve them, we shall surely perish out of the good land." Even during the Revolutionary period, when the original intensity of communal life—and jeremiads against profit-seeking—had greatly weakened, the dominant philosophy was markedly skeptical of anything that might further erode community. As conservative a figure as John Adams worried greatly about such matters as the new nation progressed. In 1819, writing to Thomas Jefferson, he entreated, "Will you tell me how to prevent riches from becoming the effects of . . . industry? Will you tell me how to prevent luxury from producing effeminacy, intoxication, extravagance, vice and folly?"[12]

In the republican ideology of the nation's founders, individual independence grounded in small-scale property or artisanal skills was to be highly prized, but private property was never seen as an end in itself. Liberty allowed participation in the public life of the self-governing community, or commonwealth. Indeed, such participation was the understanding of "virtue" in republicanism. Great extremes of wealth or the speculative sale of property, like the squandering of the means of one's independence, were seen in the most unfavorable light because of the clear danger that the community would be eroded.

Historian Rowland Berthoff has pointed out that by the mid–nineteenth century, original notions of property and virtue had been turned upside down. The ideal citizen was now the free-enterpriser: Business "character" replaced civic virtue and dedication to the common good; Horatio Alger, instead of figures from the Bible and American Revolutionary heroes, had become the model for (male) children to emulate. Yet the original communal vision retained a subterranean power in American culture precisely because the earlier commonwealth conception more nearly fit the aspirations of different immigrant peoples arriving on these shores.

America's original dream of rough communal equality, sustained by an independent citizenry, was peasant in origin. And it was nourished and reinvigorated by wave after wave of ethnic groups hoping to re-create communities of self-sufficient and self-governing freeholders. Such aspirations fit common patterns in the areas immigrants came from. Typically, immigrants were drawn from "middle peasant" ranks. Such families had worked mainly for themselves, handing over only a small portion of their produce to the nobility. They had considerable experience in a range of cooperative activities, such as open plowing and harvesting. Their land, by custom and sometimes law, was handed down over generations, with considerable security of tenure. With others of similar rank—the great bulk of male adults in the typical village—they had had considerable practice in rough self-government concerning day-to-day civic affairs. For instance, though the legal government of the English village rested firmly with the gentry and manorial court, as far back as the Middle Ages, peasants would meet in the local church to decide for themselves such matters as crops, dates of harvest, numbers of animals allowed on the common pastures, lookouts in the meadow, and regulations for hedges, common footpaths, boundaries, and so forth.

Thus, immigrants from a great diversity of cultural backgrounds often had similar dreams and aspirations. The values of the "commonwealth" included hard work, rough equality, self-government, independence, frugality, bound by a deep, strong sense of life in common, sustained by familial ties and religious beliefs. These values could be found, as well, among immigrants from cities, retaining older rural traditions and embodying their hopes in a wealth of craft, fraternal, sororal, and mutual aid societies.[13]

Such themes are strikingly evident in interviews and stories from West Siders of different ethnic backgrounds. Ralph Stacker, for instance, spoke of the community spirit he saw in all the different groups. "For the Jews, you had to help. You are your brother's keeper. Whatever you had, you had to share." But other groups had similar values in his view. "The Catholics, the Italians down along the river, they helped themselves." And such mutuality of values created the glue of the community. "Nobody on the West Side—Irish, Germans, Mexicans—nobody closed the house. Nobody had any keys. People could walk on the streets at three or four in the morning with no people around. Nobody would bother you, molest you, make a dirty remark."[14]

There is a certain roseate edge to such memories, undoubtedly. Yet for a period of some fifty years or so—from something like 1890 to 1940—a "commonwealth" of sorts existed in the West Side Flats area, weaving together different groups in ways that were remarkable, allowing people to discover what values they shared across all the differences of culture and history.

The isolation of the Flats contributed to the sense of commonality. Bounded on three sides by a river and to the south by the West Side Hills, a mainly working-class community with which there was more or less peaceful coexistence, the definitions of the Flats were clear and unmistakable. But they were also more than geographic. The rest of St. Paul "looked down" from loftier heights—in both physical and social terms—at the low-lying area across the river. And it quickly turned away. George Restler, the prominent artist who grew up on the West Side, once did a series of etchings of common people and scenes from his neighborhood. It showed in Europe to enthusiastic reviews; but it was not displayed in St. Paul until the 1970s.

Moreover, people on the West Side roughly shared common economic circumstances—"We were all in the same boat" is a common observation. More-affluent Jewish immigrants settled in the Fourteenth Street area of St. Paul, and there continued to be sharp rivalry between the two neighborhoods for half a century. And for Jews and other immigrants, the spring flooding and the social stigma attached to terms like the "Flat Rats," applied to residents of the West Side by other parts of the city, combined to produce powerful incentives to move at least to the West Side Hills, as soon as a family acquired the means to do so. Those remaining tended overwhelmingly to be poor. And most of the poor shared a further, wrenching commonality: They had been separated from their previous homelands and had come to a strange country where few understood their ways.

With all of these points in common, however, the most important factor bringing different groups of people together, according to everyone I interviewed, was Neighborhood House. It was Neighborhood House that created something more than coexistence—that allowed sustaining bonds to form among peoples of different races, religions, and cultures. Neighborhood House was called "the center of the community," or simply "the meeting ground."

Neighborhood House opened its doors in 1897, the inspiration of Rabbi Isaac Rypins and women from Mt. Zion temple who were zealously concerned that the flood of poorer Jewish refugees from the pogroms would learn American customs and the English language. The settlement drew from similar models around the country, like Hull House in Chicago, directed by Jane Addams, and Henry Street in New York. True to these precedents, the house decided not to limit itself to a Jewish population. In 1903, Neighborhood House reorganized on a nonsectarian basis and issued a stirring mission statement, pledging "to serve the residents of the 'flats' through helping the individual, through fostering family and neighborly friendliness, and through cultivating human relationships across the lines of race and language, party and creed."

"American identity is like marriage; ethnicity is like ancestry," argued Werner Solors, making a distinction between voluntary "allegiance" to the nation and shared cultural and familial heritages. Yet for most immigrants arriving in the United States in the early years of the twentieth century, the expectation was that they would trade the latter for the former. Israel Zangfield, who authored the play *The Melting Pot,* might seek to include "all races" (including "black and yellow") in his homogenized new race. But public policy and dominant cultural attitudes were more direct. Everyone was supposed to become like white, English Protestants. One survey of early twentieth-century schoolbooks found negative stereotypes used to portray every ethnic group except the English, Germans, and Scandinavians—and the imagery of the Germans changed in World War I. Dirty, shiftless, often smelly, dull if not backward, given to lawlessness, conniving, and, of course, indolence—such were the portrayals that immigrants arriving in St. Paul, like those in other places, had to confront and somehow live with and struggle against.

In such a context, Neighborhood House was a rare enclave. It taught English, gave regular "citizenship classes"—a kind of basic literacy course in American government and law—and held sessions on cooking, sewing, health care, and other subjects. And it also encouraged the diverse cultures of the neighborhood to come to expression.[15]

"Neighborhood House was the nucleus of the whole community," explained Mat Moreno. Mat is a workingman, born in the Flats in 1924 into one of the earliest Mexican families. He speaks carefully, conveying the impression that his thoughts are crafted and dignified, like his work. He describes the clubs of Mexican men that met in Neighborhood House. "Anahuac Society, an Indian name. It was a business society of the elders. If there was some problem, these gentlemen would gather." A Mothers Club was organized by Mexican women; the Aztec Club sponsored dances and other social gatherings. On the fifth of May, a parade would gather outside to celebrate the old Mexican defeat of the French in 1862. At Christmas, Anahuac held a pageant, with costumes and presents for children whose parents couldn't afford them. "We had Easter parties, summer camp, classes to speak English, mothers' clubs, cooking classes, exercise classes." Mat strings the programs together with enthusiasm. "The gym had a beautiful program of recreation. Volleyball, basketball. If there was a dance on the West Side, Neighborhood House was where it was held. You'd have to see it to appreciate it. We were people who came from every country, looking for identity."

Miss Currie came as director in 1918, followed shortly by Miss Baker. Helen Turner went to nursery school in the first Neighborhood House, at 153 Robertson. The new one opened in 1923. "I remember when I first walked into the new Neighborhood House. There was a double door. You felt a feeling of warmth. You were just enveloped. I don't know how to describe it." This is an image Helen uses all the time describing Neighborhood House—"a feeling of warmth"—but she struggles to put it into words. Rooms in the new, four-story building had fireplaces. Stairs from the first to the second story were large, black, hardwood. An elegant entrance opening onto Robertson was never used and the entryway was eventually converted into an office. Everyone filed in the side door.

Upstairs, classes were held; in 1928 a large gym was added. On the third and fourth floors were apartments for part-time instructors or interns from the University of Minnesota, and transients who had no place else to go.

Miss Currie communicated the spirit of the place: warmth and toughness. She was a ferocious disciplinarian, but occasionally she would bend.

"Helen was one of the first women's rights fighters," Bill Kuehn says with admiration. Bill, retired after years as a successful engineer and surveyor, defers a bit to Helen on matters of West Side history. He calls her "Miss Old West Side." Helen begins the story.

"The girls basketball team would practice on Tuesdays and Thursdays for one hour. The boys would practice every other day. So one Thursday I came up and said, 'Get off the court. It's our turn.' We had a tournament coming up. Nothing happened, so I went over to Miss Currie and told her. She said, 'They have to practice.' I said, 'They have every other day of the week to practice and we have a tournament coming up.' She said, 'I say they're going to play.' And I said, 'Why you dirty . . . ' "

Bill looks stunned. "You said that to Miss Currie!"

Helen continues. "Miss Currie looked at me and said, 'You get out of this Neighborhood House right now and don't come back!'

"Well, I went. I was boiling mad. But what was I going to do? Neighborhood House was my life. I was going crazy. But I was a stubborn girl and I was right."

Helen shakes her head with the memory. "Normally, I'm very easygoing," she says, in obvious violation of every fact. "Some of the girls got together and talked to Miss Currie. Meanwhile, I would walk past and turn my head the other way. It hurt too much." Finally, a week before the tournament, Helen got a note. It said, "Helen, I want you to come back to the Neighborhood House. I want you to play basketball, but you must promise not to use bad language." Helen ran there as fast as she could. Miss Currie never said a word.

"But from then on, we got our turn every time," Helen concludes.

Bill adds, "She knew you were right. She always had a good sense of justice."

The teens, twenties, and thirties were the heyday of the Flats. Sometimes the smell from the dump up State Street would mingle with the odors of the slaughterhouses farther south. Derelicts would pass through. Smaller roads like Texas and Water Streets were never paved. But for all the mud and smells and poverty, people remarked again and again on the beauty, the flowers, the Indian mounds across the way (where one could see lights at dusk—signs of the ghosts, children would be told in stories). The spot for watching the bluffs was a forest where Holman Field airport was built in the late twenties. A small spring fed a pond. A tree stump "as big as a large table" served for picnics. "One night at dusk we had a powwow," Helen recalls. "Somebody played the guitar as the moon came up. We had a fire nearby. I stood on the tree stump and sang Indian love songs and my voice echoed back against the bluffs."

During years of good harvest, West Siders could help with

crops in August and September. A few farms remained on the
Flats themselves, like Remackel's on part of the land where
Holman Field is today. Remackel's had a number of cows and
goats, and large vegetable crops. Just down Robert Street in the
Hills area were farms belonging to the Oakdales, Rupps, Mosi-
ers, and Stassens, the family that produced a Minnesota governor and perennial presidential candidate. Harold Stassen was a
classmate of Bill Kuehn's at Humboldt High. St. Michel's divided, forming St. Matthew's parish for the German population,
Our Lady of Guadalupe for Mexicans. During the depression
years when many West Siders were unemployed, New Deal
programs like the WPA, CWA, and NYA and surplus commod-
ity food were run out of Neighborhood House, along with
health clinics, nurseries, and other services.

But the community was changing. Through the thirties, the
Jewish population started to leave in growing numbers. Hoffman can remember as a child walking down Texas and realizing
he would never be as happy in any other neighborhood. But the
lure of education and success was powerful. "Learning was the
most important thing," Helen recounts. "Above everything.
You had to learn. Mothers and Fathers would save nickels and
dimes just to send the kids to school." Among Christian families,
success was sometimes defined in somewhat different terms,
but similarly it often led elsewhere. "We all read Horatio Alger
books," Bill remembers. "Sink or swim, do or die, make it." Bill
is dedicated to such principles. His admiration for the businessmen of the community "who served as role models" and provided jobs—including one for his partially disabled father—is
palpable. As is often the case, conservative instincts in a man
like Kuehn also nourish a tenacious commitment to the history
of community. But Bill is not unaware of the irony. "This is a
piece of history that in a way was stolen from us by progress,"
he remarks ruefully, thinking of the destruction of the Flats to
make way for the industrial park. The park symbolized an emp-
tying that had begun long before.

In my travels, I heard an American fable. It seems that a
doughty and determined family of immigrants, seared by ex-

periences in the old country, arrived in New York some years ago. Rather than mingling with others from their homeland, they wanted nothing to do with their past. "Never look back" was the family motto. So they moved across the country, lingering here and there for a few years, then becoming restless and moving on. Again and again this occurred. When there would be sadness or reluctance about leaving a place, they would remember their family saying: "Always look ahead, never behind."

Finally, however, they arrived in California. Standing on the beach, gazing into the Pacific, they realized that their single-minded pursuit was over. And at last they turned around to see where they had come from.

Remembering, as Jackson Lears has observed, can be a subversive activity in modern society, whatever the particular economic or political arrangement. From the vantage point of capitalists or socialists, technocrats, commissars, or corporate managers, the past is a hindrance to rational planning and calculation. And America, in a sense, is the nation of the uprooted. We are after all the society of immigrants, of people who have escaped from the Old World or have been torn violently from Africa and other lands. For most of our history, this understanding of America as new and modern, divorced from older ties, has been celebrated in the mainstream and by protesters against the mainstream. The sixties, it was said, were the "Age of Aquarius" and the "counterculture." In such terms, freedom meant an embrace of the novel and the future, *Easy Rider,* and Jack Kerouac novels.[16]

Yet even in the 1960s, such images of our destiny began to dissolve. In part, challenges to the notion of freedom as rootlessness came from among blacks, women, Hispanics, and others who, dissenting against one-sided portraits of American history, unearthed stories not normally included in the standard textbook. The popularity of the TV series "Roots" was itself a spectacular expression of widespread public sympathy with the black quest for a recovery of historical and cultural identity. The search for a new rootedness was also visible in the general rise of ethnic group consciousness; in the popularity of movies like *The Deer Hunter* or the novels of James Michener. And it was apparent in the neighborhood renaissance, detailed by studies like that of the National Commission on Neighborhoods, released in 1979. Neighborhood activism represented, in the words of National People's Action leader Gale Cincotta, a challenge "to the insidious throwaway mentality afflicting America which classifies older people, older homes and old neighborhoods as expendable—like pop bottles and Kleenex."[17]

Finally, the importance of roots to Americans in a time of flux and growing uncertainty was strikingly evident in the figures on religious commitment and involvement. Generations of scholarly predictions that Americans would eventually lose interest in religious institutions and religious values had proved simply false. Gallup surveys in 1982 found that 76 percent of the population expressed the view that they would like "religion [to] play a larger part in American society." Moreover, such public attitudes gave little support to a "conservative philosophy" based on material acquisition or simple allegiance to the status quo. Seventy-one percent simultaneously believed that there should be less emphasis on money in our culture. A survey of churchgoers in Minnesota discovered that nearly two-thirds believed religious institutions have an obligation to speak out on issues like the arms race and nuclear power. Attendance at churches and synagogues, after declining from record highs in the 1950s, had in fact increased very slightly from 1972 to 1982, when 41 percent of the population said they attended a religious congregation in a typical week. As if to certify such trends' endurance, *Newsweek* magazine organized its end-of-the-year issue in 1982 around the theme "The Bible in America: How One Book Unites Us, Divides Us, and Still Defines Us."[18]

Broad social trends take on reality in the lives of individuals and communities. During the 1980s, amid all the talk of high tech and the coming "information society," a myriad of such stories could be found.

Susan Cobin is a curriculum specialist at Talmud Torah School in St. Paul, where children—including the descendants of many Jews who once lived on the Flats—learn about their Jewish heritage and its values. Susan, a thin woman in her late thirties, wore slacks the day I interviewed her. Her glasses had thin frames and her hair was short. The effect was a kind of bookish intensity, softened with warm informality. Around the walls of her office were stacks of books, scenes from around the world, a Jewish calendar, a world map. I could feel the passion when Susan talked about "a world that doesn't nurture children." It grows from her own long history of political activism, and her family's Jewish heritage. But it was also shaped by a long, individual odyssey.

Susan Cobin grew up in Springfield, Illinois, a conservative Republican area. She felt different in a number of ways. At an early age, Susan had polio, and she wore braces in school. Her family were Democrats—Susan remembers being almost the only child she knew who was for Stevenson in the presidential election of 1952. She always identified with the Jewish holidays, especially with Passover, which they celebrated each year in her grandparents' home in Chicago. And she felt a strong attraction to the American Revolution—from an early age, she had loved the writings of Thomas Jefferson. All these things, perhaps, combined to create a rebellious spirit. In grade school she refused to say the Lord's Prayer. "It seemed to me I shouldn't have to say it." And she refused to participate in school events held in clubs that discriminated against Jews. There was a good deal of discrimination in her town, but it seemed to her that it did not make the Jewish community more closely knit. Rather "it created more of a need to assimilate." Thus her behavior found little support from anyone. "People were appalled," she remembers.

Like many of her generation, Susan became politically active in high school and college, getting involved in civil rights, protesting the Vietnam War. Through her activism, she also became increasingly angry at what she felt was the hypocrisy and conformity in the Jewish community. "It seemed to me that belonging to a synagogue meant watering the flowers and worrying about what you wore on the sabbath. I couldn't bear it."

In 1969, she and her husband, David, moved to Berkeley, on
Bastille Day, July 14, anniversary of the French Revolution, she
recalls. That day "There was a demonstration on Telegraph
Avenue, with tear gas and troops standing on corners with
bayonets." By that time both were far removed from active
involvement with any religious community. "There were a lot
of Jews we knew, but none practicing Judaism. People we knew
were making a religion of their nonreligion."

Susan taught for several years, becoming disillusioned with
the free-school movement in Berkeley. ("They used to tell me
that I was laying my trip on these kids. All I could answer was
that if you don't want me to lay my trip on these kids, I shouldn't
be here. For strictly social interaction, I'd rather be with my
peers.") She was also dismayed by the normal school system,
which she believed gave poor and blue-collar children little
feeling of their self-worth or accomplishment. As an alternative
to both, she opened a prevocational school, which taught math,
reading, vocational skills, and other subjects as the foundation
of creating self-confidence among students.

Then their own lives changed. "I had a baby. It never occurred to me that I would be so awestruck by a new life."
Having a child transformed their perceptions of the world
around them. "Before Seth, we never noticed our neighborhood much. But suddenly it became important to think about
playgrounds, the neighborhood school, the kind of rental property in the area." It also changed their attitudes about the future. "We started to think about leaving Berkeley. In Berkeley
there was a deep confusion about what it means to be a free
person, a confusion between freedom and license."

Finally, they moved back to the Twin Cities area in Minnesota, where Susan's mother's family had come from many
years before. And they rethought their relationship to their
heritage as well. "We began to think about how our children
will learn about values, and what we wanted them to learn."
With a friend, she put ads in the paper inviting other people to
help them create a community to explore "how to be Jews in
the 1980s." The group met for discussion, celebration on the

sabbath, and Hebrew lessons for their children. Susan also eventually joined a synagogue where she found support for her concerns about social justice and action.

Through this process, she came to feel they were part of what she calls "a chain." "I was really touched at seeing my nephews have their bar mitzvahs before the Ark, just as their father had and my father had." She wanted the same for both their children, a boy and a girl. The chain had formed "over a long period of time. I didn't want to be the one to break it."

Memory erodes as individuals leave behind their communities. And it is regained only as people rebuild them. Indeed, shared memories are central to community, defining its language, symbols, textures, and occasions. Susan Cobin, whose story began in a Jewish heritage, could only return through some communal effort to explore "how to be Jews in the 1980s." Her story has found many parallels through the early 1980s in America, as people have sought to weave out of the fragments of their lives and relations new common ground and continuities. In American neighborhoods like the West Side, such a process often began first in conflict.

As in other cities across the country, the early 1970s in St. Paul witnessed a proliferation of community organizations, neighborhood associations, cooperatives, and community-development efforts. Coalitions began to tie areas together across geographic and cultural boundaries and to create a sense of "neighborhood power" for the first time. "I felt it was very important to see what was going on and to try to have some effect on it," explained Kathy Vadnais, active in a coalition of St. Paul neighborhoods formed to fight a section of Interstate Highway 35.

On the West Side in 1971, a dramatic campaign for a new high school to replace the decrepit old Humboldt building brought together diverse elements of the community.[19] Ralph Brown, at that time a teacher in a Catholic school, remembers how surprised central administration officials seemed when they arrived at a community meeting called to voice neighborhood concerns. "The Italians, Germans, Poles were there. We had a conservative state legislator and his Democratic Farmer Labor party opponent, the head of the young Republicans, and the head of the Brown Berets. We had pulled buses up in front of Humboldt and got kids to come, too."

With such a coalition, the community took charge of one of the school planning districts, designed to help make long-range blueprints for education in St. Paul. School officials, originally opposed to a new high school, gave formal endorsement but declined to include money for the project in a bond bill they were offering before city voters. "We indirectly let it be known that if they put up the bond issue without our schools, we wouldn't support it," explains Brown. Finally, both sides agreed on a formula, and the neighborhood helped lead a successful effort to pass the measure.

At one point, the West Side called for a parade in downtown St. Paul in support of the bond issue. City officials were flabbergasted. "They didn't know what to make of it," says Brown. West Siders dressed in clown suits wove among the aisles of downtown stores, passing out invitations to the parade. They lined up school bands to play from all over the city. And when the huge crowd began marching across Wabasha Bridge into the heart of downtown, a contingent of militant young Mexicans, named the Brown Berets, were in front. The iconoclasm and color all seemed somehow to suit the West Side image. But it proved successful. "People had always felt we didn't have power," Brown observes. "For the first time, we were taking some power. I could see people were really getting excited."

A year later, many West Siders active in the school campaign joined in the formation of a citywide alliance of neighborhoods, religious congregations, small businesses, unions, and others, called the Organization for a Better St. Paul. The organization sought to get more mortgage money for neighborhoods from city lending institutions. It also backed local areas in particular issues. Thus when the West Siders read about plans for a new development in their community—a ski slope to be built along part of the bluffs—they turned to the alliance for help. Jim Scheibel, then a community organizer working with the Organization for a Better St. Paul, had been born on the West Side and recalled their approach: "We asked why our community wasn't involved in the decisions."

With memories of the Flats' destruction still poignant, the community gained further cohesion and confidence when they were able to block the development. Through such efforts, moreover, participants often acquired new skills and a sense of mutual accountability. "You would go around the table and ask each person how many people they could get out to the demonstration," explains Mary Crossen, vice-chair of the Organization for a Better St. Paul from the West Side. "It would be terrifying, but an incredible challenge, too." She found the experience a rare opportunity to learn in a constructive way. "If you didn't do what you said, people wouldn't put you down. Everybody would analyze what mistakes you had made and how you could do better the next time. It was very supportive criticism."

Ralph Brown, Mary Crossen, Jim Scheibel, and others decided to form an ongoing community group on the West Side to continue to seek a voice for the area in city affairs. In the fall of 1973, the West Side Citizens Organization (WESCO) officially began. The same year, they also expanded a newsletter from Neighborhood House into a regular newspaper for the entire community. They called it the *West Side Voice*. "We wanted to let people know this would be West Siders speaking with one voice, and that we had a voice now," says Scheibel. "It was a way of involving people and celebrating our neighborhood."

The victories on issues like the high school and the ski slope fed a new neighborhood élan. In the *Voice*'s review of its first year in 1973, the paper reflected on such successes and noted a new spirit of grass-roots democracy at work in the community: "Democracy works only if citizens take the initiative to know one another and together plan the future," read the editorial. "Democracy gives us all responsibility."[20]

Through the 1970s, community groups like WESCO commonly formed during battles against unresponsive bureaucracies or large economic interests. But the hallmark of the thousands of such efforts that have spread through neighborhoods in recent years has not primarily been criticism. Rather, their main thrust as they evolved has been positive, a revival of the old American traditions of community involvement and self-help once embodied in such practices as barn raisings and quilting bees. In the Bronx and on Manhattan's Lower East Side, in the barrios of East Los Angeles and the West Side of St. Paul, across the country in communities once labeled "garbage dumps" by city administrators, stirrings of a positive vision have become visible. Ron Shiffman of the Pratt Institute calls it "the same pioneering spirit that built so many communities across the country" in American history. Along with the community spirit has come a remembering.[21]

Gary Brueggerman, St. Paul's unofficial neighborhood historian, began his research into the city's neighborhoods in 1974. "At that time, city history was pretty elite," he remembers. "It would focus on the wealthy and on the mansions along Summit Avenue." But Gary had grown up in a working-class community, West Seventh Street, not far from the West Side, and he felt most drawn to what he calls "the underside of city history" —neighborhoods and institutions where common people lived and worked.

For several years, Brueggerman did a great deal of work on his own, giving a course here and there, working on a neighborhood-history calendar for West Seventh. But in 1976 or 1977, he noticed a dramatic increase of interest in such subjects. The Minnesota Historical Society's reading rooms, in the early Seventies used only by a scattering of scholars, suddenly filled up. "After 'Roots,' the television show, I think people began digging into family histories and, with them, neighborhood histories," Brueggerman says. Wherever he went, he found a new eagerness to hear about the past. In more professional and middle-class areas, he noticed that "everyone would be into neighborhood history." In working-class areas, people often had sharply negative images of history, learned from unpleasant experiences in school, but "when they found out it was concerned with the churches and blacksmiths and local businesses and bars in their own areas and lives, they became excited, too." Brueggerman felt he was part of some general trend. "I would be doing a guided tour or giving a speech and it would suddenly occur to me that this was part of something larger." America, he speculates, has always looked only to the future. He hopes people are now beginning to think about the past as well, once again.

The West Side, with what Bill Kuehn calls its "special magnetism in the soil," helped lead the interest in neighborhood history. The *Voice* found that its most popular feature was a regular column by Kuehn entitled "The West Side Story," detailing characters and stories from the old days. St. Paul's United Jewish Fund and Council sponsored an oral history project on St. Paul Jewry, entitled "A Dialogue with Our Past," which focused on the West Side, and developed a slide show that toured widely. WESCO itself developed a growing interest in historical themes. Each year it sponsored "West Side Pride Day," bringing together new and former residents of the community to talk about their experiences and memories. Many who had long departed from the area—and had been embarrassed to let anyone know they were once "Flat Rats"—showed up at such events. The organization initiated an annual "Riverfront Day" in the summer, celebrating the heritage of the river, and a "Winter Carnival Day" in January. And they laid plans for the West Side History Conference.

"A proud community celebrates its being," read the grant proposal for funding for the event. Ralph Brown, who now directs Baker Community Center—a division of Neighborhood House—helped write the proposal. He has thought a good deal about the meaning of history to a community like the West Side. "Just as individuals can be depressed and down, so can communities," Brown believes. Organizing around issues—from the early fights for a new school to more recent issues like support for local businesses, more housing, the creation of a park, food cooperatives, and other efforts—is essential to gaining some optimism and a sense of control. But Brown is convinced that an honest look at neighborhood history builds the sort of roots that hold a community together. "We need to rekindle a sense of pride in community. You can get a false pride out of a false history, but the real story is more interesting in the long run anyway. Even when you look at the warts in a community's history, you come out with a sense of pride."

Thus in communities like the West Side, recovery of a connection to the past has become inextricably linked to the effort to deal with the future. Gary Brueggerman, deeply engaged by the histories of St. Paul neighborhoods, worries that the enthusiasm for community history might prove a passing fad: "I would hate to go back to the fifties, when people didn't care." But the final test may well be Brown's: whether the stories of communities, and of broader geographic areas, are told "warts and all" or whether they are romanticized and nostalgic. In turn such authenticity depends in large measure on who participates in the telling and what values inform the narrative. Communities across the nation struggle with such issues as the 1980s progress, often with different outcomes.

3

Alternatives

At the heart of American communities, there is a restlessness that begets change. "We are all a little wild here with numberless projects of social reform," wrote Ralph Waldo Emerson to Carlyle in England in 1840. "Not a reading man but has a draft of a new community in his waistcoat pocket." The first half of the nineteenth century indeed saw an explosion of communitarian experiments across the land. Like Puritans before them, their founders fully anticipated that their efforts would inspire again a world grown corrupt and ossified by the weight of custom. A few, like Harmony and Amana, lasted nearly a century. Here and there, ventures such as Joseph Smith's Church of the Latter-day Saints, grown to the modern Mormons, began large movements. Amana's legacy remains in the refrigerator by that name.

A hundred and thirty years after Emerson's thought, young partisans of another New Age, seeking to escape "straight society" and create alternatives, flooded woods and farmlands. "Oceana may not be perfect, but it's sure an improvement over the way they live out there," remarked one member of a rural commune in Maryland. Or as one of his co-workers put it, "We've turned into a gouging society. Nothing but taxes, high prices, and red tape. Not me! You want freedom, you'll find it here at Oceana, not out there!"[1]

Something like 2,000 communes, it is estimated, were established in a single year in the early 1970s. Older alternative living communities such as Koinonia, an interracial Christian farm in southwest Georgia that had been founded in 1942, experienced rapid growth. "Everything was booming when we came," recalled Don Mosley, who with his wife Carolyn decided to investigate when they returned from the Peace Corps. Clarence Jordan, who had inspired and guided Koinonia for an often troubled quarter-century, had died just months before. But Millard Fuller, who followed him as director, was far from discouraged. "He had tremendous energy," Mosley continued. "He would travel around the country speaking, telling everybody he met they should come down and see for themselves." From a low point of four adults in 1968, the community expanded to thirty-five at the beginning of 1972. Hundreds more came to help for periods of time on the farm's diverse enterprises. "The idea was to create a partnership between poor people in the area, who had experience, and middle-class people with expertise," Mosley explained. "When we got there, everybody was talking about the concept of a new partnership, not charity but a two-way process. They were grand visions. Millard imagined a hundred thousand houses and all sorts of other Christian industries."

Such exuberance, as foreign observers have often noted, seems distinctively American. This is the land of the second chance and the fresh start. More than two centuries ago the Frenchman Crèvecoeur defined an American as "he . . . who, leaving behind him all his ancient prejudices and manners, receives new ones from the new mode of life he has embraced, the new government he obeys, and the new rank he holds."

Yet as generations of pioneers in new covenants have discovered to their frequent despair, a spirit endowed with zeal and freedom is not enough for success. Those new communities that endured, like Harmony and Amana, were rare exceptions in the nineteenth century; most ended within a few months. The utopian expressions of the 1960s' counterculture proved in the main even more transient. No more than 1 percent of communes lasted as long as six months. Most quickly fell prey to bitter internal division, economic hardship, or hostile reactions from surrounding populations.

Despite its longer history, Koinonia also experienced a crisis in the early 1970s. "It was much more difficult to carry through the projects than to conceive them," as Mosley put it. "Most businesses flopped within a year." Other problems plagued the farm. In the fifties and early sixties, internal divisions over such issues as the responsibilities of individual families to the whole had been exacerbated by external pressures. In southwest Georgia in those years, an interracial community was seen as an alien intruder whose presence could have dangerous consequences for towns like nearby Americus. "The people have had it up to here," said one local sheriff, voicing widespread sentiment after a night of violence against Koinonia. "We get reports of whites and Negroes strolling down the streets together in Americus. One report said a white girl and two Negro boys walked down the street all eating popcorn out of the same bag."[2]

Courageous witness against southern bigotry was one thing—and Koinonia acquired a national reputation during those tumultuous years in the South as a center for interracial justice. But ten years later, when surrounding whites had finally come to view the farm with something like grudging acceptance, a new wave of young people reopened old wounds. "Clarence Jordan was a prophet," said Mosley, "but he had a sense of humor that kept the farm from being shut down completely. The first years we were there, though, the phrase *cutting edge* got worn out quickly. People who had arrived only a few weeks before had far too great a readiness to assume the role of being prophetic. Any incident in the area of someone from the farm being slighted would get trumpeted as part of the prophecy."

Despite difficulties, that idealism which creates new American communities sometimes adapts and endures as well. Mosley himself seems somehow to embody the sort of contradictory qualities necessary.

Bald, in his forties, with a thin moustache, Don Mosley when I first met him struck me as someone who could easily be taken for an engineer or agricultural expert just back from some Peace Corps project. We talked at the end of a hot summer's day in Jubilee Partners, a community he helped to establish near Comer, Georgia, sitting on the porch of Jubilee's meeting hall, Koinonia House, looking over the fields.

Don's practical bent surfaces right away in conversation. He tells about working as an engineer in his father's business, and he describes with evident competence the experiments he conducted over the years at Koinonia in appropriate technology, machines designed to be more respectful of the earth and its resources. Indeed one can see the fruits of such efforts all around Jubilee. Sheds, garden structures, and buildings are put together out of cheap, easily obtained pine boards, Sheetrock, plywood, and chicken wire. All are constructed with an eye to solar energy and conservation techniques. "Koinonia became famous for appropriate technology," Mosley remarks. "One year we had five thousand visitors come by, mostly because of our roofing techniques, our solar collectors, and our experiments with cement."

Mosley, however, joins handcraft to other commitments. He was most powerfully attracted to the idea of a Christian service community in Koinonia, despite the problems. "I liked the experiments because of my engineering background," Mosley explains. "But I got sick of talking about chicken wire. What I really wanted to talk about was the kingdom of God."

I ask him what he means. He explains.

His father, child of a poor Texas family, became what is known as a "self-made man." "He was a benign employer, but if you didn't do what he told you as an employee, he booted you out the door," says Don. When Mosley became an adult, his father expected him to take over the increasingly successful family business. But his interests took him instead farther and farther away.

Don had mixed mathematics and history as an undergraduate in college, learning engineering on the side. In graduate school he majored in anthropology. Finally, instead of staying with the firm, he took his engineering skills to Malaysia as a Peace Corps volunteer. He returned for a time, met Carolyn, got married. But both were unhappy at the prospect of settling into a conventional life-style. In the late sixties, Don and Carolyn went back into the Peace Corps, this time to Korea. "In a way we were postponing decisions. We didn't know what we were going to do with our lives."

While they were in Korea, a friend who worked for IBM began sending Don tape recordings of sermons preached by Clarence Jordan. Mosley was fascinated by "this brilliant, unorthodox theologian." He had never before heard such a version of the gospel.

"Tall, high hipped, hands jammed into blue-jean pockets, floppy straw hat shading a grin, dusty from the peanut rows, greasy from the tractor shop, bespectacled from persistent study, the man was full of the unexpected," wrote Clarence Jordan's biographer, Dallas Lee, in the book *The Cotton Patch Evidence.* Jordan had grown up in Talbotton, a little town in south Georgia. He spoke with the drawl and idiom of the Deep South and the humor of a "good ole boy" telling the latest joke from the store down at the crossroads. But his message, schooled as it was by a graduate degree in Greek New Testament, scarcely comforted white southerners. "Most Christians cannot accept that Jesus was plain, sweaty, down-to-earth flesh," said Jordan. "We create in our minds an image of him as a superbeing and thus safely remove him from our present experience. Preachers by the dozens who vehemently affirm his deity shamelessly deny his humanity if he is black and poor."

In Jordan's depiction, Jesus's earthiness was radically different from ascetic self-denial. "Jesus loved the feast," as Jordan put it. "He praised the women who poured expensive perfume on his feet and he fed the multitudes." But enjoyment of the things of the world was one thing; lust for them was another. "He rebuked those people who set their lives on possessions." Indeed, it seemed to Jordan that the church had sold its soul. "We are begetting children, but I wonder if they are not bearing the image of their true father, Mammon." Only a radical change would be sufficient, what he called "metanoia," a Greek word normally translated as "repentance." But Jordan disagreed vehemently with the translation. "*Metanoia* means to go through a transformation not of the body but of the mind and soul," he argued. "It doesn't mean repent. *Repent* means to be sorry for getting caught. It's more like a caterpillar changing into a butterfly."

As usual, Jordan illustrated with a story, this one drawn from the experience of two of Christ's disciples—Matthew, the publican tax collector, and Simon, the Jewish nationalist. "If Jesus could take a wild-eyed fanatical, patriotic zealot like Simon and take a collaborating publican like Matthew and put 'em in the same sack, shake 'em up, and cause 'em to have the love of God in their hearts, the kingdom of God was there." He brought it home in contemporary terms. "The publican would be just about as popular in our part of the country as someone from the federal government trying to enforce integration." Simon, the disciple who had been a zealot, he compared to a "good ole boy" who "waved a confederate flag, saying, 'Save your confederate money, boys, the South will rise again.'" Zealots in the days of Jesus were sworn to assassinate publicans, agents of the hated Romans. "On more than one night, Jesus had to sleep between them two boys," Jordan laughed. But they ended up "walking down Main Street in Jerusalem holdin' hands and callin' one another 'Brother Matt' and 'Brother Simon.'"

But Jordan did not believe only in preaching the gospel. "Somewhere we've got to build a fellowship where men are transformed from the old thing," he said. "Before this new order can ever become a reality, it's got to take root in our lives." This was the vision behind Koinonia. The farm was to be a "demonstration plot" where Christians could seek to reclaim the true meaning of their faith.

For all its inadequacies, the attempt deeply impressed Don Mosley. "It was the first time I had ever seen people really trying to live their faith," he explains. "There was something relevant all of a sudden in what the New Testament had to say about loving your enemies and helping the poor. Up to that time, I had always felt a schism between various parts of my life."[3]

By the middle seventies, in the aftermath of disillusionment from the extravagances of the early decade, the community had shrunk in size to seventeen. But Don and Carolyn brought considerable administrative and organizational skills to Koinonia, as well as deep commitment. Don became director. Carolyn, whose deep religious convictions communicate powerfully, helped develop a number of programs, including worship drawing on the different religious backgrounds of the residents, or "partners." Don's father, who had originally reacted to their move to Koinonia with great disappointment, began to visit. He took an interest in the appropriate-technology experiments and the evident sincerity of Christian faith. Ultimately, he helped support the community financially, despite his intense conservatism. "We heard he finally began to boast about Koinonia to his friends," says Don with a grin.

Koinonia began to expand once again, growing to thirty-six. With stability came a new set of problems. As Michael Nelson, a sympathetic observer, put it, "So many people wanted to live at Koinonia that it could not accommodate them all without losing the intimacy that had made it so appealing in the first place." Thus several couples began making plans to set up a new community. After much discussion, the group decided on the name Jubilee Partners, drawn from the biblical concept of a "Jubilee Year" once every fifty, on which liberty would be proclaimed for all and land would revert back to a common pool.

Don and Carolyn made the initial move with two other couples—Ed and Mary Ruth Weir, Karen and Ryan Karis—along with the Mosley's two children and the Weirs' four—in the summer of 1979, to a 260-acre farm they had acquired with financial help from Koinonia. Their new home was on the outskirts of Comer, a little rural town along the rail lines running up the northeast corner of Georgia. "We learned from Koinonia," Don explains, telling of the initial skepticism in the local community. Apparently, rumors had circulated wildly. A local newspaper had noted their arrival with the headline "Christian Commune Moves into Madison County." Some in the largely white area had raised the specter of a reputed plot "to establish black enclaves in all four corners of the county and start moving in on the center," according to the Reverend Allan Smith of the Comer United Methodist Church. Others had feared that the new community might be another Jonestown, or the scene of uninhibited sexual orgies. According to Smith, the main reaction was to anticipate "Jubilee's coming with panic." Mary Ruth Weir remembers a hot summer night in 1979 when they retired to their tent after a day of construction. "We saw a light slowly coming down the road, and knew nobody could get here by accident. It turned out to be the mayor, looking us over."

But the newcomers worked hard to build bridges. They attended local churches and Don started teaching Sunday School in one. They gave talks about what they had planned. Carolyn began a schedule of regular visits to the local retirement home. And the mission they had finally decided upon—helping refugees from third-world nations relocate in North America—created further ties. In fact, for many Comer area residents who volunteered to help, Jubilee, as Reverend Smith put it, provided "a way of translating our Christian concern for needy people from other countries into something real, something tangible."[4]

The concept of serving as a welcome center for refugees came suddenly and surprisingly. Up until the move itself, Jubilee's broader purpose remained undetermined. They had considered building low-cost houses, or producing inexpensive solar-heating equipment; indeed, Don had spent six months before the move in an unsuccessful pursuit of a breakthrough in solar water-heating technology. But they decided to move without any final decision, devoting themselves to constructing houses and getting to know their new neighbors. Other issues had already been settled. For instance, drawing on the years of experience at Koinonia, they had decided that large possessions such as buildings and cars would be jointly owned by the whole community. Smaller items such as clothes and household goods would remain the possessions of individuals and families. The allocation of space, too, struck a balance between the need for privacy and the life of the collective: There would be individual small houses for each permanent family, surrounding the common buildings. Finally, those who, after staying for a year, made a long-term commitment would be considered full "partners." But short-term volunteers would be eagerly welcomed, normally in stays of three months. Decision-making, as at Koinonia, was to be collective, participatory, and democratic.

Then, just days before Don and Carolyn made their final move, the July 2, 1979, issue of *Newsweek* magazine arrived with a poignant picture of Vietnamese boat people on the cover. "I remember reading the article two times," says Don. The group discussed whether they might be able to help in some way. Mosley typed out a proposal in one of the unfinished lofts upstairs and passed it around. It was ambitious—envisioning Jubilee as a place where refugees could learn about American culture and find aid for permanent sponsorship. Extensive construction would be necessary and they would have to raise over $100,000 before they began, but they all agreed, with excitement. The Jubilee passage from Leviticus took on new meaning, where God tells the people that "the land shall not be sold in perpetuity, for the land is mine. For you are strangers and sojourners with me."

In the following year, their hopes were more than fulfilled. An appeal for contributions, using the Koinonia mailing list, elicited a striking response. An old friend, Harry Haines, who directed the United Methodist Committee on Relief, assured them that there was a great need for such centers, with tens of thousands of refugees entering the United States each year. Volunteers contributed more than 50,000 man-hours of work in building construction. By the fall of 1980, they were ready to welcome their first visitors.[5]

I arrive at Jubilee just after their old bus, with orange and gold letters announcing their new program, "Año de Jubileo," has returned from an unexpected emergency trip to pick up Central-American refugees in Texas. "We had driven in from three days on the road," Don recounts, telling of one of Jubilee's regular trips to Chicago's O'Hare Airport, whence they send many Central-American refugees to church-sponsored homes in Canada. "Then in the middle of the night we got a call." Jubilee's Methodist contacts along the border told a story that seemed to portend disaster. Immigration officials had taken a large group to jail for refusing to give local addresses. (Even those refugees with legal papers, as these families had, normally decline to give their temporary local addresses to avoid any possible damaging consequences to their hosts.) A trip to the border region straightened things out, however, and Jubilee was able to arrange bail. A moment of worry about whether all the papers were in perfect order evaporated when they reached the checkpoint. The guard was evidently out to lunch. They simply drove the bus on through.

We tour the classrooms and cabins where the new arrivals are staying, on the way looking at the forested area that the refugees will help clear during their six-week stay. Inside the school building, an English class is just finishing. Two children who know English help translate for their parents. Around the walls and tables are books and posters about Canadian life and customs, written in Spanish.

The history of earlier groups—300 have already come through Jubilee—imprints the community in many ways. The partners' children have many stories of friends they got to know from Cambodia, Cuba, Thailand, Vietnam. On one wall a large map has pins with paper flags naming individuals who have settled there. The southern United States especially is filled with such markers on the map. In a classroom are the strikingly beautiful drawings of Phally, a fifteen-year-old Cambodian girl who had been at Jubilee the year before. In intricate detail, she had interlaced scenes from her native land with birds and flowers.

Don conveys the histories of their sojourners with further stories. Much of Phally's family, I learn, had been killed in Cambodia. One recent visitor, Carlos, had been on a bus in El Salvador that chanced into an area controlled by a right-wing death squad. Everyone on the bus was forced out. The troops opened fire with machine guns. Carlos survived by diving into a nearby ditch.

Among the new group just arrived from Texas are refugees from several Central-American countries, and I interview the Galeano family. The father, Efrain Galeano, was once boxing champion of Central America; while we talk, his children proudly show me clippings of his fights, some years ago. When the Sandinistas took power in Nicaragua, Efrain Galeano fled, because it was rumored they would kill all the boxers—boxing had been a favorite sport of the former dictator, Somoza. He worked for a time in Texas, coaching a young boxing team, before his papers ran out. Then he brought his family from Nicaragua. They planned to settle in Canada, and Galeano was trying to find out about boxing in their future home. "I love the sport, and I would love to coach," he explains.

Jubilee seems a radical juxtaposition of worlds: a community of friendly, North American Christians from mainly comfortable, middle-class backgrounds, welcoming refugees whose stories of hardship and death are almost incomprehensible. But strong bonds have evidently formed again and again between the newcomers and the community. (Some early, nasty incidents involved refugees' reactions against their permanent church sponsors, whom they had expected to be like the people at Jubilee.) "Many come from nonmaterialistic cultures," Don explains. 'We rationalize bringing them from cultures which in some ways are more in keeping with our own values. But we also think all we have a right to do is acquaint them with alternatives and provide a compassionate entry." Moreover, the process is two-way: "We've been tremendously enriched by having them here. Sometimes they make us feel like phonies. We thank God for the color of the leaves. They thank God that their little brother escaped when other family members were killed."

Jubilee is loosely linked with a network of perhaps 200 Christian communities around the country, through ties like the magazine *Sojourners* and common work in the peace movement. "Initially I saw peace as a separate thing," says Mosley. "But we've come to believe that you can't have true peace except with justice. When we deal with refugees from Central America, we realize that issues of starvation, economic oppression, and violence are all bound together." When he speaks of his disagreements with American foreign policy in the region, his voice takes on a sharp edge, recalling the passionate indignation of Clarence Jordan before him. Mosley, too, believes in what he calls "metanoia"—the possibility of transformation on both an individual and a corporate level. And their work regenerates a sense of possibility. "We meet the best elements of American society all the time," he explains. "Some are sponsors, taking in people they have never known. Some are supporters, sending donations. Many are local neighbors who are interested

and help out." The first group of refugees were fifteen men
from Cuba, who arrived in the midst of national publicity about
all the problems new Cuban immigrants were creating. Comer
United Methodist Church symbolized the progress that Jubilee
had made in its first year, building ties to the area. Soon after
the Cubans arrived, the church held a welcoming dinner.

At the end of my stay at Jubilee, Don takes me to what he calls
their "secret retreat" down at the end of a forest path, where
those in the community come when they need to be alone or
think about something. It is a beautiful spot, overlooking a small
lake. Jubilee residents have constructed a small, simple building
there, with a single cot, a desk, and a woodburning stove inside,
and a front porch from which one can see beavers crossing the
water. The place reminds me of another retreat center I visited,
called the ARC Community, near Grandee, Minnesota. ARC's
methods are different from Jubilee's, but their aims bear note-
worthy resemblance.

Getting to ARC requires a long drive along muddy and
deeply rutted roads, and I remarked when I arrived that they
have cut themselves off from the rat race as completely as it is
possible to do in the middle of Minnesota. But if ARC seems
secluded, it is scarcely primitive. Sunlight floods the room in the
middle of the long, central building, through an enormous window to the south, rising two stories high next to the cathedral-
like living room. The walls are made of beautifully rounded
light cedar logs, interspersed with pine paneling. A fireplace,
built by a master stonemason who donated time, rises in the
center of the room, like some Gothic piling. Tapestries in gold,
burnt orange, red, blue, and brown are hung on the wall, picking up the orange and yellow and brown of the thick rug that
stretches out from the living room up the stairs to the library
and through an archway into the dining area. The cosmopolitan
cast to the place is as unmistakable as is its rich comfort: A statue
of Don Quixote, a complex African wood carving, a mobile of
driftwood, Julien china dishes, Indian cloth designs, Scandina-
vian prints—all suggest wide travel and taste.

The residents' interests are also clearly evident in the magazine racks and bookshelves that fill the middle spaces of the building. Religious, feminist, and political literature predominate: *World Press Review, Christianity Today, The Other Side, Lutheran Women, Spiritual Life, Daughters of Sara, Women in the World of Jesus,* Rich's *Of Women Born,* Heilbroner's *Human Prospect,* Schumacher's *Good Work,* and so forth.

Literature, furnishings, building, like the location in the midst of quiet pine and birch forests, all form a piece, I later learn, in support of ARC's mission of "hospitality." A quote from Henri Nouwen on the frontispiece of the small booklets in each guest room defines what they intend: "Hospitality means primarily the creation of a free space where the stranger can enter and become a friend instead of an enemy. Hospitality is not to change people, but to offer them space where change can take place." The thought seems a play with polarities. But then, I learn, ARC thrives on paradox and juxtaposition.

Driving up, I had thought of the resemblance of ARC to Puritan settlements in the New World. Like those who sought to create new "cities on a hill" away from the corruption and evil of the past-encrusted places they had left, ARC sees itself in many ways as an alternative. Indeed it is new in a fashion that surely would have horrified the elders of New England. ARC began as a feminist retreat center where people could come to reflect on the most basic of questions—relations between men and women, their images of the deity. Its religious services, held morning and evening for any who wish to come, are full of the most wide-ranging experiment—using male and female images for God, rotating leadership, mixing ritual and conversation. And from the beginning, ARC has defined itself as an alternative living arrangement to the nuclear family. Permanent residents include not only Ruth and Loren Halvorson but also Sister Judith Stoughton, member of the order of the Sisters of Saint Joseph of Carondelet, and several other unrelated individuals.

Though it diverges from tradition in many directions, ARC claims many ties to the past and to the surrounding rural folk. The Puritans had imagined themselves set down in "a hideous and desolate wilderness full of wild beasts and wild men," as Governor William Bradford of Plymouth once put it.[6] For ARC,

its setting is a priceless resource, not only for the beauty and
solitude but also for the history, "exact site of an Indian community created one thousand years before." When they cleared
the land to build buildings, the members of ARC went about
assiduously cultivating ties with local residents, in the manner
of Jubilee. They attended local churches, populated mainly by
Baptists of Swedish origin. They gave talks. And they hired local
artisans to oversee the construction work. "It was quite a culture clash," Loren describes. "There were local masons there
with their country and western music, who had never seen
women in construction crews. And students in a summer work
camp helping out, up from the city. At the end, the students
made an enormous cake to look like a building, and sang the
songs they had composed about the masons. It was great."

Finally, ARC believes in returning to things that have been
lost or marginalized. "Much of the wisdom that has been ac-
cumulated through millennia of life together in tribe, family
and village seems to have been forgotten," wrote Loren in an
unpublished manuscript about the base community movement
around the world. The task that led to ARC is what he called
"replenishment . . . not rupture. There is no new virgin land to
be settled or stolen from the natives." The challenge is instead
"the recovery of ancient roots."[7]

One time I attended a workshop led by Loren on "maleness,"
which was full of juxtapositions like "We are most male when
we are most feminine; and most feminine when most male";
"The church is most relevant when it is most reverent, and most
reverent when most relevant." They seemed interesting, but a
bit arcane. His basic point sought to amplify his book's argument that, paradoxically, "our own struggle for justice and social change should have led us to the woods." Loren explained
that through many years of education work in the institutional
church, trying to deal with social-justice issues like world hunger, he had come to realize that "you can't shake the tree for
the fruit when the apples have already fallen off." To illustrate,
he drew a model of a tree on the board. Ground level divided
"the organic root system" from the "inorganic."

In Loren's depiction, aboveground represented the language

and terms of the modern world: products, systems, management, marketing. "Belowground," in contrast, was the realm of relationships, households, birth, and death. He argued that, in the main, biblical imagery is "organic"—about things like mustard seeds, washing feet, living and dying, the unseen. The problem with the modern world was that the organic and inorganic had moved dramatically away from healthy balance; instead, in a society where "the system is the solution," human relationships, histories, and idiosyncrasies are mainly considered "problems" that potentially intrude upon efficiency.

It was arresting metaphor. But ARC and its purpose began to take on life when I heard the stories of Ruth and Judith, and found out how the Center had evolved.

When I interview Ruth, I think somehow of pioneer women of the Midwest, traveling by wagon, birthing at home, milking cows, growing things, and raising children. As she talks, her own childhood on a North Dakota farm comes through, along with the values of farming: the land, animals, family. So does a certain feistiness. She tells how she used to challenge her mother as a child. "My father had to be right and was the vocal one, even though she was the real strength of the family. In order to preserve peace, she would ignore things or move on to something else." From the vantage point of the farm, Minneapolis seemed the place to go. "As a young person, you always think the city is better. The cosmopolitanism, the lights and the glitter and the fast pace." She laughs. "Now I've come back to the country!"

Ruth and Loren had what both called "a good but traditional marriage." As she recounted, "He was expected to go upward in mobility and I was expected to ensure that he could, and take care of the kids." But she was extensively involved in community activities like her church and the League of Women Voters. Then in the early 1960s she read Betty Friedan's *Feminine Mystique.* "I thought, How could anyone have articulated my situation so well?" But few of her friends agreed. "That simply compounded the notion that I was weird."

For several years she continued to feel "like I was going

upstream." Then she went on a weekend retreat shortly before they were to leave for Geneva, Switzerland, where Loren was going to work on international programs. The retreat was the yearly event of the American Lutheran Church's Board of Higher Education, held each year for board members, staff, and their spouses. But unlike most years, this time the group itself was to determine the agenda, and wives were invited to have input. Nervous but determined, Ruth decided "to talk from my personal experience."

She gave a long presentation on women in higher education and the ways she believed their options were limited. "I said I thought we were kidding ourselves if we dealt with issues of justice and equality only over there somewhere and weren't willing to deal with this basic question in our own lives, with ourselves and between ourselves." As she talked, she drew on her own experience, including her marriage—with Loren in the room. "It couldn't have been any more difficult if I had undressed before everyone." But she felt she was speaking from the center of the Christian faith. "Jesus had given his life in order to break down the walls that separate people. This was a wall that had never been broken."

Her presentation stirred the whole group, including presidents and executives of a number of Lutheran colleges and universities. Moreover, the meeting produced results: the establishment of a special church task force on women's role in college education. But Ruth herself, ironically, could not participate. "We were supposed to go to Geneva. I thought to myself, Here is something exciting about to happen and once more I'm asked to give it up."

When they arrived in Europe, Ruth accepted an invitation to the sort of individual retreat she had previously declined, perhaps because she felt at loose ends and angry. It was held at a place called Communauté du Grand Champ, directed by Catholic sisters with what she calls "a low-key and noninterventionist approach that gave you the space to deal with your own agenda." For her, the stay proved a profound experience. "I began to see how the notion of a retreat could address the whole person, how times of solitude can help you deal with yourself

in a way that nothing else can." When they returned to the
United States, she organized a group called Women Concerned
for Wholeness. And she and a friend, Sister Judith Stoughton,
began holding ecumenical women's retreats.

Sister Judith is a neatly dressed woman who describes herself
as "a crazy artist." She teaches in the art department at St.
Catherine's College in St. Paul, commuting back to ARC as does
Loren, who also teaches several days a week in the Twin Cities.
When she talks about people who have stayed at ARC, or the
"changes" and "healing" she has seen there, sometimes
marked, she is calm, thoughtful, warm. As she describes the
process that brought her to ARC, her voice becomes intense.
"Vatican Two was an enormous step back into the real world
after a very protected environment," she explains. Traveling
around Europe in the early seventies, she found religious communities everywhere in turmoil after the Catholic church's call
for engagement in the world. "We had just taken off our habits.
Many experimental communities were forming, looking at new
forms of live-in communities. Women did what they chose. To
somebody growing up in a traditional Catholic community, that
was very radical."

Judith continues. "My own mind was in ferment, trying to see
what my life was going to be in the future." She decided not to
live any longer as she had, in an all-women setting. But the
changes in her order and in the church meant that she could
stay a nun and part of the Sisters of Saint Joseph, a community
in which she had found many resources, religiously, personally,
and intellectually. "I knew that if I thought something was a
good idea, people would hang with me."

When she returned to the United States, she and Ruth began
talking about the changes that women were experiencing in the
church in response to the growing women's movement,
"women who wondered if they were crazy, who didn't know
whether to believe or not believe the people who were putting
them down when they asked questions." So they decided to
hold a retreat for women from various denominations. "We
called it 'feminist' so we would not draw people who would
react negatively to that concept, and 'Christian' to draw women

who were religious. We saw it as a place for people to talk who were very puzzled about the connections."

They didn't know what the response might be, but they rented a place for a weekend along the St. Croix river and printed a flyer, which they circulated. Drawing on her experience in Grand Champ in Europe, Ruth put in time for people to be together, talking, and time to be alone. "I was convinced that a contemplative setting was the way to deal best with issues of both feminism and also our own spirituality, and how they were related." Response proved extraordinary—they had a waiting list to draw on for the next retreat. And the group that weekend opened space where people could talk openly and find community for the first time. "People had wondered if they were crazy. There was a lot of pain and anger. But ultimately there was a feeling that they had a right to be part of the church." Friendships forged during that weekend continued, across every denominational line.

After the weekend the two knew that there was need for such retreats on an ongoing basis, and with Loren and a few friends they began to talk about a permanent center. Then suddenly a retired couple who had thought for many years about creating a retreat center themselves heard of their plans. They donated fifty-six acres of land, and construction started in 1976.

Planning the Center, it became clear that several ingredients would be essential. The patterning of space, for instance, would shape the nature of relationships and experiences. "If it was to be a retreat center, it had to provide individuals with private space," Ruth explained. The need for psychological and physical space for individuals meant private rooms with a personal touch: Each guest is taken to the place she or he is to stay and finds her/his own name on the door. The group also developed the concept of a permanent community, which would live at ARC year round. Thus there had to be private spaces for residents as well. Two ends of the main building now hold small apartments on three floors, one end for the guests and one for the community itself. "In between," Ruth continued, describing the rationale for construction, "there needed to be common space for living, dining, hospitality, reading."

Moreover, space needed a quality of "freedom." Partly, *free-dom* meant openness for wide-ranging discussion, for experiment with worship, for time to be by oneself as well as with a group. Partly, it defined the relationship with outside institutions like the church. "We're not anti-institutional and we're not underground," Judith elaborated. "We are a free space alongside institutions, moving in and out of them. The Catholic church or the Lutheran church has nothing to say about what we do here, but we value the riches in those traditions."

As they talked, they also broadened their understanding of the purpose of the retreat center. Ecumenical feminist meetings would continue to be a mainstay, but others would be invited to use ARC as well. In the years since its creation, ARC has become a widely used place where staff from denominations, faculty from seminaries, lay members of congregations, ministers, and individuals all can come for varying lengths of time. During their stay, guests eat with ARC residents and, if they choose, can draw on their help for their workshops or program activities. The week before I came, a church group from Cambridge, a rural town down the road, had held a meeting there.

Looking through the book in my room where people are encouraged to write their thoughts, if they wish, before they leave convinced me of the impact of such retreats on many. Sometimes there were simply hints: "Suddenly, a perfunctory benediction within my liturgical tradition has come to life," wrote one. Other authors talk in more intimate, if usually anonymous, detail about things they had kept buried or not realized they felt, using poetry, song, prayer.

It seems clear that ARC taps deep needs in many who come. But what impresses me most is a down-to-earth quality to the Center, something of the populist radicalism of a Clarence Jordan in midwestern idiom, which avoids the sentimentality or excessive piety I sometimes associate with spiritual centers. Ruth conveys such a spirit when she talks about the need to see laity as the foundation of the church. "When we get a collar around our neck or a degree, we somehow get this notion that we have the answers that you need to have. We don't understand that ordinary people in the pews have a lot to offer." ARC worship, she explains, is designed to maximize opportunities for different people's participation. "We see the kind of empowerment it gives to people when they feel like they personally participate."

Sister Judith, in different terms, also raises a similar imagery of ARC as "a normal, healthy environment in which people have space to work out their own problems." It is not, she explains, a "radical alternative" to their lives (though Ruth uses the word *radical* positively in the older meaning of the term, as a "return to roots"). Rather it is "ordinary, not in the sense of the way people actually live most of the time but in the sense of being how they want to live."

I realized that ARC connects to other communities I visited, in ways that were not obvious at first glance. With comfortable space to talk, good conversation, and quiet time in the forests, it creates a place where people can think about what is most important in their lives, gaining the sort of perspective that allows wiser action. Reflective moments and places take many forms. Indeed, they can be found, too, in the middle of cities like New York or St. Louis, where people think about the values they wish to live by and begin to develop the capacities to act upon them.

4

Bakesales, Barn Raisings, and Bootstraps: Helping Ourselves

A long the commercial strip that forms the arterial hub of Williamsburg, the old Italian neighborhood in Brooklyn, a large change has taken place in recent years. Graffiti and chipped paint are gone. Instead, the steam-cleaned brick facades and painted cornices on the storefronts complement new brick sidewalks and streetlights in the style of gas lamps from the neighborhood's distant past. A sign in a large vacant lot announces the shopping mall soon to be constructed. In front of each store, painted Styrofoam sculptures add whimsy to the business of attracting customers. A boy on a bicycle hangs over the door of Albert's Bargain Store. An old-fashioned wishing well adorns the entrance to Special Occasions. Customers shopping in the Grand Bazaar walk underneath a smiling teddy bear. For those dining at the barbecue place, a large pig out front gives anticipatory welcome.

The changes I saw in Brooklyn were elements in the revitalization plan for Williamsburg that had been developed by the St. Nicholas Neighborhood Preservation and Housing Rehabilitation Corporation, a community organization to which all neighborhood residents belong. In concert with the merchants group that St. Nick's helped set up, the organization combined such physical improvements with an aggressive public-relations campaign, sending out postcards, calendars, using advertisements and other devices to lure customers back to the Grand Metro Shopping District, as the area has been labeled. It all succeeded far beyond expectations.

Most of the funds for the community efforts came from the

local area. A city grant for the commercial district's improvement, which required local merchants to add a dollar to every two provided publicly, precipitated a rush of private capital. For every dollar the public authorities put in, local merchants themselves ended up spending eight. Federal funds played an important role. St. Nick's obtained a grant from the National Endowment for the Arts to help with the Styrofoam sculptures. Seed funding for the shopping mall came through a neighborhood self-help program at the Department of Housing and Urban Development, begun during the Carter administration.

On the face of it, one might well have imagined that such local entrepreneurial zeal and initiative would find even warmer reception from the appointees of President Reagan. The entire endeavor, after all, would seem to embody precisely that "American spirit" which candidate Reagan had pledged at every opportunity to renew, and on no subject was the campaigner more articulate. Taking the lead from the top, the Republican party platform of 1980 pledged a government "committed to nurturing the spirit of self-help and cooperation through which so many neighborhoods have revitalized themselves." And through his years in office, President Reagan has justified proposals ranging from budget-cutting to the New Federalism by invoking the need for increased local control and a rebirth of voluntary community initiatives.

Thus, St. Nick's encounters with the government after January 20, 1981, contained no small irony. "We couldn't even get our phone calls answered," recounted Gary Hattem, St. Nick's executive director, describing the organization's efforts to work out details of the self-help grant already secured. "It was like we were Godzilla. Everyone in the bureaucracy ran the other direction." Moreover, the St. Nicholas Corporation's experience was scarcely unique. Across the country, neighborhood projects —many of which had taken the rhetorical commitments of candidate Reagan to neighborhood self-help at face value—met with brusque indifference when the new officeholders reached Washington.

To evaluate the effects of the administration's budget cutbacks on neighborhoods, the United States Catholic Bishops' own self-help funding program for communities, the Campaign for Human Development, conducted a survey of the organizations with which they worked. All eight government programs that the bishops' group judged most useful to community self-help—from economic development to jobs programs based in neighborhoods—had been directly designated for elimination. Associate Director Kathy Desmond, who conducted the study, concluded wryly, "When you demythologize the rhetoric and look at the specific things the administration has cut, you find that they've specifically targeted all those programs that we think of as essential components of self-help." In the view of observers like Desmond, the administration's basic stance was simple aversion to anything that resembled community organization or independent, "trickle up" citizen initiatives. "The Reagan people didn't want the government to fund groups that were going to stir things up," she concluded. "Anything that was organizing or advocacy."[1]

Neighborhoods getting together to help each other out—and at points "stir things up"—is indeed an old American tradition. When the French observer Alexis de Tocqueville visited the United States in the 1830s, he marveled at Americans' propensity to organize themselves: "Americans of all ages, all conditions and all dispositions constantly form associations." Barn raisings, quilting bees, voluntary fire departments, rural cooperatives, and farm organizations had such urban counterparts as immigrant mutual aid and burial societies, fraternal and sororal orders, and trade groups. In view of such hallowed practices, it is perhaps not after all surprising that image makers would find rhetorical usefulness in an appeal to local initiatives in the mediagenic politics of the 1980s.

Yet whatever the oratory of politicians, powerful forces had long undermined self-help and local control, and any call for return to such traditions that took no account of the changed situation was bound to smack of cynicism after a time. On the simplest level, for instance, a vast concentration of wealth and power vested in large corporate and bureaucratic institutions had long been gathering momentum. In 1955, 44.5 percent of all manufacturing and mining employees in the United States worked for the largest 500 companies. The percentage had risen to 72 percent by 1970. Four companies controlled an average of 42 percent of the market in the 213 major manufacturing industries. "By the year 2001," predicted Judd Polk, the former senior economist for the United States Chamber of Commerce, "200 giant corporations will own 54 percent of all the productive assets worth owning on the planet Earth."[2]

In concert with economic concentration, big government has similarly grown, from 28 percent of the GNP in 1962 in America to more than one-third in 1978. Between 1965 and 1972—bridging the administrations of Lyndon Johnson and Richard Nixon, alike—total federal spending on education, health, and welfare rose from $7.6 billion to $43.3 billion. Somehow, almost everyone felt abused and diminished by such a process. "Welfare recipients find it difficult to express gratitude for small favors, often thoughtlessly, even cruelly administered," pointed out political theorist Peter Clecak; "working people frequently resent the burden of such payments; and welfare professionals feel underpaid, frustrated and unappreciated."[3]

More subtle, perhaps more insidious, processes fed such a sense of grievance, undermining peoples' *capacities* for self-help and problem-solving even as the new aggregates of power assumed a growing number of functions. In counterpoint to the erosion of community life, a new class of experts and professionals increasingly controlled and directed ordinary citizens' child-rearing practices, food preparation, recreational activities—even their day-to-day interactions with friends and family. Supposedly apolitical ideologies of the "helping professions" in fact mask operations of well-developed industries with a vested interest in expansion of their areas of control. Whole new aspects of life become defined as "problems" in need of professional help: old age, for instance, or baldness. Indeed, there is now one famous clinic where people who don't feel anything is the matter with them can go to find out what their problems are, so professionals can then attend to them.

Thomas Dewar, professor at the Humphrey Institute of Public Affairs in Minnesota, has pointed to two quite different models of "helping." In the sorts of helping approaches found among friends, family, or neighbors, the exchange is between equals and peers. People draw on common bonds of experience, tradition, and shared values. Those "being helped" may well need new skills or ways of dealing with problems, but the expectation is that roles might be reversed at another time. The result is a strengthening of ties and an increase in confidence in common capacities.

In contrast, what Dewar terms "technical" approaches to problem-solving are based on an assumption of sharp and qualitative differences between the helper and the person being helped. The helper "knows" how the problem is to be described; what problem-solving method ought properly to be deployed; and what a "healthy" outcome looks like. "A physician's patients, for example, learn about health in terms of the medical model, about *having* a body rather than *being* a body. . . . They learn that health is something you *get* rather than something you *do.*" In such a setting, being a "good client" means accepting without question the superior wisdom of the expert—trusting and obeying: "anything less is apt to be viewed as unwise or irresponsible, not only by their helpers but more importantly by the clients themselves and their peers." Thus, the most debilitating aspect of the technical model, in the end, is the erosion of trust in our own capacities to judge, to act, and to assert control over our lives. "When the capacity to define the problem becomes a professional prerogative," concludes social critic John McKnight, "citizens no longer exist."[4]

By the 1980s in our increasingly service-oriented society, such processes are far advanced indeed. Yet they have also begun to call forth countertrends as an integral part of the revival of community life.

Among Americans of all ages, races, income levels, and situations, an explosion of self-help groups was observable. Self-help observer and chronicler Frank Riessman pointed out that the expansion included groups of all sorts: "Health and mental health groups have been growing as well as the more directly activist women's groups, gay groups and handicapped groups. . . . In the United States alone there are 500,000 mutual aid groups with a total membership of 15 million that is climbing rapidly." In other terms, 41 million Americans currently spend several hundred million hours each year on do-it-yourself renovation, the retail value of which, $28 billion a year, equals or exceeds the value of the same work done each year by professionals. Thirty-four million families are involved in gardening, including more than 2 million who work in community garden plots. In New York City during the 1977 power blackout, while many communities experienced widespread looting, those blocks where neighbors had begun urban community gardens remained relatively untouched.[5]

The new neighborhood activism was a striking example of the revival of American traditions of self-help. Indeed, whatever resources might be lavished on communities, the evidence was clear that neighborhoods could not be rescued from outside; renewal had to begin within. As Carl Holman, president of the National Urban Coalition, put it, "City services and strategies can prevent decay only in neighborhoods that have confidence in their own future." For poor communities, self-help to be effective entailed not only a revitalization of their internal spirit but a powerful challenge as well to all those outside power brokers who circumscribed their possibilities and took away pride, resources, and self-respect. Examples of such renewal, self-help, and challenge could be found even against the most overwhelming odds and in the most devastated of circumstances. They furnished models of inspiration for people in similar straits everywhere.[6]

I first met Bertha Gilkey in the lobby of the new Sheraton Inn in downtown St. Louis. She was wending her way among groups of costumed Shriners whose convention that weekend was bringing something like $17 million into the city according to the local newspaper. (In downtown St. Louis, everything seems to be expressed in multimillion-dollar terms: The "$42-million Sheraton" is across from the "$47-million Cervantes Convention Center." Down the road an enormous mall is under construction—"another $150 million." Tens of millions more have gone into renovation of the Mississippi waterfront. Where once old industrial buildings crowded the water's edge, a maze of walkways, parks, and shops now testify to the vigor of down-town redevelopment.)

Bertha Gilkey was a contrast to the Shriners. A striking black woman, she looked, even on a Saturday morning, as if she might just have stepped off the pages of *Vogue* or *Ebony,* gold neck-laces and elegant rings and flowered dress. "I look like them," she later tells me, talking about downtown executives. "They don't know what to do with me." Not that "they" haven't tried. Bertha is the leader and symbol of the tenants' organization in St. Louis public housing projects. Her own, Cochran Gardens, is just down the street from the Sheraton and the convention center. "When I was a little girl," she recalls, "there wasn't nothing here but industry. Now it's the place to be. The only problem is we're here." Bertha smiles, as she often does, a wide grin that lights her face. "I have no problem with the condos, the hundred-and-fifty-million-dollar mall, the Sheraton or the mercantile tower, which is about fifty million. I think it's all gorgeous. We're sitting right next to these highways, able to get in and out. People pay for all of this. I understand that. It's fine, as long as they understand that we ain't going nowhere. We're going to be here to enjoy all the different highways, and to take walks right on over here to the inn."

Now, corporate support downtown for Bertha Gilkey and tenant self-help endeavors is most often enthusiastic. Only a few years before, business leaders' maps of the future down-town area held no trace of public housing; tenants were slated for inconspicuous "relocation." The chief executives did not know what they were getting into.

A block or so down Cole Street from the Cervantes Conven-tion Center and the Sheraton Inn is a row of luxury condomini-ums. Brick walls are tastefully matched outside by walkways; a circular-cut motif adds a distinctive signature to the develop-ment. Across the road, attractive high-rise buildings surround-ing a large courtyard pick up the circular pattern, amplify it in designs and walls, creating the feel of some urban mountain range, a nice effect.

The high-rises make up Cochran Gardens, one of four public housing complexes in St. Louis that are managed by tenants themselves. In the case of Cochran, the project itself is the centerpiece of an extensive maze of housing developments, businesses, and services that the Tenant Management Council owns and operates on a nonprofit basis through its development corporation. At a glance, one could identify the residents' involvement in reconstruction of the buildings around the courtyard. Each apartment looks out over the common space. Wide walkways on the lower levels, here and there forming gathering spots where wicker chairs left in the open suggest their frequent use, lead up to apartments on the first several floors. Rows of flowers and trees can be seen among children's play equipment. Even on a summer morning in the notoriously hot year of 1983, the area is full of people. It forms a pleasantly congenial scene. "Either you plan or they plan for you" is how Bertha sums it up. She waves across the view. "Isn't this beautiful? Isn't this the way poor people are supposed to live?" These are questions she asks again and again as we tour the changes that have come to Cochran Gardens and the surrounding area.

Bertha Gilkey grew up in the high-rises "before the changes." We pass the building where she lived as a child along the way. It forms a radical contrast to the others, like some monument to a past that might otherwise be impossible to conceive. Huge piles of rubbish surround the doors. Broken windows and graffiti testify to the rage tenants felt as they abandoned the building. "We're saving that one to fix up for last," Bertha explains. "Just to be a reminder."

Norma Bell joined us. She also grew up in public housing, and her own individual history lends poignancy to her accounts of "the old days." Her project, the widely publicized public housing 'failure' Prewitt Iago, which was blown up by city officials after they declared it irretrievably damaged and deteriorated, offered constant "peer pressure to go the wrong direction," in her terms. One after another, she saw childhood friends get involved in drugs, crime, prostitution. "You had to be very strong to resist the pressure," she says.

As soon as she could, Bell left the projects, going off to Germany with her husband, who was in the service. She worried about her brother, still there ("I could see the changes in him," she explains). Finally she asked their uncle in Chicago if he would help out. "He came down, gave him a good whipping, and took him back with him. Now he has a nice home and a job. But everybody didn't have that chance."

In the sixties and early seventies, after returning to the United States, Bell directed social-service projects for the poverty program in Cochran Gardens. "It was just like Prewitt Iago," she recalls. "There was shootings out in the open." She shakes her head in amazement. "You'd hear the shots and fall flat on your face like they do in the movies to avoid getting hit."

Like others I talked to in Cochran Gardens, Bell remembers the attitudes of police angrily. "They had an image of Cochran" is how she puts it, which meant they assumed guilt no matter who you were. "Police would come in with drawn guns. If you wasn't a suspect before, you might be one by the time they got through with you." What made her angriest was their periodic shooting when children were around.

Yet there was indifference, born of fear, among residents themselves. "It wasn't nothing to be going on the elevator and you see someone laying down," she continues. "You'd say, 'What are you doing?' They don't say nothing. They'd be shot. People would just pass by the body. Nobody would even call the ambulance. 'He's just been shot,' they'd say. Nobody even got upset." She remembers older people barricaded in their rooms. "One old lady hadn't had a bath in months. She met me at the door with a gun. She was eating out of cans." Bertha interjects, "You could see the fear in the children's eyes when it got real bad. On a real hot day like today, you wouldn't see anybody outside. You could *feel* the crime, almost cut it with a knife."

Drugs, crime, prostitution, garbage and urine in the halls, broken windows, graffiti—the tales go on and on, like stories of vast squatters cities of the dispossessed one reads about in some third-world country, climbing the hills of Seoul, perhaps, or Hong Kong. Upper floors of buildings had been abandoned to criminals and drug dealers. Sometimes people would stay in apartments and remain anonymous, never paying rent (the Housing Authority's contact with much of the project was minimal). "The only people who could walk through this neighborhood and not be afraid were the criminals," says Bertha. "If you were a person that didn't get out a lot, you would get mugged or raped or assaulted. If you was white, you just got murdered."

We walk around a good deal more before Bertha begins her story of "the changes." Security still remains a concern. Each building, for instance, has a locked outer door; a special pass is needed to open it. But the fear is strikingly absent. I notice one time Bertha leaves her apartment without locking it and ask her about it. "Sometimes I do and sometimes I don't," she says.

In each building we enter, people greet Bertha with great warmth. Here and there a white family is visible, mingling with others—a statement in itself, since the days when whites rarely entered the project at all. In the air-conditioned high-rise for senior citizens, two elderly women in the laundry room talk with pride about their apartments and the various activities they help organize. I ask one how she likes living here. "It's wonderful," she says. "Better than your house!" In another building, Nancy Sisley, an older woman in a wheelchair, takes me around to look at the building, which has been made accessible to the disabled. Ms. Sisley, friendly and hospitable, is the elected captain of her building, which means she runs the monthly tenant meetings, oversees the laundry and recreation rooms, counsels residents, and attends to the community in a dozen other ways. She has lived in Cochran Gardens for twenty-five years. She, too, has many stories of how Cochran "went down," and I ask her why. "The people didn't have much of a say. The manager really had the say-so," she replies. "Now people have a chance to a voice. If you live here, you're going to be interested in the place."

From the top of one twelve-story high-rise, we look out over the surrounding area and Bertha points out the fruits of battles over the years. "See that old Catholic church? We helped them save it when the city was going to tear it down. Conventioners didn't want to go past Cochran if they wanted to go to church, they said." I see a large park, tennis courts, Cochran Plaza town houses that Bertha's tenant committee built as replacement housing for families in Cochran after renovation of the buildings had started and the number of residents per building—the "density"—was being lowered. "We said, 'No one is going to be displaced,' " Bertha recounts. She turns to Norma Bell. "But we had to fight the Housing Authority on that one, too, didn't we? When we got Cochran Plaza built, they said it was too beautiful for people from Cochran and started moving other people in. So we took them to court. The judge wrote a whole decision about how incompetent the Housing Authority was. It was beautiful."

Everywhere, there is grass. "The grass is really important to me," Bertha explains. " 'Cause when I watched Cochran go down, the most significant thing was there was no grass. Nothing but dirt. Bottles. The grass wouldn't even grow." When Bertha describes these memories, she often raises her voice until she is almost shouting. "It was so bad, when you'd pass under steps, water, eggs, even a stove might come down at you. People would be shooting up on porches." She pauses. "The horrible thing was, kids got to accept that." When the changes began, the tenants brought in topsoil. "We brought in a gardener, too, to teach kids how to grow flowers. When have you seen flowers in public housing? We made flower boxes out of old railroad ties. I got the mayor to give me some tulip bulbs."

Bertha Gilkey came from a family of sixteen children. Fifteen are still living. Her mother, married at eleven, spent almost all her life trapped in the house. "My mother would be glad if some of us didn't come home, it was so crowded. We had nine girls in one bedroom." Only recently have her children taught Bertha's mother to read. "Any excuse we might have not to go to school," Bertha remembers, "she'd say, 'Fine. Stay home and wash the clothes. Watch the children.' She didn't have an education, so she didn't see the value of it."

These stories of Bertha's childhood, like the accounts of Cochran in years before, accent the incredible transformation that has taken place. It is a story Bertha loves to tell. "This goes against the grain, doesn't it? Poor people aren't supposed to manage. Poor people are to *be* managed. Only people with degrees and credentials can manage." She smiles. "What I've done, what we've done, is cut through all the bullshit and said it doesn't take all that. People with degrees and credentials got us in this mess. All it takes is some basic skills, knowledge of finance, management, how to screen. And then, a different attitude. You can't deal with public housing unless you're willing to deal in a totality." And begin from the perspective of the tenants themselves.

Bertha's "befores" and "afters" usually contrast the devastation of Cochran Gardens with its current renewal. But her story begins with an earlier "before."

"My mother was one of the first black families to move into public housing. It was very segregated in those days. That was thirty-two years ago. But public housing didn't have the stigma then. We moved from a cold-water flat, and public housing was like heaven. We used to sleep outside. There were bicycles outside. We had laundromats. Mailboxes. Nobody got vandalized. I gradually watched a beautiful community turn into a jungle."

Deterioration, Bertha recalls, came over time and accompanied a gradual racial transition. As Cochran Gardens became more and more black, the Housing Authority withdrew services. "By the time it was twenty percent black, you'd see small things. They didn't spend the same attention on the plants, maybe. Then when it was seventy percent white and thirty percent black, they reduced security. Then when it was sixty percent white and forty percent black, they stopped spending any money on flowers or landscapes at all. By the time it was eighty percent black, maintenance was cut to the bone."

To Bertha as a young girl, the world outside seemed overwhelmingly dominated by whites. Perhaps the most damaging forms of domination were the most subtle, like that found in the church nearby, which was all white. "They held meetings for the tenants, but they'd set the agenda. And they'd have programs for kids from the projects. There would be a little module of a white house with a picket fence and a two-car garage. The problem was, our kids didn't live in that kind of house." From Bertha's perspective, such images offered no hope to kids who could expect to live their lives in public housing, and thus laid no foundation for change. Public school was similar. "It didn't tell us there was nothing wrong with living in public housing.

What was wrong was the garbage, the rot, and all the rest of it. The question was, What can we do to change it?"

Tenant control over the buildings—first informal, then officially recognized (in the case of Cochran, in 1976)—has been the key element in the renovation, in Bertha's opinion. I asked her how the Housing Authority relinquished power over various policies. "Cochran Gardens was so bad they didn't care," she replied. "They didn't want it. They couldn't get union contractors to come down here to do work if they wanted to."

An older black woman named Mabel Cohen, whom Bertha calls "my mentor," was one of the few residents from the project hired by the poverty program. She was a "homemaker"; her job was to visit different families and give advice. And she identified Bertha as someone with great leadership abilities, even as a young teen-ager, encouraging her to attend tenant meetings at the church across the street. Bertha was frustrated by the domination of the meetings by whites who lived outside the project, and she was frustrated by the various poverty programs of the sixties as well, which seemed to her "just a way to buy off the leaders. The community didn't benefit."

In 1969, when she was twenty years old, Cochran tenants elected her to chair the Cochran tenants' association. With a base—and a determination fueled by rage at "seeing good housing go bad"—she and several others started out "to turn things around." They had few resources—"nothing but dreams," Bertha puts it. People had to bring their own chairs down to the meeting room in her building, since the room had no chairs of its own.

Though some residents had moved from the project out of fear, others had stayed, claiming Cochran as their home. There was much apathy, born of hopelessness, but a few people believed things could change. The group had a simple initial strategy: "the short range and the long range," Bertha describes it. They started with small things, "things we could change immediately. We met and said, 'What can we do? What are the things that can give some hope?' "

Everyone wanted a laundromat, for instance. "But the laundromat was torn up, it was kicked in and vandalized. So we said,

'Can we get the door locked?' " She adds, "When we took over, there was no locks. There was no *doors!* All the doors had been taken down." One "little thing" was getting doors back.

Tenants in the building held a fundraiser to raise money for a lock. Then they raised more money for paint for the halls. "The elderly who couldn't paint prepared lunch, so they could feel like they were a part of it, too." Key to each step was rebuilding a sense of responsibility to the community. "Everybody who lived on a floor was responsible for painting that floor. If you didn't paint that floor, it didn't happen. Kids who lived on a floor that hadn't been painted would come down to look at the paint and then go back and hassle their parents. It was kid pressure. Parents would start begging us for paint."

The demand for a new sense of community responsibility was also overt. Bertha traces the deterioration of Cochran Gardens most specifically to the end of any screening process for tenants coming into public housing. She says that when such screening ended, the projects became "dumping grounds" and people felt things were out of control. Along with early changes in physical appearance, tenants in Bertha's building set up a screening committee. Tenants elected monitors on each floor to see that the rules established for behavior—no disruptions, fights, clothes hung outside, garbage, and so forth—were being followed. They renamed the building (1121 North Seventh) Dr. Martin Luther King. And they took the rules with utter seriousness.

After renovation of the whole Cochran Gardens complex began on a large scale in 1978, "one group of people wouldn't change their behavior," Bertha recounts. "So we moved them into another building to give them a chance to think about what they were doing wrong, but we wouldn't move them into any of the new apartments. They were fighting, lying, creating disturbances in the building. We're not going to tolerate that. We told them, 'We're going to put you in one of the old buildings, and when we finish the next four we're renovating, we hope your attitude and behavior has changed. Because if it hasn't, the next move is going to be out.'

"They called the newspaper on me. I told them they could

call God. The newspaperman called up and said, 'Miss Gilkey, is that the decision your community made, that these poor people couldn't move into new apartments?' I said, 'You're absolutely right. They're not lying one bit. They're not moving to the renovated buildings on account of their behavior.' I said, 'The taxpayers have invested millions in Cochran. All we're asking them to do is buy into the standards that the tenants created. Not me. *They* created. They sat down and voted on whether certain attitudes and certain behaviors were acceptable and to be enforced. Now are you telling me that they should move [into a new apartment] when they're urinating on the elevators and creating a peace disturbance?'

" 'No, no, Miss Gilkey,' he said. So I said, 'Well, let me tell you something. I don't care if they call God. You can quote me. The next move is going to be out of Cochran. Our community has given them another chance. *But we will not have that kind of behavior!* That's all there is. We will not have it. We've worked too hard to turn our community around and either you're a part of the solution or you're a part of the problem.'

"They changed. They cleaned up their act. They're ready now."

Bertha Gilkey combines toughness with a wonderful sense of the ways people need appreciation, especially people used to lifelong abuse and belittlement. "Everything we did, we had a party and a celebration. There would be a dedication, a ribbon-cutting." When tenants won a community center from the city, each room was dedicated to someone who had died but had aided the community. The boxing room was named for an older resident, a former lightweight boxer who spent years working with teen-agers on different teams. The ballet and dancing room was graced with the name of a woman who helped tenants upholster old furniture. "Their families were there. We had celebrations and gave them roses. It was beautiful," Bertha remembers.

Small steps built on a sense of the totality of community life that needed to be changed. "Working with low-income people is like opening Pandora's box," Bertha observes. "Poor people got all kinds of problems. Housing is just one. Unless you're willing to deal with them all, it just doesn't work." I asked her what was at the heart of it. "Self-respect," she replied immediately. "And giving people the right to have a say-so over their life like they should. Just because we're poor doesn't mean we don't have a right to a say-so."

Bertha emphasized again and again that people would believe her or follow her lead because she "understood." As she put it, "I come from the projects and am one of them." She has applied her sense of the need for respect and appreciation for the life of the community to every phase of the community's transformation.

A major foundation of Cochran Gardens' changes has been programs for young people. "We felt the school in the community was not a part of the community," Bertha explains. So with the aid of a federal program designed for public-housing children, they developed a curriculum. "Kids wrote papers on what I like about living here, playing up the positive. In the art class, they took cardboard and built a model of a housing development with the streets and the playgrounds. The principal put it in a glass dome with a sign that said 'Cochran.' Then kids could say, 'I live in that building.' Gradually, in an indirect way, we were rebuilding self-esteem, telling the kids that it's all right to live in public housing."

Teachers and students planted trees and flowers in the project. "You can bet they didn't get torn up, because the kids did it themselves," Bertha points out. She saw such a process in a straightforward way: "The problem was kids did not respect life 'cause they had seen so much brutal killing and murder. There was no grass and no trees. We wanted to bring that back.

"So we had kids take a plot of land. We fenced it in. They made a garden, planted the food, and they'd care for it. They'd tend it. And after it grew, they cooked it in the home-economics class. It showed that you start with a seed, you grow a plant, it produces food. Now it gives you nourishment, keeps you living." For Bertha, everything has pedagogical possibility. "I'd tell them, 'The same thing happens when you shoot and kill somebody as would happen if you killed that plant. That person could have ended up becoming a doctor or a poet or an artist or a singer or a dancer. They could have saved your life. They could have put something back into the community. That's why life is so important!' "

One program took students, parents, and teachers for a several-day trip to the countryside. The point was to teach cooperation. "Most of the time, we're taught self, not us, not we. Mine. I. Me. We wanted them to understand that you by yourself could do nothing. But once you do linking with other persons, there's a hell of a lot you can do." Another program paired students with jobs in the project: building manager, janitor, and so forth. They would then organize skits to solve various problems: unruly tenants, conflicts with the Housing Authority, family conflicts. Through the school programs, like other activities, the principles of self-respect, participation, and community responsibility ran as the central threads.

"We have a parenting program, Share-Care, that provides day care for very young mothers," Bertha continues, making the point. "It opens at six in the morning and closes at seven at night. The agreement is they've got to go back to school. They pick what they want to be." She shakes her head. "You know, Harry, the saddest thing is they have such low self-esteem. They say, 'Well, I want to be a nurse's aide.' I say, 'Why don't you want to be the doctor?' "

This kind of program opened a window into the despair and frequently self-destructive fury of young unwed mothers. "We found a great deal of resentment," Bertha describes. "The young mothers resented their mothers: 'She doesn't have any education. She wears a rag around her head all day,' they would say. But they're becoming an exact replica of their mothers. The girl may be eleven and pregnant. Then we met with the young grandmothers. They hated their daughters and their sons who had children and left them on them. 'Well, Bertha,' they'd say, 'when does our life get started? All I can remember is having babies. When can I lose weight, find a job, do some of the things I want to do? I resent them because I tried to tell them not to get pregnant like me and they wouldn't listen.' "

In the Share-Care program, the young grandmothers also were able to leave their children's babies and go back to school.

But mothers and grandmothers alike not only have new opportunities; there is also a kind of "payment." Bertha tells them, " 'We don't want money. The cost is that you've got to buy into the parent concept. You are a parent whether you like it or not. Attend meetings, encourage the fathers to come in. We make children's toys. Do fun things like go to the zoo.' You know, Harry, sometimes they've never had fun with their kids. 'Think about family planning.' I say, 'You've got to sit down and do some peer training with other teen-age girls who are not pregnant yet. Say to them, "Hey, this is not the way to go." 'Cause they're not going to listen to me, but they'll listen to you, one of their peers who's been there.' "

Bertha and other community leaders have used every activity to rebuild community ties. "We got a grandparents-as-foster-parents program," she continues. "I got young grandmothers who are twenty-nine who don't want to be grandmothers. And I got older women who want to be mothers and don't have anything to do. They'd love to tell younger women, 'Don't do this. Burp the baby like that.' So we match 'em up. Young women with older women, maybe fifty-five, who become like their adopted mothers. They talk to them about their problems. They come in and rock the baby. And they feel like they're doing something worthwhile. It takes a lot of pressure off my young grandmother who is being used as a scapegoat by the young mother."

For Bertha, the more role models young people have, the more they can "put back into my community." In the day-care centers (she has established four in Cochran and three other public housing projects, and for ten years directed one herself), all the teachers are residents. "They know where these babies come from. They know the residents. They can provide good role models. The child will say, 'I can see my teacher 'cause she lives downstairs. I don't have to be a drug pusher or dope dealer or thief. I can be somebody.' Then when they get to the age of twelve or thirteen, they can take another course."

There is a kind of drivenness in Bertha when she talks about keeping teen-agers from "going bad." She sees it as a process one must check from the beginning. "When a child comes in from a very poor home," she says, describing the procedures at the day-care centers, "we got a bathroom. We bathe them, comb their hair, get them a set of clothes so when they go into that classroom they look just like the other kids. They feel good about themselves. They don't have to turn over a chair or slap another kid to get attention. The teacher will hug them and kiss them, not just the kids who smell good and have little ruffled panties." Bertha is now shouting and she pounds the steering wheel of the van we are riding in. "That's why I hire residents. They know that! I set up day care because we had to stop producing children who end up incarcerated, end up vandalizing the buildings, end up selling drugs. It starts when they're very young. The day-care centers are meant to begin to deal with that, so the next generation will put into our community instead of taking from it!"

For all her tremendous empathy with her neighbors' feelings of isolation, discouragement, and self-hate, there is also a steely determination about Bertha. It comes out in different ways. Shortly before we met, she had fired one entire janitorial crew on the spot. The manager of the janitorial service, one of several businesses owned and operated by the Cochran tenants' community corporation, was hospitalized. The crew had used his absence to not clean an assigned building. Bertha wouldn't stand for it. "It's the kind of thing which hurts the reputation of the whole service," she explained.

Then there are the stories about how she has stood up to the rich and powerful on behalf of poor, black tenants. The classic tale recounts the way Cochran Gardens finally got funds needed for a wholesale renovation.

By 1977, a tenant management committee officially ran Cochran Gardens, part of an experiment initiated by the Ford Foundation, which had led to four tenant-run housing complexes in St. Louis, out of nine. Bertha was president of the Cochran Gardens committee, and also president of the citywide association of public-housing tenants. Because of her visibility as a "community leader," she was called to a meeting that year at which the city's major political figures and chief business leaders were gathered.

"The city was going to submit a proposal for a UDAG," Bertha says. UDAG—for Urban Development Action Grant—was one of the federal initiatives established in the 1970s with the avowed intention of aiding urban revitalization. Under pressure from neighborhood groups around the country, the legislation had stipulated the need for "community involvement" in the planning process. Put simply, city leaders felt they needed Bertha's signature on the proposal.

"They were all there," she remembers. "The city fathers. The bankers. They said they were concerned because poor people had to live in all these high-rise buildings. They said they wanted to move Cochran."

Bertha shakes her head. "We'd been here for thirty years and no one was concerned, right? So I said, 'Well, where we gonna move?' They said, 'Oh, we're going to build you some houses up the street.'

"Remember," she continues, "we'd been working real hard to turn things around. We'd started in 1969. But no matter how much we organized, we could not change the physical appearance to make Cochran fit into the new St. Louis. So I cried a couple of minutes. And then I said, 'Over my dead body.'"

This is evidently a story often told, and Bertha relishes it. "We were concerned, too, that Cochran didn't fit into the new downtown." She told the officials, "We want to fit in. In fact, we've been concerned for twenty-five years that we were going to be displaced. We knew when you people continued to build all these new buildings and you weren't spending any money in our community that there wasn't any intention of keeping us here. So we were just waiting for you to come to us and say what you're saying to us today. But let me tell you, we're not going anywhere.' I said I would go back and tell all the tenants that they were going to put us out, and we would march on them downtown. 'I can't be responsible, you know, for the anger that may come out.' They said they felt I was threatening them and cared not to speak to me anymore. So I said, 'Fine,' and left.

"God, was I scared!" Bertha remembers with a grin. "I went back and told my people, 'Look, if they kill me, don't move. If they think I'm the only thing keeping them from taking over the community, who knows?' Three days later they set up another meeting. 'Miss Gilkey,' they said, 'we thought about it and we're going to let you people stay here.' They said, 'We hired an architect and we've redesigned your buildings.' They were going to move the large families down to the little buildings where our playground and parks are. Then they were going to convert all the buildings at one end to elderly apartments. Those were their conditions.

"I said, 'No. If I don't see Cochran in the UDAG, I don't sign nothing. What are you going to do for Cochran? I need an architect and a planner.' They said, 'We've got an architect.' I said, 'No, he who pays the piper calls the tune. We want our own. We might need millions of dollars of work before it's over.'

"Well, they'd been working on this plan for the last twenty years, and they gave us two weeks. But we got a planning grant to hire our own architect and we had representatives from each of the twelve buildings in Cochran meet over those two weeks to make up our own plan. That's where we got the original money for all this rehabilitation—five and a half million dollars. No more Band-Aiding. We wanted to start from the beginning. We wanted a community center, rooms, first-floor apartments, wrought-iron fences, doors, walkups for the large families, courtyards, playgrounds—all of it. Everyone was involved, saying what they would like.

"We wanted people to face each other over the courtyards so there would be more of a community feeling. People sharing, talking—you know, like a real neighborhood, something that's here to stay. We had two weeks to plan it all. Then we had a meeting of everyone, in four-below-zero weather. Everyone approved it."

Bertha Gilkey is an amazing leader and champion of her community. She combines such leadership, moreover, with a street-wise savvy about entrepreneurial possibilities and city politics. A tour of Cochran Gardens these days not only encompasses the renovations in the original twelve public-housing buildings; it also takes one by O'Fallon Place, for instance—an elegant, 500-unit town-house complex partly owned by the Tenant Management Committee. ("In this one we wanted a share of the profits," Bertha comments. They have used their share partly to subsidize the Share-Care program.) In O'Fallon, subsidized housing at $25-a-month rent is mingled with market-value units at $350. "Both have plush carpets, central air, chandeliers, walk-in closets, stoves, refrigerators," Bertha points out. The only difference is a dishwasher in the market-rate apartments.

We pass the building in which Cochran Tenants' Catering Service is housed (grossing more than $600,000 a year, "the only nonprofit black catering service in the country"); the health clinics, swimming pools, sites for the planned shopping mall and training school . . . the litany of businesses and constructions goes on and on. Nearly 400 young people are employed each year in community jobs, funded partly through government programs, partly from profits of other businesses ("so we don't have to meet the crazy government regulations," as Bertha puts it). An extensive training program in building trades began with the top floors of the Cochran buildings that had been abandoned.

"We took some of the hard-core youth when we took over managing Cochran," Bertha remembers, "and we used jobs-program money to train them in apartment renovation. These were the kids that were kicking in the apartments and vandalizing them. We had them renovate them instead. For three years these kids did that. We hired journeymen painters, carpenters, plumbers, and so forth to supervise them. When we got ready to start building housing ourselves, we shot them right into the apprentice programs 'cause they was right. Once they become an apprentice, they don't need a Bertha Gilkey. Those hard-core youth that people have given up on are now living in our communities, working, paying rent, running our baseball teams. They provide a role model for the other kids that are coming up. Those kids know there's hope for them 'cause they *know* what this guy used to be like."

Money made in various projects is returned to the community in different programs. Often the aid they receive takes the form more of loans than outright grants. In the O'Fallon project, for instance, Cochran tenants received a million-dollar grant from the city under the Community Development Block Grant Program one year; they returned $600,000 the next. "Eventually this will be a self-help program in its totality," imagines Bertha. "We will be able to finance our programs through the profits. Food, rent, buying shoes—whatever; profits will all come back to provide supportive services."

The tenants have skillfully maneuvered. For many years, for instance, they have been allied with small businesses in the downtown area, and Bertha serves on the board of Downtown, Inc., the business organization. Out of 18,000 tenants in public housing, 16,000 are registered to vote. One city councilwoman lives in the projects. "You do what you need to. It's just important to be clear about your goals," Bertha remarks when asked whether she is worried about the tenant programs becoming co-opted and losing their independence.

At the base of Cochran Gardens' independence, however, is a clarity and dedication unusual in much community organizing about the goals and values that inform their efforts. Bertha admits her own needs for recognition clearly enough. "We have a strong youth council that works with smaller kids," she tells me. "One time when I asked them what they wanted to be, some said, 'President'; one said 'a buyer at a big store'; and one said, 'I want to be Bertha Gilkey.' I liked that. I really did." But it also becomes indisputably clear, talking to Bertha Gilkey and other tenant activists in public housing, that her deepest loyalties are to her community and she has set an example others follow. In an extraordinary way, Bertha Gilkey is a leader who cannot be bought. None of the elected leadership receives compensation for their efforts. Indeed, she speaks of the "motto" that neither she nor any member of her family should be employed by tenant businesses. "We view that as a conflict of interest. One thing we always want to project is that there is no clique, no favoritism. That's very important. A lot of times you start off opposing the system and you become the system, do the very things that you were fighting. I'm always conscious of that," she explains. All elected officers—and every officer in Cochran must regularly stand for election by secret ballot—sign a code of conduct that they must live up to. "How could I tell a manager to evict someone for antisocial behavior if I had antisocial behavior? Leaders are supposed to be role models," she concludes.

Bertha contemplates running for the city council and eventually higher office. "I'm convinced that the people we put in office have to be people with principles who cannot be bought," she says. But her reasons for waiting so many years before running, when many opportunities for public office have presented themselves over time, are as important as her current aspirations. "We had to get Cochran together first," she explains. "And the other thing is leadership. I wanted to be sure when I leave, people have the same standards. There are leaders who will carry it on."

Bertha Gilkey now consults with tenant groups around the country and even abroad. She is co-chair of the National Congress of Neighborhood Women, a group that sponsors programs in dozens of communities. The city of Louisville, Kentucky, has hired her as a consultant to help set up tenant-managed public housing programs. She believes that the principles that have proved so successful in Cochran—self-help, dignity, empowerment, community responsibility—are transferable to any community. "If we can do it in public housing, it can happen anywhere," she argues. "Public housing is so impersonal. Buildings are designed to cut off communication."[7]

It is not simple, however, for poor and disadvantaged communities to undergo the sort of metamorphosis that is evident in Cochran—what Clarence Jordan surely would have described as "metanoia." To generate such a sense of one's own capacities and to effectively challenge the powers that be required in the United States of the 1970s and early 1980s a rare combination of circumstances: leaders with great skill and talent, resources that could be mobilized, no small measure of good fortune, and a deep loyalty to communal values in a society that constantly tends to corrupt and undermine them. But other models could nonetheless also be found in far different settings. Like Cochran, they involved as constituent elements the refusal to accept definitions of "the problems" imposed from the outside. To regain capacities for self-help and self-reliance, people somehow had to find the courage to define their own situation for themselves.

In certain instances, self-help communities could help precipitate far-ranging movements for social change. Such has certainly been true in the case of the Center for Independent Living in Berkeley, an institution formed, developed, and run by disabled people themselves.

By the later years of the 1970s, the disabled in America had gained a striking new visibility, mainly through their own assertiveness. Their sit-in at the offices of the Department of Health, Education, and Welfare in San Francisco in 1977, demanding that the government actually enforce the laws against discrimination that Congress had passed in 1973, brought international headlines. "We had support from Safeway Stores to the Black Panthers," remembers Judy Heumann, a leader in the demonstration. In the first four months of 1978 after adopting implementing regulations, the department received 377 complaints of discrimination against the disabled—considerably more than those of race and sex discrimination put together. Blind people battled airlines who proposed to take away white canes during flights, while employees at a workshop for the blind in Cincinnati joined a union, the first time such a work setting had ever been successfully organized. "The handicapped are emerging as a vocal political action group," ran a special report in the *New York Times.* "Emboldened by civil rights legislation that is just going into effect, they are demanding fundamental changes in the way society treats them."

Access to public accommodations, jobs, educational institutions, and community facilities of all sorts made up the movement's agenda. But more intangible themes formed its central animus: a challenge to fundamental cultural standards of beauty, attractiveness, competence, and worth. "An incredible amount of paternalism has always greeted the handicapped," explained Mrs. Milk, executive director of Mainstream, Inc. "People say, 'We will protect you from yourself. Stay on the first floor of the world and you'll be safe.' " Similarly, Dr. Frank Bowe, director of the American Coalition of Citizens with

Disabilities, defined the goals of the new movement as achieving "to the limits of our abilities, not our disabilities. We should be defined by what we can do, not what we can't." But to demand such changes required not only a willingness to take on conventional American wisdom; it meant overcoming the pervasive and often pernicious myths that disabled people had often themselves absorbed about who they were and who they could not be.[8]

Certain images hold powerful sway over the culture as the yardsticks to measure what is "normal." Indeed, in cultural terms the struggles of blacks, or women, or other groups defined as subordinate and marginal constitute a wrestling with precisely the dominant definitions of what constitutes "the mainstream."

In these terms, the label of a disability poses a different order of problem. As John Gliedman and William Roth, authors of the Carnegie Council report *The Unexpected Minority: Handicapped Children in America,* have pointed out, at an elemental level there is simply the matter of pride: "No one argues that mental retardation is good, that blindness is beautiful, that doctors should stop research into the causes and cures of cerebral palsy." Blacks may challenge the lower social roles assigned to them by asserting that "black is beautiful." "The stigma of handicap, on the other hand, hampers its bearer's ability to assume virtually any positive social persona." In contemporary health-conscious America, we remember such figures as Franklin Roosevelt (in a wheelchair) or Julius Caesar and Alexander the Great (both epileptics) as great men whose handicaps were incidental or entirely invisible. In contrast, those we think of *as disabled* have little or no role at all.

The disabled have at times been radically excluded. Chicago once had an ugly law that prohibited anyone from appearing in public who was "diseased, maimed, mutilated or in any way deformed so as to be an unsightly or disgusting object." In supposedly more enlightened settings, the disabled were seen as objects for pity, dependent upon protection and charity. Policies in this vein aimed at total-care institutions, with provisions for rehabilitation for a few who might achieve certain kinds of employment. The language to describe such care revealed, sometimes starkly and crudely, society's judgments: "villages of the simple made up of the warped, twisted and the incorrigible, happily contributing to their own and the support of those more lowly—'cities of refuge' in truth, havens in which all shall live contentedly, because no longer misunderstood nor taxed with expectations beyond their mental or moral capacity," read one description.

From the perspective of the disabled themselves, perhaps the most overwhelming obstacles in the way of independence and dignity were the great pressures to become "good clients," in Dewar's terms. Or as Adrienne Asch and Lawrence Sacks put it in their study of the autobiographies of blind women and men, "Lives Within, Lives Without," "playing out the [disability] role's requirements entails being helpless, submissive, dependent, uncomfortable with nondisabled people, asexual—in short, unable to perform any adult social function."

In traditional terms, escape out of the ghetto created by pervasive social expectations and assigned roles has almost always meant *individual* attempts to deny or render irrelevant one's disability—not to challenge the expectations themselves. Asch and Sacks found, studying the autobiographies of blind women and men, great difficulty (especially for the men) in identifying with other blind. Even rarer, moreover, was any attempt to redefine "the problem" itself: "What is tragic and astonishing is that virtually all believe that, unlike their sighted families and friends who take membership in the world for granted, they must prove themselves and their worth *before* they enter. . . . It never occurs to these authors that they should never have been excluded in the first place."[9]

Thus the story of how a movement of self-assertion among the disabled emerged in the 1970s and continues today involves an exploration into changing *self*-perceptions as well as dominant social attitudes. In this process the Center for Independent Living (CIL), located not far down the street from the University of California on Berkeley's famed Telegraph Avenue, has played an indispensable role.

CIL grew out of a community living situation for disabled

students at the University of California, originally housed in Cowell Hospital. Cowell reflected the complexity and ambiguity of many disabled-community settings in the 1960s: It simultaneously proscribed the lives of residents and nurtured new feelings of community, strength, and assertiveness.

Summer camps for disabled children and teen-agers were the classic model. Such camps often brought people together in a relatively egalitarian peer setting for the first time. Adrienne Asch did well in public schools, feeling she belonged and, properly, had a *right* to be there. But sometimes her public-school experiences had also infuriatingly made her feel simply "different." "In sixth grade I remember saying to my father in despair, 'I have 33 guides and no friends.'" Camp for the blind in New Jersey included a diverse mix of children, ranging in age from six to sixteen, of all races and with many forms of disability: "It was really amazing. You had white upper-middle-class kids and black and Hispanic kids whose common denominator was blindness. You also had kids who were blind with other disabilities, with cerebral palsy, mental retardation, with hearing problems." Strong friendships formed among many children. As they became teen-agers, some would date each other. But the camp also had sharply hierarchical and constrictive aspects that cut across the sense of camaraderie.

Blind children who were sent to special schools during the school year seemed to embody the worst fears of the majority who attended public school: "They hadn't made it in public school for some reason; we knew we worked very hard to get to public school and stay there." In different years, rules would be more or less restrictive: "There were some years when you were encouraged to be as independent as you wanted to be; other years when you were encouraged to rely on people with partial sight, depending on the counsellors or the administration." Certain divisions remained throughout. Cabin counsellors, for instance, all were sighted. When teen-agers began dating, they would often be discouraged. "I remember being very angry and saying to a counsellor I was very fond of, 'How can you say it's fine to be blind and then object to blind kids dating each other?'" Asch remembered. Adrienne Asch is now a therapist and a university teacher, but she has struggled with such questions all her life. "If it's all right to be who you are, why is it so important to go where someone else is?" she asks. "I was younger than 15 when I was trying to pose that."

For Judy Heumann, who became associate director of CIL, camp for the physically disabled had restrictions that grated over time: "As you got older you became aware that counsellors were always nondisabled," she remembered. But mainly it offered the space and freedom to build a warmly supportive community of peers: "It was the only time I spent with other disabled kids, where we could talk about how we felt, the personal pain and feelings of rejection," she explained. "It was difficult to discuss it at home. There wasn't anybody else who had a disability. My nondisabled friends always said when you get older, people will see you for who you are. The disability won't matter." But Heumann's actual experience was the opposite: "The older you got the more ingrained these things were." Camp provided a place through teen-age years to develop not only supportive relations but also political perspectives. "The discussions became more and more sophisticated. We began to make distinctions. While we were definitely into integration of disabled people into society, we understood that from a political point of view there needed to be organizations which disabled people controlled."

In 1970, her friendship networks formed from camp became political companions when she and others created the Disabled in Action, the first group in the nation to bring people with different disabilities together to press for change in an activist, public way.

Such a process of community-building and growing political sophistication in the face of outside control developed at Cowell. Phil Draper, one of the founders of CIL and for many years its director, pointed out the contradictions of the program. "It allowed students to go to school and relieved them of day-to-day worries so they could channel energies into the school end of it." But problems multiplied over time. This was, after all, Berkeley in the late 1960s. Students all over campus were growing their hair longer, experimenting with new life-styles, trying out new ideas. "The social atmosphere of Berkeley was very important," Draper believes. "There were move-ments going on like free speech, the women's movement. Dis-abled people realized that, 'Hey, we're no different than other disadvantaged groups. We want to be considered as equal.'" Cowell, however, reflected the condescending and restrictive social attitudes about the "disability role," stipulating when stu-dents could come and go, how long they could wear their hair, whom they could invite in as guests, even how they should behave. But it did create a space for student solidarity to de-velop as well, fired by the restive, assertive spirit of the broader Berkeley environment. "The residents talked, interacted," ex-plains Draper. "And they found strength among themselves. They began to believe they could control their environment."

Finally, a confrontation with officials resulted in increasing independence for the program, now called the Physically Dis-abled Students Program (PDSP). Students moved off campus, found an old building where they could set up an office, and began providing services not only for students but also for some from the community. With control of their own program, at least in relative terms, the disabled students quickly identified needs that normal rehabilitative services had completely over-looked, such as wheelchair repair. "At that time, nobody was fixing wheelchairs," Draper remembers. "People would wear out their wheelchair and then send it back to the factory. If you didn't have a backup—and most didn't have second chairs—you were immobile." At that point, Draper got involved.

Phil Draper is an imposing man who uses an electric wheel-chair to get around. He radiates a kind of indomitability and independence—for some time he had been "getting along on my own as best I could, hustling attendants, meeting with the welfare system, trying to find my own transportation," but he didn't like the hassle, and he had a natural instinct as an organ-izer. As he puts it, "I've been on both sides of the fence" (Dra-per was disabled after reaching adulthood) "and I wanted to get back to the side where things were happening." Going to school, connecting up with the PDSP, he envisioned a program that involved people after they graduated as well. "One person can try to get along, but they're not going to get very far."

The vision he and others discussed was an expansion of the sorts of services they were already beginning to provide for people from the community, "a program that would be an advocate for disabled people, that would be a spokesperson for dealing with the institutions and systems that affect people's lives, and at the same time it would be a service program to provide services disabled people need to survive on a day-to-day basis." He recalls the excitement such a vision generated. "We would sit around and talk and realize, 'Hey, there has to be something better than this, a way to work, to live in the community, to do those things that everybody else takes for granted!'"

The Center for Independent Living officially opened in 1972. It drew on the supportive friendships that had developed over time through Cowell and the PDSP, and it was funded partly through the help of Edward Roberts, director of the State Department of Rehabilitation, who himself had been one of the first disabled students to graduate from Berkeley. The concept of "independent living" involved full participation of the disabled in the life of the community—and a definition of the disabled that cut across the normal segmentation by specific disability. Indeed, such a redefinition in itself was a profoundly political act, a shift from the way the *society* defined the issue (the disabled are people with specific sets of limiting problems) to a definition that reflected the point of view of the disabled themselves. "I really think that was key," remarked Bob Funk, one of the theoreticians of the disabled movement who later worked with CIL as a lawyer in its Disability Law Resource Center. "If it had only been providing services, it would have been less important. It was providing a community of different people"—commonly afflicted with the constricting expectations of the broader culture.

Another radical notion was that CIL would be controlled by disabled people themselves. For many service providers who had always seen the disabled as people to be "helped," the concept indeed was disturbing. Phil Draper described the hostility they met in the beginning from many in Rehabilitation Services: "The counsellors saw us as a threat to their jobs. Here were some disabled people who didn't know what they were doing or what they wanted to do, they thought, stepping on their turf." Others in Berkeley simply saw the Center as "a long-haired hippie group" that was sure to fail with rapidity.

But rather than fail, CIL quickly established a reputation for competence and innovation in a broad range of service areas, from new wheelchair design to van modification, legal representation, and peer counseling. Moreover, its very existence as a success was its most important characteristic. "It took me years to feel at home in Berkeley," said Judy Heumann, who arrived in 1973. "But to feel at home in CIL was automatic. The spirit and energy was always high. Disabled people who had been considered have-nots were setting up an organization, getting money, providing services to people who we really believed were the severely disabled in the community. We were able to gain that sense of self-respect that we didn't have otherwise." Put simply, the Center helped people rebuild the sort of self-confidence they needed to claim their full and complete identities. "You could be a lesbian or gay or black or Hispanic or any other thing, but for many of us we have really known that the rest of the world sees us as disabled," Heumann continued. "CIL has allowed us to be all of our parts because we had our *own* community. To gather the different parts and then go deal with this community or that community. We had this real sense of power."

One can feel the activist spirit. CIL is housed in a spacious, well-lit building. Tulips outside and colorful wall designs create a vivid background for the posters that are everywhere, exhorting, challenging, demanding, and encouraging: "See Me for Who I Am, Not What I Appear to Be!" "Full Participation and Equality!" "Eliminate Stereotypes and Handicappism!" "Show New Pathways to Social Esteem, Liberty and Competence," "Show that Everyone Makes a Contribution to Our Lives." As striking as the activist sense of the Center is the reversal of normal roles when one enters. The nondisabled visitor is given directions by someone who is blind; asked to take a seat by a receptionist with some evidently severe back problem; offered coffee by a woman in a wheelchair.

The current director, Michael Winter, like Draper before him, communicates a pragmatic organizer's style. He tells stories of past experiences in the disability movement—at college in southern Illinois, as a director for an independent living center in Hawaii—with obvious delight in the minutiae of organization tactics, strategy, and maneuvering. "My first love is community organizing," Winter explains. "When I think of building a movement, that's my first emphasis." (His interest is inherited: His mother is a longtime leader in the welfare-recipients movement in Chicago.) But Winter came to the Center as director because of his considerable skills in administration and finances. In differing terms, the combination of effective organization for provision of services and organizing spirit shaped CIL from the beginning.

Organizing stories—many of which are now legendary in the disability movement—weave through reminiscences of those involved with the Center over the years. "Our first big battle was in 1972," Phil Draper recounts. "We approached the city, going through proper channels, with the idea to make Berkeley as accessible as possible. We suggested a program of making curb cuts [for wheelchairs] in the sidewalks. The public-works department said, 'You don't know what you're saying. There is no way this is going to happen.'

"Someone from CIL wrote a resolution for the city council and we got support from neighborhood groups in Berkeley. We organized all sorts of transportation, and disabled people came out of the woodwork. We had the meeting moved from its original place, which was up one flight of stairs, to the Berkeley Community Theater, which is accessible. It was one of the largest turnouts they ever had. The resolution was approved, thirty thousand dollars a year for curb cuts. The places to put them would be identified by disabled people through CIL. It made Berkeley perhaps the most accessible place at that time."

Symbols of CIL—like the great big lumbering van called "the Pumpkin" that would bring people to demonstrations—became commonplace. Other communities in the state and around the nation looked to the Center for leadership on different issues, like the campaign for HEW action to implement antidiscriminatory laws in 1977. Along with organizing, furthermore, came pioneering models for social services that built people's confidence and self-respect. "Peer counseling was an important service that CIL provided," explains Phil about one innovative program. "In peer counseling, a highly disabled person who had similar disabilities to the person they were dealing with and had learned ways of dealing with the problems would meet on a regular basis to share experiences and find out how to get things done." In such a program, learning how to deal with "simple" things like pouring coffee or shopping could be major advances toward freedom and self-help. "Many disabled people can't go out and buy their own clothes," Phil continues. "But that's an important part of your personality, being able to choose the clothes you want. People can get shut in, not know how to manage money or buy groceries for themselves."

With growing reputation, CIL made Berkeley a kind of mecca. "People would come to Berkeley from all over the country. Hitchhiking. People coming on their vacations, seeing what was happening and not wanting to go home," Draper remembers. In some ways, the Center overextended itself. "We tried to do everything at once," he says. "We couldn't wait to get going on everything."

Mary Lou Breslin, who worked with the Law Center begun out of CIL, also remembers a certain unalloyed optimism, but points to the results it achieved. "There was a naïveté in ways but also an incredible amount of energy and a tremendous spirit of cooperation. People thought you could get anything done. Volunteers would come in all the time to stuff envelopes, help with mailings, do whatever had to be done."

At its peak size by the late 1970s, CIL employed more than 200 staff and had an operating budget of $3.2 million. National and foreign news media ran features on the Center—networks from England, Ireland, and Japan sent crews to do special documentaries. Yet a collision between the Center's explosive growth and an increasingly austere fiscal mood in politics was perhaps inevitable. Eventually the Center opened a large deficit and the fiscal crisis forced major cutbacks. By 1982, the budget was less than a quarter of the maximum funding— though it had begun to increase slightly, once again; programs with the schools, with computers, with minority youth, with transportation services, and in other areas had been dropped.[10]

The Center for Independent Living, however, remains a remarkable model, one that has inspired hundreds of similar centers in the United States and in other nations (twenty-seven others in California alone). Moreover, its impact at the simplest level cannot be measured by numbers, yet it remains profoundly subversive of stereotypes in America. "CIL has told disabled people that they are not crazy," Judy Heumann concludes. "Our perceptions of how we are being treated are more likely than not correct. Given that premise, you've got a right to fight."

Indeed, the new self-respect and self-assertiveness incubated in places like Cochran Gardens and the Center for Independent Living turn our very notions of "charity" and "normalcy" upside down. They force a questioning of our basic and inherited notions of whom "the community" includes, and also such core American values as individual success and achievement without regard to communal implications. In sum, these stories prompt a new attentiveness to the values of living communities as the very ground of freedom and human dignity. They challenge us to take seriously principles that are often given only lip service.

If this sort of challenge is ever to impact in a significant way on the centralized structures and large bureaucracies of the modern world, it must acquire, simply, power. The organization that has pioneered new methods for harnessing the values of democratic community to the exercise of power in the broader society over years, on a continuing basis, is to be found in San Antonio, Texas. There, through the efforts of Communities Organized for Public Service—a community organization based largely in the barrios of the south and west sides of town —Mexican Americans who once were afraid to enter City Hall or the agencies of government now claim them as their own.

5

Empowerment

With the rain in San Antonio used to come the fear. "We would sleep in shifts at night," remembered Helen Ayala, a child of Edgewood, the Mexican-American community on the sprawling West Side of the city. Mrs. Ayala, now middle-aged, still shivers a bit when she describes the scene. When the rains continued through the night, it would mean a hike without shoes through the muddy stream flowing down her street. The Mayberry drainage ditch behind the houses would turn into a lake, spilling over its banks, lapping the white adobe walls where one can still see faint mud lines from past floods. Families down on Inez Avenue would pack what they could and leave their homes, sometimes in Red Cross rescue boats. A major downpour, continuing for a day or more, would turn Apache Creek into a torrent, pouring south and eastward into the Mexican neighborhoods around the stockyards. Major rains usually claimed the life of a child, sometimes more than one.

The city had developed a plan to improve the drainage system on the West Side in 1945. It was an urgent need—flooding regularly affected more than 100,000 families—yet by the early 1970s, no money had been spent. One could travel for miles through the winding, muddy roads of the West Side and never see a storm drain. Those ditches like Mayberry that existed were overgrown, cluttered with garbage and debris.

"This is the twentieth century, but it seemed to me like another world," says Andres Sarabia. One can see Sarabia's anger when he remembers what it was like to grow up as a Mexican American in the 1950s in San Antonio. Drainage problems were part of a pattern. "Things seemed to me wrong. I graduated twenty-fifth out of my class of four hundred. But our school was basically vocational. When I wanted to go to college, they said I didn't have enough credits." He became active in his parish at Holy Family and began to get involved in other community efforts, such as the Model Cities Program, in an attempt to do something about the community's problems. "But nothing would happen. We'd just talk."

Sarabia also tells about the day when Mexican Americans began to do more than talk. The city manager, Sam Granata, had refused to discuss the drainage problem with West Side residents. At last requested to meet by an embarrassed city council, Granata came to the West Side just after an enormous rainfall in 1973. One bridge over the Mayberry ditch had collapsed. An old woman with a fever of 105° had been forced out into the mud. The crowd that greeted him, brought to the meeting by a new organization called Communities Organized for Public Service, was large and angry. Confronting Granata with research about the history of broken promises and unimplemented legislation, they asked him why. "If you want something, you have to ask" was his weak response. Sarabia chuckles. "We've been asking ever since!"[1]

These days, no feature story on San Antonio appears without some discussion of Communities Organized for Public Service (COPS). Pablo Eisenberg, a major architect of the federal War on Poverty in the 1960s who now directs the Center for Community Change in Washington, described COPS to me as "the Sugar Ray Robinson of the community-organizing world" and "the most effective community group in the country." I remembered the special on San Antonio I had seen the spring before on the NBC "Today" show. There, inserted among segments on Mexican-style country music, food, and the political future of Henry Cisneros—"the first Mexican-American mayor of a major American town," as the media likes to describe him —was another sort of story. "When you have trouble with City Hall in San Antonio, you call the COPS," ran the tag line. Sonia Hernandez, COPS president, appeared next to Jane Pauley, describing the organization and its accomplishments and purposes. She caused some consternation, I later discovered, by saying that the city had been run ten years before by a group of wealthy white North Siders, members of the exclusive Texas Cavaliers Club.

But the federal study of American communities commissioned by the National Commission on the Neighborhoods made much the same point. It detailed the hundreds of millions of dollars' worth of improvements in streets, drainage, public facilities, and cleanup that COPS had won for poorer neighborhoods in San Antonio. It described the five, six, or seven thousand delegates who come each year to the COPS annual convention. And it concluded: "There has been a major shift in power from wealthy 'blue blooded' Anglos to the poor and working Mexican-American families of San Antonio. COPS has been at the center of this shift." I was eager to see for myself.[2]

Arriving in San Antonio, one finds signs of COPS's presence easily. The cabdriver told me at some length about the organization on the way in from the airport. On the evening news were scenes from a COPS Independence Day rally, celebrating the organization's tenth anniversary. Mayor Cisneros called COPS "the most powerful community group in the country" and "the voice for 150,000 families." With the practiced and polished oratory that has become his trademark, he exclaimed that "COPS has made a declaration of independence for the poor people . . . for all the people in San Antonio!"

It was the sort of recognition a community group might dream about. But the scene was made all the more remarkable by the calm, skeptical reply to the mayor by Ms. Hernandez, who remained clearly in control of the program. She welcomed Cisneros but was entirely unimpressed with one of his new ideas for citywide "goal-setting," which she thought was mainly a public-relations gimmick: "We reject expansion based on boosterism," as she put it. And she defined the relationship in a different way: "We rather call upon our public officials to challenge us as we challenge them—to be reciprocal, collaborative and consultative as we cooperatively forge a new vision and new consensus for San Antonio."[3]

Behind this kind of exchange, I later learned, was a specific organizational philosophy: "Politicians' work is to do your work," Hernandez explained. "When you've got somebody working for you, you don't bow and scrape. It's not meant to show disrespect. When politicians deliver, we applaud them. Not until then." The point of COPS, she continued, was not "politics as usual. COPS is about people, mainly poor people who have decided to do something about their lives. There isn't anyone around, not a Mayor Cisneros or a Governor White, who is going to come in and do anything for them. People are doing it for themselves. If we ever lost that touch, we would cease to be COPS."

I had had an introduction to COPS's public reputation. What the organization was, and how it came to be, proved a longer story.

Like Andres Sarabia, Ernesto Cortes grew up in San Antonio in the forties and fifties. He remembers decay in the Mexican community's spirit. "The struggle was to become American," Cortes explains. "If someone called you a Mexican, you were supposed to beat them up." (Helen Ayala, too, recalls the deterioration, not only in the houses but in the community fabric on the West and Southwest sides of town where most Mexicans live. "Our children were leaving for the North Side. There were not jobs or good housing. It was very sad.") In the sixties, Cortes went to the University of Texas at Austin and earned a degree with a dissertation exploring different approaches to "dealing with poverty." War-on-poverty strategies. Educational strategies. Fiscal strategies. None of it seemed very convincing. But the statistics were clear enough as Cortes profiled the Mexican community in his hometown. Median family income hovered just above the poverty line. More than three-quarters of the teen-age population dropped out of high school before graduation. "It brought home to me on an aggregate level what I had known personally," says Cortes. It also led him to begin thinking about organizing.

In Austin, Cortes did some work in electoral politics and later helped with the United Farm Workers, the migrant union organizing project headed by Cesar Chavez. Coming back to San Antonio in the late 1960s, he developed an economic development strategy for the Mexican American Unity Council. But none of it spoke directly to his perception that the problem with the Mexican-American community in San Antonio was its lack of power. No matter how many plans were developed or how many politicians promised a better day, there was not the clout to get much done. He decided to spend some time with the Industrial Areas Foundation in Chicago, the training school for community organizers started in 1969 by the legendary craftsman and dean of the tradition of organizing, Saul Alinsky.

Saul Alinsky had grown up in Chicago. Raised by poor Jewish parents who emigrated from Russia, Alinsky's childhood stories conveyed his favorite activity—thumbing his nose at authority. "I was the kind of kid who'd never dream of walking on the grass until I saw a sign that said, 'Keep Off.' Then I'd stomp all over it." For more than thirty years he practiced his attitude by helping poor communities around the country "organize themselves for power." Over this time, moreover, his reputation in local power centers frequently caused panic. "Alinsky is hated and feared in high places from coast to coast for being a major force in the revolution of powerless people," the *New York Times* put it. On hearing that he had been asked to visit Oakland's black ghetto, the city council once passed an ordinance barring him from the town.[4]

Saul Alinsky's approach was straightforward. He came to communities where he was invited—normally by a "sponsoring committee" of local institutions such as churches, small businesses, and civic associations—and he learned the community's agenda. "The first thing you've got to do in a community is listen, not talk, and learn to eat, sleep, breathe . . . the problems and aspirations of the community." He had considerable disdain for those he called "do-gooders," out to help the poor. The goal in his view should be to assist the poor in helping themselves, through building what he called "mass power organizations" that would apply leverage and win a new voice. Only through such groups, he believed, could people who were accustomed to humiliation and defeat all their lives experience a new self-respect and gain hope. On the South Side of Chicago, for example, in the large black ghetto called Woodlawn, Alinsky helped create an organization that won numerous victories from City Hall, and blocked an urban-renewal plan that threatened the area. But he argued that "our most important accomplishment was intangible . . . we gave the people a sense of identity and pride. After living in squalor and despair for generations, they suddenly discovered the unity and resolve to score victories over their enemies, to take their lives back into their own hands."

Alinsky counseled poor people's "power organizations" to operate on a "power basis" instead of appealing to values or ideals. They had to know their opponents, use the establishment's rules against them, ridicule, embarrass, and do whatever else was necessary—with nonviolent and reasonably legal limits, and the experience of the group taking action—to win. His tactics became famous. Chicago mayor Richard Daley once agreed to meet with a delegation from Woodlawn after they threatened to occupy all the bathrooms in Chicago's O'Hare International Airport. In response to the Oakland City Council, he sent the group a box of diapers to show his opinion of their "level of maturity" and invited the news media to accompany him across the Oakland Bridge, birth certificate in hand.

By the end of the 1960s, Alinsky had become convinced that more was needed than helping communities organize, one by one, to get "a piece of the action" in their areas. "There's a second revolution seething beneath the surface of middle-class America," he maintained in a *Playboy* magazine interview in 1972. High inflation, declining services, rising crime, distrust of public officials, and a general deterioration in people's lives bred fear that made Americans ripe for demogogic appeal from the Right. "The Right would give them scapegoats for their misery—blacks, hippies, Communists. And if it wins, this country will become the first totalitarian state with a national anthem celebrating the land of the free and the home of the brave." But he also believed that the middle classes—those he called "the have-a-little, want mores"—could come to understand the actual sources of their problems, which he identified especially as unresponsive and out-of-control corporations. Before his death in 1972, he experimented with a new model of organization, the Citizen Action Program in Chicago, bringing people together across older antagonisms—poor and middle-income, white ethnic, professional, black—around common problems like utility rates and pollution from the steel mills. [5]

Cortes came to Chicago in the summer of 1971 in a period of considerable ferment and change in the world of community organizing. Veterans like Ed Chambers, Tom Gaudette, Dick Harmon, Father John Egan, and Peter Martinez, who had worked with Alinsky for years, were trying out new forms of organizing. A younger generation of activists from the Sixties movements, such as Heather and Paul Booth and Robert Creamer—who would eventually play important parts in the creation of the Citizen Action network of community organizations—was learning skills of practical organizing and ways of translating moral fervor into lasting organization.

In Cortes's opinion, perhaps the most important education he gained with the Industrial Areas Foundation (IAF), was insight into his own personality. "I had a tendency to jump down people's throats, which could intimidate people," he reflects. Indeed, Cortes is often gruff, challenging and exhorting those around him, demanding people's best efforts. In Chicago, he believes, "I learned not to allow my anger to get so vociferous, to get more focused." Drawing on the fundamentals of Alinsky's approach, Cortes also no longer felt compelled to dominate discussions: "I learned the value of listening," as he puts it.

Cortes also radiates what might best be called a "populist" sensibility. It is evident sometimes in small ways. When we passed through a restaurant in San Antonio, he greeted old friends with great warmth, stopping to speak for a few minutes with a Mexican veteran disabled in the Vietnam War ('He won a Medal of Honor from Reagan, and then lost his disability," Cortes tells me as he comes over). But it is most striking when he reflects, as he often did in our discussions, on the importance of forcing organizers themselves into situations where they can "rekindle energy and passion" from the inspiration of ordinary

people. "If you're a lead organizer for COPS or any powerful
organization, you're into heady arenas," he remarks. The challenge is to constantly go back to "see new possibilities in the
people . . . to see them in a different way."

But for Cortes, drawing inspiration from ordinary people
does not mean superficial relations. Cortes is an indefatigable
reader who communicates an intense intellectuality. He regularly carries around a briefcase overflowing with the books he
is currently studying, and conversations with him range widely,
from theology to ancient history or political philosophy. What
he means by drawing inspiration is to create new ways for
people to learn to express themselves in the whole of their
personalities—their values, traditions, aspirations for the future.
Cortes brought not only the tough and skillful mind of an organizer to the IAF; he challenged traditional notions of what organizing is all about, at just the moment others, like Chambers,
were also beginning to ask such questions.

"There is a war being waged on television and in taverns, in
local stores and massive shopping centers, in corporations and
congregations, over who will shape the values of our society,"
begins the basic training manual of the Industrial Areas Foundation, *Organizing for Family and Congregation.* "It is about
this fundamental question: Who will parent our children? Who
will teach them, train them, nurture them?" Such questions
now frame the leadership-education program of the IAF,
taught to leaders and organizers from all the affiliated community groups with which it works around the country. But they
add a strikingly different dimension to the discipline of community organization from that of the past. "From 1940 to 1970,
where was the political education in community organization?"
is the way IAF's current director, Chambers, puts the problem.[6]

Saul Alinsky at his most reflective and visionary moments
could eloquently identify himself with the American democratic tradition, the tradition of those who "forced the addition
of the Bill of Rights to our Constitution," who labored "in the
shadows of the Underground Railroad," who stood "in the van-
guard of the Populist Party," or who organized among "the
thousands of packing house workers" during the days of the

Great Depression. But his normal organizing style pushed any explicit discussion of values or ideology to the sidelines. Instead, his rhetoric tended toward the wry and cynical: "In the world-as-it-is what you call morality is to a significant degree a rationalization of the position which you are occupying in the power pattern at a particular time," he wrote. "Man moves primarily because of self-interest. The right things are done only for the wrong reasons and vice versa." When longtime associates such as Father Egan suggested more discussion of religious values, he dismissed the idea." 'You take care of the religion, Jack,' he would say," Egan remembers. " 'We'll do the organizing.' "[7]

In many ways, Alinsky simply mirrored the world in which he operated. Like trade-union leaders in American history, he was driven by the desire to see poor and marginal people get more from the system in the terms the system understood. Moreover, whatever he *said*, he sought out places to organize "where there were pockets of values, and people who would take risks for their values," according to Chambers. Father Egan pointed out that the Back of the Yards community in Chicago where Alinsky first experimented with his methods was "a neighborhood with the richest kind of roots; where there was in every home a love of the family, of peoples' traditions, their customs, their religion; where age and wisdom were respected; where the neighbor was an important person; where you were not anonymous." But whatever Alinsky's own instincts, much of the organizing that claimed his legacy gained a reputation for the narrowest of concerns and vision. "Organizing for power" was often described as the end in itself—with little or no reflection about how power was to be wielded, or for what purposes.

Ernie Cortes had once considered becoming a minister and had a strong interest in theology. He brought such a perspective to the IAF. "I thought a lot about a conversation I'd had once with Cesar Chavez," he remembers, "that every organization needs an ideology if it is to continue. The United Farm Workers' was Christianity." For the Mexican community in San Antonio, too, it was hard to imagine effective organizing that did not draw explicitly on the religious language and stories of the people, and build on the Catholic church as an institution. He saw "the church [as] the center of strength in the community." Moreover, he found that priests, while strongly interested in the financial health and physical survival of their parishes, had often a deep engagement in questions of values and broader purpose. "They questioned the ministry, their faith; they challenged you and themselves. That's what gave them energy, made them interested and interesting. If you took Alinsky literally, you'd never probe below the surface."

Thus Cortes helped the IAF to broaden its understanding of people's motivations. It continued to stress the importance of "self-interest," that organizing poor and working people required working on questions of immediate, visible, and pressing concern. But it began to distinguish between "self-interest" and "selfishness," arguing that people's basic concerns are not only financial but, perhaps more fundamentally, intangibles in their lives—the happiness of their families, the well-being of their neighbors and friends, the vitality of their faith, their own feelings of dignity and worth.

As the IAF training school developed through the seventies, it came to regularize its relations with the community organizations with which it worked. Local areas would ask for aid in helping to organize; IAF organizers would in return ask for the formation of a sponsoring committee that would raise initial funds and guarantee legitimacy for the organizing effort; and as the community organizations grew, leaders would continue to be trained, not only in their areas but also in regular ten-day sessions held in different parts of the country, where they would meet leaders from other communities engaged in similar efforts, often around similar problems.

In 1973, Father Edmundo Rodriguez invited Ernie Cortes and the Industrial Areas Foundation to help the Mexican community in San Antonio try to get itself together. Cortes brought back with him the organizing skills he had learned, and a great zeal to see his own people gain power and new dignity.

There were traditions of collective struggle and communal life that could be drawn upon: a strike by Mexican pecan workers during the Great Depression; the election of Congressman

Henry Gonzales, friend of the Cortes family, whose fierce integrity had long proven a model and inspiration to many; the sense of solidarity that the circuit of Mexican festivals and celebrations generated across neightborhood lines. He knew these were there. But Cortes's basic approach was to listen. "I began to interview pastors and from them got the names of lay leaders in the parishes," he remembers. "I kept records and tapes of each conversation."

Through the course of perhaps a thousand interviews during the first year, Cortes gained a detailed sense of what mattered most to people in the neighborhoods. It turned out not to be the more visible issues that politicians or Chicano militants usually talked about—things like police brutality or racial discrimination. Rather, it was the problems closest to families and neighborhoods, such as housing, utility rates, and drainage. Father Rodriguez, who had worked for many years with only modest success to try to get Mexican Americans involved in political issues, later said it was "like one of those light bulbs that suddenly appears in cartoons." Prior efforts had failed because of their approach. It wasn't that people were unconcerned, it was that they themselves had rarely been asked what they were most concerned about.[8]

Thus the issues that COPS initially addressed broke the mold. So, too, did those who became the leadership. "One of the remarkable things about COPS," observes Sister Christine Stephens, the warm and intelligent woman who is now staff director of the organization, "is that it builds around the moderates, not the activists on the Left or the conservatives on the Right. It didn't begin with people who were the politicos or who were in public life, the people who wheeled and dealed. It grew from the people who run the festivals, who lead the PTAs, whose lives have been wrapped up in their parishes and their jobs and with their children. What COPS has been able to do is give them a public life, the tools whereby they can participate." Her observations, ten years after the beginnings of the organization, brought to mind people such as Sarabia, a civil servant at Kelly Air Force Base, active in his parish and community. And Janie Gonzalez, once a shy, quiet housewife and mother, who became executive vice-president of the organization and one of its most powerful leaders.

Janie Gonzalez is the sort of person known as the "backbone" of her community. Well dressed, middle-aged, she seems someone to turn to for advice or consolation in time of trouble. She remembers the beginnings of COPS well. "When Ernie Cortes was in the process of interviewing people in 1973, he always kept coming back to me. I always said, 'Why?' " Gonzalez speaks softly, with a marked Spanish accent, and I have to listen closely. "Ernie used to say you have to speak loud, from your stomach. I'd say, 'I'm sorry, I'm not that way. You take me the way I am!' " Cortes said he was looking for community leaders. Mrs. Gonzalez protested that she was not a leader. It shows the problems with the normal definitions.

For many years she had been active in her parish and in the school's PTA. Even when her children had gone on to secondary school, she continued to work on the school's problems because she remembered the migrant Mexican children when she was a young girl and how bad their education had been. In her own neighborhood, too, the schools were in terrible shape. "They put trash cans on the tables when it rained to catch the leaks. The teachers would get tingling sensations from touching the refrigerator. The urinals were leaking. The benches on the playground were broken with pipes sticking out." As an officer in the PTA, she regularly asked school officials to do something. Finally, she asked for a copy of the requisition for repairs. The principal of the school could not produce one. So even though she doubted she was the sort of "leader" that Cortes was looking for in the new organization, her frustrations with school officials led to involvement. "When I went to the meetings, it was what I wanted," Gonzalez explains. "I felt this was a way of putting my faith into action."

The fusion of work on specific issues with discussion of faith and other values gave a distinctive, powerful cast to COPS from the beginning. "We'd talk about what values come from our families and our faith," Gonzalez describes. "Love, caring. Then we'd talk about the pressures on the families nowadays.

Drugs. The media. Peer pressure. Alcoholism. And we'd talk about how the church should respond."

I got a more detailed sense of the sort of discussion she had experienced from a training workshop that Cortes conducted for leaders of community organizations around the country. Cortes drew a diagram on the blackboard. In the middle was a circle representing people's "primary relations"—friends and, above all, family—through which most people learn the basic lessons about relationships, reciprocity, nurturance, identity, habits, work, personal roots. He called these the "foundation experiences," which people share beyond differences in race, ethnicity, sex, and so forth. Then he made two additional points. In the first place, according to Cortes, the family cannot be seen as "everything." People's private lives cannot exist only for their own sakes. "I think there is only one sin," he commented. "The sin of idolatry. What the 'Moral Majority' does is make an idol out of the concept of family."

Second, people's activities in the broader world have to be anchored in a private life. Ed Chambers explained to me later that in his view the personal lives of organizers themselves have often been slighted or ignored in the community-organizing tradition, with injury both to themselves and to the community group as a result. Cortes maintained that if the public world "does not exist for the private" as well, totalitarianism is the outcome. "There must be a constant tension in values between public and private."

Surrounding the circle of family, he drew other circles to represent what he called "mediating institutions," a concept drawn from the work of social theorists like Peter Berger and John Newhaus. Mediating institutions are voluntary groups, neighborhood organizations, and, in the Mexican community, especially the church. If properly understood, they nourish, support, and empower people's primary relations, linking them to the broader world.

Big government has often been seen as the enemy of such "mediating institutions." Cortes, too, saw an intrusive government and unresponsive bureaucracies as undermining mediating structures. But he invited the group to list other pressures on primary relations and mediating institutions and wrote down a much longer list as well: economic forces like inflation and unemployment; cultural influences like TV; drugs; lack of day care; community problems such as crime, redlining by lending institutions, and urban renewal. Differing from the emphasis of conservative social theorists, Cortes traced such pressures primarily to the functioning of large corporate institutions. He maintained that corporations dominate our society, controlling vast sums of money, communications systems, and huge political resources. In the 1970s, most people's response to the pressures on families and mediating institutions was withdrawal into private life. He suggested that such a strategy was "idiocy" in the classic Greek meaning of the word—the inability to function in a public life.

Finally, Cortes divided the blackboard into two columns. On each side were to be clusters of values, or what he called "guides to action." On the first side, he asked the audience to list the "ways of the world"—the values most prized in the corporate system and large bureaucracy. "Do your own thing," "Look out for number one," "Never give a sucker an even break," "If it feels good, do it," and so forth formed the list. Those values, he argued, were what the corporate system makes *operational*—most effective in achieving results. On the other side were values that groups like COPS believe are the foundation of citizen organization, values Cortes traced to Judeo-Christian and American democratic traditions: cooperation; participation; integrity of the whole person; free expression; concern for others; reciprocity; respect for the past; love; concern for the weak; justice. What citizen organizing accomplishes if it is successful in empowering communities according to their best values, he concluded, is to make operational *those* as the alternative. At the end, people crowded around, talking excitedly: black welfare mothers from New York, white hard hats from Houston, priests from Los Angeles—for them all, it was plain, the discussion touched a deep chord.

In San Antonio, the connection of basic issues of immediate concern to people, Mexican and American traditions, and the extensive grounding in values produced some amusing moments early in COPS history. "Once we were accused of being Communist," Sarabia remembers. "This fellow talked about Alinsky and communism. I told him that I'd never met Alinsky. 'Why don't you worry about Jefferson and those guys? They're the ones who wrote the basics for this stuff.' " The combination also called forth tremendous response from thousands of people who had never before experienced success.

George Ozuna, now twenty-six and an area leader of COPS, was seventeen when his grandmother took him to one of the organization's first "actions," a large-scale protest in classic Alinsky style held at the largest department store downtown, Joske's. While several hundred Mexican Americans slowly tried on clothes, carefully took them off, and put them back on the shelves, store officials rushed around in consternation. A delegation went up to try to meet with the head of the store, whose help they planned to seek in setting up a meeting with the business community, those COPS considered to be the "real leaders" of San Antonio. ("We were naïve in those days," Sarabia laughs. "We thought they would meet with us because Mexicans had run up so much credit at the store!")

From the perspective of a high-school student, the event seemed mainly bewildering. "When we got downtown, I saw some kind of demonstration," Ozuna recalls. "So I told my grandmother that we'd have to walk around. She said, 'Oh, no.' It turned out she was part of the whole thing."

George continues, recounting the event with pleasure. "People started putting on clothes. So I said, 'This is a good price. Let's buy it.' She said, 'No, we're not going to buy anything. We want to see their eyes.' Their reactions," George explains, "she wanted to see their reactions." He stops and his voice lowers. "You know, I've never told this story before about my grandma.

"When we came back from that action, I asked my grandma some questions. She was getting some opposition in the neighborhood because of COPS, and I said, 'Is it worth it? Why are you doing this?' " Ozuna shakes his head. "She told me, 'I'm doing this because we're winning. Your grandfather and I came from Mexico to try to build something. But we were losers.

There were things that always worked to keep us down. In Mexico, it was the government taking away our animals and chickens. In was poverty again. Grandfather working at Fine Silver with no union. All my life I've worked very hard to win, to find something where you're really winning. We've always lost. Now I'm winning. *We're* winning. And we have a say-so in what's going on. And we're going to have more of a say-so.' "

During my stay in San Antonio, I heard many stories such as George Ozuna's. Ten years before, it was as if a quiet people on the margins suddenly walked off the pages of tourist brochures where they had been "background color," and out of the chamber-of-commerce promotionals where they were described as a "cheap labor force." The city did not quite know what was happening.

"Do Gooders Become Do-ers," ran the headline for a column by a local reporter, under the byline "Don Politico." COPS's first annual convention was held in the auditorium of Jefferson High School on November 23, 1974. Over 1,000 delegates jammed the auditorium, adopting a constitution, a plan for seeking $100 million in city improvements in sidewalks, streets, libraries, parks, and other items, and strategies for fighting problems such as air pollution. "COPS did not simply grow; it exploded on the scene last July after a flood which devastated West Side homes for the umpteenth time," wrote Don Politico.

Tracing the victories that the organization had been able to achieve in its brief history—a $46-million drainage bond, another $8 million in neighborhood improvements—Politico went on to say that "COPS didn't disappear with the receding of the floodwaters," despite many peoples' predictions. "It is an organization of organizations," he said, which gave it a certain solidity: "parish clubs, church societies, parents' groups, youth clubs, senior citizen groups, neighborhood associations and block clubs—and any others interested in seeing 'nonviolent change for the betterment of their neglected neighborhoods,' " he quoted one member as saying. He noted the apparent effectiveness of COPS tactics—the "controlled anger" of the "slightly unruly groups" that had become common at city council meetings—and he speculated that the group "won't go away soon."[9]

"We got a reputation for confrontation in the beginning," explained Andres Sarabia, elected the first president of COPS. "But that wasn't me. I would have done things with sugar. We learned." He illustrated the point with a story of an early meeting with the city council, when COPS delegates planned to make a presentation suggesting that utilities' excess charges, ruled a "windfall" by the Utility Commission, should be returned to the consumers. "I went up to the podium. The mayor said, 'What do you want?' I said I wanted to speak to the motion on the floor, which would put the windfall into the city budget, not return it. He said, 'Wait just a minute.' Then he proceeded to take a motion and vote. He turned and said to me, 'What did you want to say?' We were stunned." Sarabia still communicates amazement. "From that point on, whenever we got to that podium, we started talking. They could say we were out of order or whatever the hell they wanted. They taught us."

To an outside observer, such meetings may have seemed spontaneous and "slightly unruly," at the least. But behind the events were weeks of planning, discussion, research, and role playing that taught people to express themselves in a new way, simultaneously articulating and controlling their buried anger.

For people like Janie Gonzalez, expressing anger was extraordinarily difficult. "We'd been trained to be polite, to say please and thank you," as she put it. Or as Sarabia explained, "The ethos was work within the system. The schools and even the church to some extent told us that. They would say you were supposed to fight injustice, but never how."

Workshops addressed the issue of anger, drawing on biblical examples to show how such a feeling could be expressed in a positive and "controlled" way. Sonia Hernandez illustrated the sort of questions she asks in training new groups. "When was Christ really angry? When he found the den of thieves in the temple, he didn't ask them politely to leave. He threw them out because the people who came had very little means. They were forced to think they had to pay to use the temple. We talk about how Christ was not meek and mild, but a man with real emotions, a man who would challenge. If anger is repressed, it can be dangerous and destructive."

Janie Gonzalez soon had an opportunity to test the sort of assertiveness discussed in the workshops. With others in her parish and PTA, she organized a meeting with the superintendent of schools in her district to talk about the need for repairs. When the man got there, he found a large group of parents, and also the media, taking pictures. "The lady who was supposed to speak for us froze," Gonzales recounted. "She was afraid because her children were in school and the principal had threatened them. So I took over." It brought results. "This was Friday, Labor Day weekend. The next Tuesday, the repairmen were out there!"

Values and emotions were important themes in the initial workshops. Important, too, was education about the simple nuts and bolts of organizing. Such education, like the other discussion topics, was extraordinarily rare in the traditional community-organizing approach.

In rhetoric, the role of the "community organizer" has been classically posed as "organizing oneself out of one's position." The notion held that the organizer is catalyst and facilitator for communities getting themselves together; after training community leaders to take on more and more responsibility, the organizer finally leaves the scene. The reality is often different. For many, perhaps most, community groups, the paid organizer is the central actor. He—or, rarely, she—does the fundraising, knows the whole community, has had experience and training in how to analyze issues, chair meetings, deal with the press, think through strategies that are the lifeblood of practical problem-solving. Often such skills are complemented in citizen organizing by differences in class background and education: College-educated young people, coming in from the outside to "organize the people," may well displace local leadership, without being conscious of the process.

Moreover, the informal ideology of community organizing traditionally tended to reinforce the myth of the organizer's difference from the people he worked with. As Chambers put it, the traditional organizer had a "have-gun-will-travel style," imagery suggesting a Lone Ranger character without personal needs or concerns, coming in to rescue the poor and downtrodden. Training procedures also reinforced such myths. "The mistake of the past was that we trained the organizers but we never took time to train the leaders," he continued.

But in the 1970s, IAF-connected organizations such as COPS began to take the time. "Our iron rule of organizing now is that you never do anything for people that they can do for themselves," said Chambers. In San Antonio such an approach meant that Cortes conducted dozens of training workshops on subjects like doing research, chairing meetings, keeping leadership accountable, dealing with the press, breaking down problems into manageable parts, and so forth.

I arrived in San Antonio when COPS was hosting a meeting to plan a statewide campaign on education. The organization the previous year had drawn up a Texas-wide plan with planks such as increased aid for school districts with low student achievement scores, state money to help schools cope with immigrant students, and increased funds for bilingual education. A number of organizing efforts around the state, modeled on COPS, had also backed the plan, and the Democratic gubernatorial candidate had pledged his support, following up with a renewed pledge after the election. But before the education effort was ever formulated, extensive discussions had occurred in each parish of the organization. People had reflected on what schools were like in biblical times. They had looked at how schools had changed, and the needs of poor people for education today. Through such discussions, people had gained detailed knowledge of the educational system and its problems— and the organization had developed a rich repertoire of stories that would later be of use in taking the case to the public. "One gentlemen in one of our discussions said that the great trial of his life is that he has three children who graduated from high school," Sonia Hernandez described, "but none could fill out a job application the right way. He passed away, but we often use his story for reflection."

Behind such discussions, moreover, is a particular approach

to the organization's membership that offers another clue to its great strength. "We never talk about people in terms of 'masses,' " Hernandez explained. "We don't think in terms simply of getting out numbers of people. Each is an individual, and you address people as individuals. You make sure each person has an understanding of what we are going to do and why, and what their role is."

Treating each member as an individual, capable of making a contribution, soon generated the reputation that the organization was amazingly well prepared. As reporter Paul Burke put it in the *Texas Monthly,* it soon became apparent that the COPS rank and file knew more about the issues than did supposedly expert public officials: "The authorities weren't so smart after all." Even regular adversaries of COPS, like banker Tom Frost, a symbol of the city's power structure, developed admiration for the group. "They're good for the city," as he put it. Developer Jim Dement accused COPS of "fostering hatred." But he also welcomed its presence. "There's more hope and conversation in this town than in a hundred years . . . This is a town where you can have nothing and be somebody. Now don't tell me COPS is bad." Meanwhile, from the inside of the organization, COPS seemed an educational process all its own. "It's like a university where people go to school to learn about public policy, to learn about public discourse, to learn about public life," described Cortes.[10]

Successes on issues such as the drainage ditches and neighborhood improvements were important. But a central problem remained: how to change the broader patterns of development in the city that were more and more transferring resources, schools, services, and jobs to the North Side suburbs, away from inner-city and poorer communities. The organization developed a "counterbudget" plan for the city's development, opposed to city government's plans, which favored the suburban areas. But they remained thwarted by a business-oriented city council majority, and the corporate community in San Antonio formed an organization, the Business and Industrial Political Action Committee, in 1976 to ensure their continued clout. The stage was set for COPS's intervention in the political process itself, in direct challenge to the city's most powerful interests.

"COPS Leader Lashes New Political Group," read the headline in the *San Antonio Light.* "Some 5,000 members of Communities Organized for Public Service elected a new president Sunday. She immediately attacked a newly formed business political action group." The article continued, conveying a sense of a polarizing community: "Retiring president Andres Sarabia also lashed out at the business group . . . 'Who is going to elect the next city council? Will it be the power of money or the power of people?' he asked the third convention."

From the editorial pages of the other daily, the *San Antonio News,* came similarly alarmist tones. Noting that the organization had won a number of recent victories—defeat of a "super shopping mall" over the city's water supply, a project that COPS and environmentalists had joined in opposing; and changes in city zoning to encourage inner-city development—the editorial lauded "participatory democracy" but protested that "COPS's disruptive meeting tactics have become predictable, tiresome and increasingly unnecessary. . . . " It accused COPS of "creating devils to be attacked for the benefit of the crowd."[11]

The relation between community organizations and elections has long been fraught with controversy. Community groups in the main have shied away from election campaigns for a number of reasons. On the one hand, the nature of the election process—putting a premium on politicians' personalities and public-relations "packaging"—seems a far cry from the concerns with organization-building and empowerment at the heart of community efforts. On the other hand, community groups, focused on building the inner resources and unity of their areas, have been fearful that involvement in normal "politics" would splinter their membership and engage them in issues not immediately relevant to their goals. COPS began with such a premise. "Pressure is our weapon and we have to have the ability to apply pressure equally to everyone," explained one leader at the first convention. "If one of our members is thinking of running for office, he will be asked to resign. We will never divide or dilute our numbers by endorsing particular candidates, but we will hold all elected officials responsible for their actions. We will be the conscience of public servants."[12]

COPS made a single, pivotal departure from such a policy in the spring of 1977. Having won district elections for city council —a change from the at-large elections that in the past had meant an overwhelmingly white and business-oriented city council majority—it decided to work for a council majority pledged to support the organization's counterbudget. It interviewed all the candidates for city council and endorsed those who made firm commitments. With its enormous base, the organization was able to register more than 18,000 new voters. It mobilized and educated tens of thousands more. In the election, every COPS-backed candidate won, and several politicians who had strongly championed the organization, such as Henry Cisneros, gained considerable visibility.

Yet the organization drew back from such activity in the future. "We became concerned not to tie ourselves to any politician's career," Father Albert Benavides explained. Future electoral work would be more indirect: education among voters about what politicians' positions were on crucial issues and how they might react to forthcoming controversies. The continuing expansion of the organization's political power gave formal testimony to the continuing effectiveness of COPS's approach. Governor-elect Mark White, for instance, after pledging his support for the COPS education plan in the 1982 election, paid his first postelection visit to the organization's convention, pledging again his support.

Behind organizational fears of direct electoral activity and its continuing capacity for having political impact, COPS had been evolving a positive understanding of itself as a "political" alternative to "politics as usual" in America, combining several principles in a distinctive blend of grass-roots democracy on a continuing basis.

Independence. At the first convention, parishes and community groups affiliating with COPS paid dues amounting to $11,000, supplemented with funds from a grant by the Campaign for Human Development, the community justice arm of the Catholic Bishops. By 1977, dues brought in $46,000. The larger parishes paid $2,000 a year, while small local neighborhood organizations paid from $250 to $500 to join. The remainder of the $109,000 annual budget was raised through sales for an ad book. Even some of the organization's most intransigent opponents on local issues paid for ads, and revenues amounted to $63,000.[13]

Behind such internally generated funding was a specific principle: Community groups that look mainly to outside sources for their funds suffer a loss of independence. Equally damaging, the membership loses its sense of "ownership" in the organization over time. Chambers discussed the IAF philosophy about the financial base of "value organizations": "Social change is not some kind of abstraction that happens out there. It happens to people. And the first ingredient of an organization is money. If they don't pay dues, they don't own it. What is valuable and important to you, you pay for."

Such an approach meant for COPS certain specific prohibitions: The organization did not seek funds from any government or foundation or corporate agency, for example. It meant also an appeal to the self-interest of community institutions like the church. As Sarabia explained, churches needed an organization like COPS for the most obvious of reasons: "if the neighborhood dies, the church dies. Then there's nobody to put money in the collection plate on Sunday." From the beginning, the organizing effort had enjoyed the support of the leadership of the archdiocese, such as Bishop Flores—a key ingredient in its success. A combination of appeal to direct self-interest and broader purposes signed up many parishes as well. Thus Father Dan Hennessey, an early COPS vice-president, argued to his fellow priests that it did not make sense to pay thousands of dollars a year for insurance on their buildings and not pay $2,000 dues to an organization that would be more effective in creating stability. By 1977, thirty-five parishes had joined, along with community and other groups.[14]

Participatory Democracy. Even the best and most vital of community groups, in the opinion of COPS leaders and organizers like Sister Christine Stephens, can become stagnant, parochial, and inbred over time. Thus the organization has also stressed from the beginning the development of new leadership. Every local is free to take on local neighborhood issues it chooses. On larger issues, it can ask for aid from the whole organization. At every level, leadership is elected, with a central executive committee meeting twice a month—once for specific business and once for more reflective, strategic discussions or training. Each year before the annual convention, the four areas hold regional conventions at which delegates from participating groups choose their own priorities, select their own area vice-presidents, and make plans for presentations to the convention as a whole. Finally, the organization has strictly adhered to its principles that top leaders and staff directors alike must regularly change. Cortes left in 1977 for Los Angeles; he now works in the Rio Grande Valley. Hernandez is the fifth COPS president.

When Sister Christine described one parish where she had helped organize an infusion of new leadership, Cortes used the story to point out the need for constant change. "I could never have done that," he argued. "I would have been too attracted to the old leadership whom I know, who had built the organization in the beginning. In one sense, all organizing is reorganizing. There has to be that ability to go in and shake things up."

In an organization with the size and power of COPS, it is remarkable how many surprises "shake things up." Sonia Hernandez, for instance, the new president, broke a previous pattern that presidents of COPS came from the ranks of executive vice-presidents. She had been secretary of the organization, chairing the organizational committee that opposed the South Texas Nuclear Power Project, a campaign that had proved often dramatic. One week when several other leaders had been out of town, she had had to step into their roles on other issues when public controversy broke out. "At that point I started thinking about running for president," she said. "At the convention, we got in a whole new slate of leaders. If you're predictable, there's something wrong." From Hernandez's point of view, the organization has both continuity and differences with the past. "To outward appearances, this is the same organization: We're still talking about culture and values, and the importance of community life. But if you look within, you'll also see a whole new set of leadership, learning from those who went before but also making history in a new way. It's as if the organization shed an old skin, and sure enough, there is a beautiful new skin there."

Community Renewal. In classic community organizing, even the most effective and large-scale groups tended to atrophy after five years or so. In 1977 and 1978, COPS leaders also began to wonder how the organization would stay vibrant and responsive. "Frankly," admits Cortes, "we knew we couldn't keep parishes involved only on public issues."

New leaders were important, as was the rich value discussion in the organization. But the experiences of some parishes in San Antonio, and Cortes's work in Los Angeles in a new group, United Neighborhood Organizations, suggested other elements as well.

In Saint Timothy's church, for instance, new catechisms connected biblical and Mexican historical and cultural themes with the current issues COPS was working on. The results had proved very positive: People's interest in the church educational program markedly increased. Then the church added music as well. Father Benavides, the pastor, said, "I was told at the beginning that there were no musicians . . . [but] I felt every community has its artists just like every community has its leaders. The trick is to find them." When the parish issued a call for a choir, forty people volunteered, to everyone's surprise. "The results were incredible. People responded to the music in a total, exuberant way, and our liturgies were immensely improved. People appreciated hearing and singing songs that carried good messages and sounded good as well." Other elements were included. Each month couples celebrating their anniversaries stood and received recognition. "Never before had all of this been brought together," Benavides observed. "It was as if what we reflected on and celebrated reached into the soul of the people and touched them."[15]

From such experiences, the organization developed an ongoing process of community and parish renewal. Organization leaders—no longer mainly staff—would begin with a program of value discussion and training for the leadership of a parish, for instance. They would train the parish leaders in interviewing techniques—how to listen, how to elicit people's true concerns. Then the local leaders would interview residents in the surrounding area, whether active members of the church or not. The whole process would culminate in a parish convention. The total life of the area would be recognized and celebrated —the different church societies, elderly groups, girls' and boys' organizations, and so forth—and the meeting would develop priorities for the coming year, often in a festive spirit.

Hernandez described one process, in a new parish that had recently joined COPS. People began with value reflection and theological discussion, before any action. "For seniors, for instance, the concern was with being left alone." The seniors traced such a problem to broader ones. "They see the Mexican culture being watered down. Kids don't speak Spanish anymore. There is money pressure, television, pressures on personal relations." When Hernandez challenged people about what they could do, however, they were initially hopeless. "We can't do anything. It's Madison Avenue doing it to us." One woman, however, who had been a leader in a famous pecan workers strike in the 1930s, brought newspaper clippings of the marches and a photo of herself carrying a sign. "She said, 'We used to do this. We were fighters a long time ago. We can do something now.' That created a spark. People said, 'You know, you're right.' They would remember the neighborhood history, their old German neighbors, how different pastors and nuns behaved. And they said, 'It's about time the church became responsive again.' "

I asked Hernandez how people responded to such a process. "They love it," she replied. Pleasure takes tangible forms. Young people who once would have moved to northern suburbs began to stay. Parish attendance picked up. There was, in short, a changing of mood, the sort of transformation one sees in Cochran Gardens, interweaving COPS with the fabric of the community itself. A tour of the housing projects makes it vivid. Instead of graffiti, stunning wall murals depict the COPS emblem, a red-white-and-blue circle with an eagle, suggesting both the American symbol and the ancient Mexican one as well.

"COPS Declares S.A. 'Wage War,' " read the banner newspaper headline after the fall convention in 1977. As COPS's base in the Mexican communities of San Antonio deepened, the fight with the city's business establishment came to a head. During the winter of 1977–78, the anxious tone in local press accounts acquired a note of near-hysteria.

In a lead editorial, the *San Antonio Light* warned darkly of the coming "Mobocracy": "In every city Alinsky organizers have entered, they have left a legacy of hatred, division and polarization. San Antonio, it is becoming increasingly apparent, is to be no different."

What created the panic in the white establishment was a new campaign by COPS to encourage businesses coming into the community to pay a "decent wage," mentioning the figure of $15,000 as a minimal salary for a family to support itself. Beatrice Cortez, an organization leader, described the rationale. "We realized that you could only do so much with neighborhood improvements. We did research that found out San Antonio paid the poorest wages of any major city." Indeed, according to the *Commercial Reporter,* San Antonio wages were between 20 and 40 percent lower than those in other areas of the country. "We compared wages to what it takes to clothe a family and feed them." At the convention, COPS members performed a skit on the cheap-labor theme. Four evil dukes ruled a kingdom where everyone worked for peanuts. The dukes represented easily recognizable characters—a banker, a general, etc. "And there was Pedro, who never gets cut in," said Ms. Cortez. Finally, Super COPS came to the rescue. It saved the kingdom and slew the cheap-labor dragon. "We got blasted in the press after that," she laughs.

Columnist Don Politico reported that the business-development group mainly responsible for bringing new businesses to town, the Economic Development Foundation, "has already responded with vigorous and indignant denials of the organization's charges that established businessmen in San Antonio want to see wages kept low." Every day, charges and counter-charges flew back and forth, and national publications like the *Wall Street Journal* and *Forbes* began to cover the battle. But the city establishment's protestations of innocence turned sour when COPS released a copy of the secret study it had somehow obtained called the "Fantus Report." Commissioned by the Economic Development Foundation (EDF), the "Fantus Report" lauded the city's "relatively underorganized" labor force and concluded that "development personnel must be careful not to attract industries that would upset the existing wage ladder. . . . This would tend to dissipate the comparative and competitive advantages enjoyed by existing manufacturers."

COPS began demanding a meeting with the EDF to change the slogan from "cheap labor" to a more positive theme and change the approach for attracting business to the city. Other elements of the community, including the once hostile press, joined the appeal. By late February, agreement had been reached on a kind of cease-fire. Its terms could only be considered a significant victory for COPS. The development group dropped its cheap-labor approach, and later backed a COPS plan for inner-city economic and residential development, Vista Verde. Although COPS refused a number of business and city-government invitations to join in formal "consultations" of different sorts, it had achieved regular access, at the least, to any development planning the city would henceforth engage in. When Henry Cisneros became mayor, he and Beatrice Cortez flew to Mexico City to meet with Mexican officials about development; and just before I arrived in San Antonio, he had agreed to back the organization's ideas for major economic development in the poorest community, Edgewood.

Meanwhile, the specter of "mobocracy" disappeared without a trace. The organization had not only withstood the sharpest of attacks, but had emerged strengthened. Outside observers such as Tom Gaudette, one of the old-timers in the field of community organizing, marveled. "The key to COPS's victories has been its depth," he said. "It involved the whole fabric of the community."[16]

To tour the west and southwest areas of San Antonio with COPS leaders is to witness visible and tangible monuments to organizational clout: housing projects going up, new businesses, libraries—five built in the Mexican communities over the past ten years—parks, roads, enormous drainage systems. But again and again, people return to self-respect. Helen Ayala, who takes me around, points to the murals on public-housing walls. "Can't you see the pride?" she asks. "Our children are not going to be complacent. I hope to be able to sit back and watch. They will be leaders because somebody is standing up now, and there is a vehicle." In a similar vein, Janie Gonzalez says simply, "Our children have new heroes, people in the community now, that they can look up to."

Children in Mexican communities now also learn distinctions. For COPS, there is a crucial separation between "private life" and the "public world."

In one's private life—shared with family, close friends, and neighbors—belongs much of what the ARC Community refers to as the "organic roots" of things: love, intimacy, play, informality. There are no agendas. Behavior is not primarily aimed at achieving things. One seeks reciprocity, sharing, ties nourished and sustained over time through daily experience. In the public sphere, in contrast, there is respect, accountability, goal-oriented behavior. Meetings properly start on time. Strategies are developed. Leaders are those who get results, who deliver and who articulate the community's interests honestly and effectively. In the public, there is a constant process of testing, refinement, and improvement in techniques, skills, and abilities: One does "reflection" and "critique," evaluating performance in a supportive but also tough and vigorous way, asking whether people perform as they promised, how they might do better the next time.

In COPS's philosophy, one never finds the public or private in pure form. "There's always a tension," as Janie Gonzalez puts it. Marriages and families have "public aspects," where members choose goals and try to put aside the most personal of reactions. Public meetings have playful, warm, communal dimensions. Enrique Velasco, one young man I interviewed, made a distinction between "two publics" and "two privates" —"There is a public where I'm objective and a public where I socialize; and there's a private where I have many friends, and then a private of my family." But there is also a constant sorting out of what is appropriate to each realm. It produces remarkable changes in behavior.

Rudy Enriguez is a heavyset man with curly hair who speaks in soft, deliberate tones. Enriguez worked for a packinghouse for more than twenty-five years. He saw many people hurt on the job and more laid off in recent years, and he feels deep anger that the distant owners do not know or care about the men with whom he has spent those years in the plant. "It seems to me that sometimes people can get so greedy they just don't care anymore," he says with bitterness. "In the world out there, it's dog eat dog, go for it, get the gold enchilada." Enriguez's voice drops almost to a whisper. "It seems to me that some people enjoy seeing other people down. If I wasn't a Christian, I think I could make a list and I would blow some brains out, not for myself but for people I've known who cannot defend themselves."

But Mr. Enriguez has been involved for some years in COPS, ever since he heard a woman describe how it enabled her to control her anger in a positive way. It has changed his sense of what is possible. "It's a very good thing there are organizations like this; otherwise we'd have another South America here," he says. "You can take only so much lying down." In his opinion, COPS has given people a vehicle not only for controlling anger but for learning a different set of values from those in "the world out there." As he describes it, "Over the years, I've seen people who join 'mellow.' In the early years, it was 'hey, I want my street fixed first!' Now people wait for communities that need it more." Indeed, Enriguez believes that the norms in COPS have become so strong that people rarely have to be brought into line in any overt way. "When somebody gets greedy, nobody says nothing to them. They just realize and drop it. It's like a silent language, like something tells you in the air you're out of line."

Others voiced the thought that COPS generates a new culture, or alternative values, from different vantage points. For young leaders like George Ozuna and Enrique Velasco, the organization had the effect of drawing them back into the community after they had, in varying ways, thought they had left it behind. Velasco described himself as previously "something of a free spirit," spending his respectable income as a carpenter in partying and other recreation. "COPS came just at the right time for me," recounts Velasco. "It gave me a sense of doing something good, something important, something that gets respect from other people." Ozuna, an area vice-president, had once planned a career in radio-television and later in political science, attending graduate school at the University of Texas. "I came back finally because of what my grandma told me," he says. "You can go to college to get away from your community, or you can learn some things to come back and make a contribution." George Ozuna sees his education as useful, and he continues to love political discussion and reflection on the broader implications of COPS. In other areas, he feels he gains great insight from leaders such as Rudy Enriguez, who never went to college.

A striking feature of COPS is the strong leadership roles women have taken on—a rarity in both community organizing and also in Mexican-American organizations. The last four presidents, for instance, have been women. I asked Beatrice Cortez if she felt that the stress on "public life" in COPS, and its accompanying emphasis on rewarding leadership for results, not for charisma or other superfluous reasons, made a difference. She thought it did indeed. "Women have community ties. We knew that to make things happen in the community, you have to talk to people. It was a matter of tapping our networks."

Finally, the organization has clearly impacted on the church itself, training a new generation of assertive leadership in many parishes, generating a clarification of the pastor's role and a new self-consciousness about mission among the laity. Indeed, such a redefined sense of mission is reflected in the archdiocese's

"New Pentecost" vision, the official statement of the church issued by Archbishop Patricio Flores. Paralleling COPS's stress on lay leaders, the document entrusts "the laity above all" with the task of changing "the institutions of our society and society itself . . . to reflect the values of the Lord of Life." It declares the church's purpose "in all it does and in all it says [to] extend its arms and reach out to those who are oppressed, afflicted, lonely, poor. . . ." And it outlines a process of parish development drawn directly from COPS, that "calls people to a reflection of what it means to be Church, builds relationships within the parish and between parishes as well as other faith communities, and causes action for justice." Beatrice Cortez, now one of the staff in charge of development for the archdiocese, believes this sort of renewing involvement with the world will revitalize the faith. "I say if the church continues to do what it is with COPS, it has nothing to worry about. You're going to have the next crop of priests. And laity is going to take on leadership roles, so you don't need a priest."[17]

COPS sees itself as a new kind of public space, not walled off from private life but a vehicle for advancing the values of family, faith, and community. Moreover, it also seeks to refashion how *public life* is defined by the broader world. "We talk about the world as it is and the world as it should be," explained Sister Christine. "What we try to create in actions is a world in which leaders are in control of the agenda for the space of the meeting. It is the people talking and the politicians listening. A lot of time is spent making sure the leaders are prepared, making it clear it is the leaders' meeting, not the politicians'." Joe Sekul, a political scientist at the University of San Antonio who has studied the organization for a number of years, told me that in his observations "politicians have the most difficult time with the COPS notion of public. None of their normal techniques work. They have to change their behavior, just like people in COPS change theirs."

Stories make the point. For instance, Sonia Hernandez grew up with the mayor, Henry Cisneros, and attends the same parish. Yet she insists on clarity about proper roles in any public settings. When the mayor came into a COPS gathering soon after his election and said, "Hello, Sonia," she replied, "That's Ms. Hernandez to you, Mr. Mayor." Beatrice Cortez recounted another tale to illustrate how children quickly get the point.

While she was president of COPS, from 1981 to 1982, Cortez had a special COPS phone put in her home. One day Cisneros called on that line. In a playful mood, he greeted her young daughter, Victoria, warmly and said he would like to speak to her mother. "Who should I say is calling?" asked the young girl. "Tell her it's a special friend," Cisneros replied. Victoria at this point recognized the voice. "Oh, you're not a special friend. You're the mayor—I know who you are." She asked her mother if she had done right. "You've got that right, honey," Cortez answered. "I answered the phone," she continued. "Cisneros said, 'Boy, you're training them early!' "

"Happy Birthday COPS!" ran the feature story in November 1981, in the *San Antonio Light*. The following year, in a similar vein, the paper editorialized for the organization's ninth-anniversary convention under the headline "COPS Continues Its Accomplishments." "What is perhaps one of the most misunderstood organizations in this part of the country—yet, one of the most effective—will hold its ninth convention at the Convention Center Sunday. Communities Organized for Public Service has been a positive force in this city in bringing about needed capital improvements and in making the quality of life better for many San Antonians. . . . We salute COPS in its ninth year of service and invite all community leaders to work with COPS members for a better San Antonio." In the spring of 1983, as a large alliance modeled on COPS formed in the Rio Grande Valley, the paper similarly voiced its support: "An organization such as Valley Interfaith certainly can be the catalyst to get things moving to solution."[18]

I interviewed Joe Rust, editor at the *Light*, about the organization. He was embarrassed at points. For instance, he believed that Hernandez's comment about the Texas Cavaliers hurt the city's image on the "Today" show, and he also seemed at pains to explain his own membership in the all-white male club. Yet Rust was also candid about the way he and others had changed their opinions of COPS.

"COPS was originally seen in negative terms," he commented. "But I suppose its tactics made sense. The way you get a mule's attention is to hit him over the head." In Rust's view, COPS is an organization grounded in churches and communities, "representing the mainstream, not the fringe. I have great respect for COPS, even though they still don't obey rules of etiquette." He believes the organization has given Mexican people a voice in the city, drawing on Mexican cultural values as well as religion. And it also represents a trend he sees all over. "COPS is populist," he explains. "I see populism gaining all across the country." Rust pauses. "You know, I have a lot of populism in my own background. My grandfather fought for roads in his part of the state, central Texas. He was a farmer and a county commissioner. They used to call them 'road commissioners' in those days."

Thus the impact of COPS on the broader community cannot be measured only in dollars and cents. It produces a kind of populist contagion, representing the paradoxical but powerfully magnetic blend of radicalism and conservatism—the dignity and example of ordinary people who take values that are widely and facilely espoused with the utmost seriousness, giving them discipline, depth, and clout.

For people involved in COPS, there is a life change that can never be reversed. Thelma Cosper, the secretary in the office who has been there since the beginning, put it simply: "People have learned how to go down to City Hall and get things done." To Ernie Cortes, such a process amounts to what he (like Clarence Jordan in a far different setting) calls "metanoia." "It means moving from the selfish to the self-interested, from the set-apart to the relational. It means to be reciprocal, to be collaborative, to develop a new kind of cultural consciousness. That's always been the vision of COPS, the hope." But he sees the process as still just beginning, paving the way for a powerful "neopopulism" that will take up such questions as the dignity of labor and the need for working people to gain the fruits of their work.

Meanwhile, it is certainly a vision and hope that spreads, as many realize. George Ozuna said that "the COPS idea works for any community. It could be a Mexican community, or a black. Some might consider it blasphemous, but I think it can work for unions or gays in San Francisco."

I told him I knew an organization called the San Francisco Organizing Project.

6

"God's Laboratory"

E arly in the history of the San Francisco Organizing Project, a community alliance that models itself on the approach pioneered by COPS in San Antonio, the Reverend Rich Jaech did a surprising reading. The organizing effort, still more than a year away from its founding convention, was in the stage of people getting to know each other. One technique was to begin each meeting with a few minutes of discussion, led by a different person each time, who would discuss a particular document or concept from his or her own tradition. Once, a Jewish rabbi talked about the Hebrew concept of "righteousness," illustrating with passages from the Torah. At another meeting, a labor leader read the preamble to his union's constitution, which described the goals of working people.

Jaech, a young and charismatic Lutheran minister, had thought at one point about becoming a writer. He remains fascinated with literature. Instead of reading a religious passage, that day he quoted from William Shakespeare's play *Henry V,* from a speech the king gives to his beleaguered, small group of troops, telling them how fortunate they are to face the enemy on the holiday of the Feast of Crispian:

> He that outlives this day, and comes safe home
> Will stand a tip-toe when this day is named, . . .
> And Crispin Crispian shall ne'er go by,
> From this day to the ending of the world,
> But we in it shall be remembered;
> We few, we happy few, we band of brothers.[1]

The group discussed a future time "when people will remember this day, too." Hearing the story, I was doubly glad to have arrived in San Francisco in time for the official "founding convention" of the San Francisco Organizing Project, more simply known as SFOP.

The organization's press release gave a sense of the diversity they expected: "This convention marks the formation of a unique coalition of Roman Catholic parishes, Black Pentecostal Churches, labor unions, Jews, and others . . . 19 churches, 12 labor unions, 3 synagogues, and the Citizens Action League will be attending." It seemed a curious mix indeed. I was somewhat skeptical.[2]

COPS's style of value-based, community-renewing citizen organizing has since spread to a number of other areas. From groups like East Brooklyn Churches and the Queens Citizen Organization on the East Coast to United Neighborhood Organizations and Denver's Metropolitan Organizing Project in the West, perhaps twenty or so large-scale projects in various settings have evolved new methods for revitalizing communities and community institutions such as churches, while they simultaneously gain a voice for ordinary citizens in political and economic arenas. But SFOP's design—to involve not only religious congregations of different faiths and community groups but also labor unions—was rare indeed. I knew well the tensions that often had arisen in American cities between neighborhood organizations and unions over such issues as housing rehabilitation and downtown development. The gap between labor and religious groups seemed, on the surface, even larger. Divergent vocabularies and concerns, and a host of other developments, have long eroded the sort of close ties that once existed between churchmen and women and labor activists—during the great union organizing drives of the 1930s, for instance.

The convention turned out to be unforgettable. Though called a "founding convention," in fact it reflected more than two years of patient organizing work, training workshops, value discussions, and several organizing campaigns. One such campaign found its way to the front steps of Everett Middle School where the meeting was held. There, huge, ungainly garbage dumpsters sat overflowing with litter, symbolizing the coalition's support of public-housing tenants who were seeking to reverse a Housing Authority action that had replaced their individual garbage cans with the large containers.

Inside, more than a thousand people jammed into the first floor, while observers from several dozen organizations (including several organizing efforts in earlier stages in other cities) looked down from the balcony. The school, in the middle of the city's Mission District, had a sort of gaudy ornateness that somehow fit. Huge vaulted ceilings, inlaid tiles, green and gold gargoyles around the walls, and spiraling staircases found complements in the colored banners that covered the walls with the names of different organizations and the enormous letters on the curtains on stage, spelling out "SFOP: A New Vision—Integrity and Justice for All."

The event was a living statement of the range of communities that had already become involved. The SFOP Gospel Choir led the audience in songs that ranged from "De Colores," a migrant field workers' song about gold at the end of the rainbow, to a labor anthem taken from the preamble to the United Mine Workers Constitution of 1870 and "Pass Me Not, O Gentle Savior." For each issue that the audience decided to undertake as an organization-wide effort—ranging from the dumpsters to campaigns for securing more police in lower-income neighborhoods, for guaranteeing that more jobs would be generated by businesses which located in the city, and for protecting a group of restaurant workers who were being harassed in their attempts to organize a union—a candle was lit on a Jewish menorah, symbol of freedom.

The room was partitioned into sections with colored balloons and ribbons. One hundred and thirty-nine members of the black church, True Hope of God in Christ, sat in front of the delegation from the Department Store Employees Local 1100 and the International Ladies Garment Workers Union. Congregation Beth Shalom delegates were across the aisle from Local 6 of the International Longshoremen's Union and Saint John the Evangelist, an Episcopalian congregation with many gay and lesbian members. In front of Saint John's was Saint

Theresa's Catholic parish, which had sent a large delegation of mainly blue-collar Italian-American families.

Donneter Lane, the black woman who heads the San Francisco Council of Churches, proclaimed to the audience that "the whole globe is in a revolution, in a struggle to determine what it is to be human." In San Francisco, she continued, "we see some of all God's creation. San Francisco is a global village . . . a laboratory of our times for the creation of a new humanness." And SFOP, in her view, represented a "giant step" in such a grand drama, a return of the church to its proper, prophetic role.[3]

Archbishop John Quinn, who had just returned from helping to draft the widely publicized Catholic pastoral letter on the nuclear arms race, was similarly enthusiastic. "This proves it can be done," he declared. "What we have here is people of different races, different religions—Jews, Christians. We have people of different languages, people of different backgrounds, all collaborating in the service of humanity." He concluded dramatically: "What a model this is for the world! If we can only expand this circle wider and wider, we wouldn't need to worry about wars anymore."[4]

It was indeed an exhilarating moment as the audience broke into thunderous applause. Even skeptical observers could not fail to be impressed. Deputy Mayor Hadley Roff, sent by Mayor Dianne Feinstein to convey her greetings, seemed visibly surprised, saying he had "never seen a more impressive coalition." Yet the most exciting gathering is only a small step toward building lasting ties among groups with divergent histories and inherited conflicts. Moreover, the new organization not only proclaimed its diversity, it aspired to major impact. True Hope's pastor, the Reverend Arelious Walker, recalling the struggle of the Hebrews for freedom from bondage in Egypt, thundered: "We come here today to let those who have power, those who have wealth, those who have denied justice and integrity know that an organization has been formed to speak to that question!" It was eloquent and powerful oratory, but I could not help reflecting on the ironies as well.

"Part church service, part rally, part kickoff of some major campaigns," the advance publicity had described the event. With its kaleidoscopic range of groups, with gospel organ, electric rock guitars, and general exuberance, the meeting seemed to me to have an unmistakably San Franciscan style. I remembered descriptions I had read from the city's history: scenes of the parades, the dances, the bazaars, fairs, exhibitions, the jazz, blues, and ragtime, even the beer joints, card games, and saloons, and the sailors, railway workers, gold miners, longshoremen, and fishermen and women who mingled in them. One black newspaper's description of an evening on Market Street near the fabled Tenderloin district before World War I seemed somehow apropos: "like the Fairway of an enormous circus or carnival. Color, lights, crowds, music, candy, hawkers . . . Thousands of every race: Hindoos, Japanese, Black men [with] wide shoulders, slim hips, loose relaxed gait, Jews, Swedes, Spaniards, Chinese, lean Englishmen mingling in the drift . . ."[5]

Yet the city had been dramatically transformed since the days when "thousands of every race" might gather in the evening on Market Street, or when the downtown areas were home to sailors, dockworkers, fisher families, and a myriad of small shops and industries. Blacks, Mexican Americans, and white ethnics who attended the SFOP convention arrived from areas to the south—from Hunterspoint, Potrero Hill, the Mission District, Noe Valley, and even farther.

Around World War II, the city began to attract the headquarters of such multinational corporations as Southern Pacific, Standard Oil, Transamerica, Bank of America, and the worldwide construction giant Bechtel. With their arrival came the need for land for support facilities like offices, convention centers, and hotels. And such appetite for space meant inevitable pressure. "If San Francisco decides to compete effectively with other cities for new 'clean' industries and new corporate power, its population will move closer to 'standard white Anglo-Saxon Protestant' characteristics," read the corporate-sponsored Planning and Urban Renewal Association report of the fifties. The city's Redevelopment Agency director put it more simply: "This land is too valuable to permit poor people to park on it."

Skyscrapers began to crowd the shorelines, like some giant

thicket slowly overgrowing the once spectacular view of the San Francisco Bay. "San Francisco was once light, hilly, pastel, open. Inviting," said a middle-class neighborhood alliance formed to protest the high-rise construction. "In only twelve years it has taken on the forbidding look of every other American city." More than view was involved. Land speculation and housing shortages fed a major crisis. Rents soared—$500 or $600 dollars for one-bedroom apartments were not uncommon in lower-middle-class areas; affluent families could expect to pay over $1,000. The price of a modest-size house soared to more than $100,000 in a typical sale.[6]

The SFOP convention spoke determinedly of developing "a housing plan to make available and affordable low- and middle-income housing in San Francisco." But the scale of the problems seemed impervious to any quick or simply remedy.

Labor's presence at the convention also recalled legendary episodes in San Francisco history. This was the city where the Workingmen's party formed in 1877, demanding the eight-hour day, free education—and severe restrictions on the Chinese. (For decades, labor's restrictive policies hampered the entrance of blacks and Chinese into many trades. W. E. B. DuBois found only four black carpenters among 2,500 union members at the turn of the century.) This was home for labor leaders like Andrew Furuseth, the Norwegian sailor who headed the sailors' union from 1885 to 1938, and of course Harry Bridges, nemesis of the city's elite through the 1930s, who could be found planning strategy or talking to the men down at union headquarters in Eagles Hall near the docks, "dark, razor faced, with the quick lithe movements of a fencer and a nasal Cockney twang," as one newspaperman described him. The citywide strike of working people, sparked by a bloody raid on the docks when the governor ordered the National Guard to break a Longshoremen's strike, shut the whole downtown area down in the last half of July 1934. The victory for unions in that epic confrontation had helped inspire the organization of the CIO, the organization of industrial trade unions.[7]

In the 1980s, the city remained the most unionized in the

nation. Yet economic changes had steadily decimated its manufacturing base, and the "strategic plan" for the city's economic
future issued by the chamber of commerce paid scant attention
—its emphasis was almost entirely on white-collar expansion. At
the SFOP convention, Walter Johnson, president of the Department Store Union Local 1100, gave a speech that recalled the
vigor and zeal of San Francisco's labor traditions. Picking up on
a comment from the president of the Housing Authority, who,
in a confrontation with SFOP members some months before
over the issue of the dumpsters, had called the alliance a "fledgling group," Johnson pointed to "fledgling groups" that had
changed the course of American history—the revolutionaries at
Valley Forge; civil-rights activists in Montgomery, Alabama;
investigative reporters during Watergate. Johnson helped
bring many of the labor unions into SFOP and is deeply com-
mited to its success. But he is also candid about the problems
that remain to be solved before lasting bonds will form between
religious groups and unions. "The bridge has not been crossed
yet," he put it. "There has to be a deeper understanding of the
two points of view."

In fact, the dumpster controversy with the Housing Authority itself had caused problems—several building-trades unions
initially opposed the tenants' effort to get the dumpsters
removed, after officials claimed they created jobs. At the convention, many unions' participation could best be described as
spotty: Unions with thousands of formal memberships sent dele-
gations of a handful, while tiny churches like True Hope or
Saint Theresa's had a third or more of their congregation in
attendance. Like the housing issue, it remained to be seen what
real effect SFOP would be able to have on the changing economy of the city, or what jobs for the city's working people its
campaigns might ultimately produce.

Thus the buoyancy of the meeting contrasted with obstacles
confronting this sort of undertaking. At such an early stage,
SFOP could be considered an interesting and important experiment whose development bore watching. But those involved in
the organizing knew well enough the complexity and difficulty.

They had had many years of successes and failures in the field of grass-roots organization.

SFOP shares office space with the Organize Training Center (OTC), a training institute for people interested not only in the nuts and bolts of community organizing but also in its broader implications. OTC in recent years has also helped staff a number of community organizing efforts directly, including the San Francisco Organizing Project.

The Center is directed by Mike Miller, a soft-spoken veteran of many years. In the 1950s, Miller organized a student reform effort at Berkeley, SLATE. He later became active in the civil-rights movement in Mississippi, and eventually began working with Saul Alinsky, dean of the community-organizing tradition. Full of anecdotes and lore about organizing, Miller is also one of the key theorists of the community-organizing movement. His writings on "mass-based multi-issue citizen organizations" in the early 1970s were widely reproduced and read by a new generation of young organizers who came from Sixties protest efforts. They helped direct many into organizations that reached beyond the campus into "Middle America," tapping the growing anger of ordinary citizens at the unresponsiveness of large-scale corporate and government institutions.

In 1979, Miller, Larry Gordon, Josie Mooney, and others on OTC staff began talking with Arnie Graf, who had recently come to the Bay Area to teach after a period as staff director for COPS in San Antonio. What Graf described about the COPS approach—the grounding in values, the renewal of community life at the foundation of the organizing process—made immediate sense. "I had been frustrated by seeing people pass through citizen organizations like a sieve," Mike remembers. "A few would stick with the organization and grow and learn, but they also tended to lose touch with their own bases. People wouldn't go back to church, for instance—they thought the new group was 'more exciting.'"

Moreover, Graf's descriptions brought back a flood of memories from the civil-rights movement. "As soon as he talked about what was happening in COPS, I remembered Friday-night black Baptist meetings in Mississippi. People like Fannie Lou Hamer. The small farmers who had a piece of land. The civil-rights movement drew deeply on southern black religion and on people's love for the land." Knowledge of such wellsprings had stayed with Mike intuitively, and it led to an eagerness to build an organization for empowerment of ordinary people on such foundations in San Francisco. Larry Gordon, staff director for the SFOP project, amplified. In his view, community organizing "had traditionally been in defensive posture." Organizing began most often *against* something—an expressway, an intrusive development plan. In such terms, organizing is what he calls "reactive." People may come out in large numbers for demonstrations "in reaction." But energy will dissipate over time.

Gordon himself, from a Jewish background, had recently been reflecting on his family roots and the close ties he believed existed between religion, ethnicity, and family history in his case. Thus the discussion of an organizing approach that drew on such traditions in San Francisco meshed with the thinking he had been doing about his own life, and he knew it had possibilities for building something longer-lasting and more powerful than the community organizations he had worked with in the past. "Isaiah said, 'People without a vision will perish,' " Gordon explained. "But if organizing has a positive vision that it can articulate and strive for, the glue that keeps people together is much stronger. I know there is something in what makes people care that has to do with morality, their own traditions, their stories of themselves and how their families came to this country. A lot of that is expressed in the life of religious institutions."

Larry Gordon and Josie Mooney began talking with different religious leaders in San Francisco about the idea of an organizing effort similar to COPS. They found a good deal of enthusiasm for the idea. What was unique was that they also talked to people about including labor unions as well.

In San Francisco, with its rich labor history, such an idea made organizational sense. Labor remains a strong power in the city as a voice for low- and middle-income working people. It commands respect and attention. Yet labor in a number of ways has also become isolated from parts of the community. And there has been an erosion of support and participation for labor even among the rank and file of the unions themselves. As Walter Johnson put it, "People coming up in our unions now don't know what was fought for in the past. It's a hard thing to organize these days." He believes there is urgent need for a revitalization of the labor movement "from the ground up," and he fears for the future if such a change does not occur. "We're going to have the most cold-blooded society you've ever seen." His worries, moreover, reflect a widespread anxiety among many around the nation who remember the labor unions in their days of spirited movement, have seen how such an ethos has ebbed in recent years, and believe the moment in American history calls for its renewal.

As the recession of the early 1980s haltingly ended, social critics and workers themselves sensed major changes under way in the American economy. *Newsweek* ran a special feature, "Left Out: The Human Cost of the Collapse of Industrial America." NBC correspondent Edwin Newman hosted a documentary on the long-term unemployed and the economic transformations. Columnist David Broder summarized these discussions in the *Washington Post:* "Even if the recovery continues," he argued, "we can expect a higher level of unemployment . . . than we have endured since the Great Depression. Equally troubling, the technological changes taking place in the economy . . . are compounding, not easing, the severe loss of the high-paying skilled and semiskilled production and lower level management jobs." Illustrating the point in detail, an AFL-CIO report entitled "The Future of Work" found that the number of jobs in so-called high-tech industry would be relatively small —perhaps 600,000 through the 1980s—and most would be in low-paid and low-skilled assembly occupations. Growth sectors of the economy were concentrated in services, but the jobs that were most characteristic in these areas—health care, food service, clerical, and so forth—also tended to be low-paying, with little advancement opportunity.[8]

In human terms, the cost was often confusion and agony. Steve Max, a union and community organizer for many years who now conducts training sessions for rank-and-file workers and community leaders, talked about the mood he had recently seen. "People feel a devaluation of work, especially manual work, on the assembly line or in offices. And people who have been brought up to believe that if you worked hard, if you were punctual and loyal, you could get ahead are suddenly without a job or a trade they can pass on. It means a monetary loss, but also something more. It's like the rules have changed in the middle of the game. You can't support your family. People feel betrayed in what they thought the whole country was about."

In response, champions of the labor movement argued that there must be a new wave of union organizing conducted in offices and service occupations, analogous to the organizing drives of the 1930s. Moreover, unions embarked on a series of experiments in such work. In Houston, Texas, for instance, twenty-nine AFL-CIO unions joined together in a single effort to make a breakthrough in the largely nonunion Sun Belt, combining sophisticated computer techniques with more than a million dollars a year in funding. Unions such as AFSCME and the Service Employees International Union highlighted the acute problems of discrimination and harassment many women face at work in efforts to organize clerical workers, and an alliance of working women's organizations developed around the country, "9 to 5," for which the Jane Fonda movie was named. Yet despite the discussion and new activity, major obstacles limited labor's capacities for expansion.

The facts were stark. From 1976 to 1983, for instance, the three major industrial labor unions together lost 1,264,000 of their 3,576,000 members. Though most of this loss was attributable to the recession, the economic changes were also weakening these traditional labor strongholds. And public perceptions of unions exacerbated the problem. Public ratings of labor-union leaders had dropped to near record lows: Their honesty and ethical standards, in the public's view, ranked below those of insurance salesmen and realtors, near the bottom of the list of occupations. Despite its large budget, the Houston Organizing Project of the unions had only slight successes. An aggressive wave of corporate antiunion campaigns succeeded in decertifying a growing number of union locals already in place. By 1980, 902 decertification elections took place, with unions losing 656 of them.[9]

More was at work than changing economics. The vitality of the trade unions draws directly upon the vitality of communities of working people, inside the workplace and outside, alike. As such communities eroded, labor's spirit faded as well.

Nellie Stone Johnson, a veteran black leader in Minnesota who organized unions during the Great Depression and remains their ardent champion, told me that much of the old sense "of brotherhood and sisterhood is missing today." In the thirties, she said, the union and farmer movements of the Midwest had been sustained by a vision of a "communal society where people helped each other out"; she said this represented "the vision of the commonwealth, which people have forgotten today."

Moreover, the spirit of community that she saw in labor grew out of the mutual aid in the community. "During the Great Depression, everybody's house was open. Nobody had anything, but you'd share the pot of beans or whatever as far as it would go."

Similarly, Richard Metcalf, on the staff of the Amalgamated Clothing and Textile Workers Union, pointed out that in older days the unions cared about the "whole person. They didn't have a view of workers as appearing at seven in the morning and disappearing from the map at three-thirty." Unions would hold dances every Friday night, open storefronts (Nellie Johnson had worked in one "with a potbellied stove and a food shelf"), and champion the unemployed in their dealings with government bureaucrats or landlords. "But our vision has narrowed now. We have to get back more to the spirit of a labor *move*ment," he concluded.

In San Francisco, the destruction of working people's communities in many parts of the city was already far advanced and it was certain to make the revitalization of labor difficult. For example, the fabled Longshoremen's Union along the city docks had drawn its strength from the rich, intricate life of the waterfront areas and from work patterns that encouraged a spirit of workers' cooperation, linked to pride in craft. Herb Mills, a union activist, longshoreman, and historian of the area, described the scene as a maze of storefront churches, missions, reading rooms, saloons, newsstands, and other small shops catering to the waterfront workers. The nearby neighborhoods of fisher families added to the color and spirit of the waterfront. Small boats, cats, dogs, parrots, bait and tackle shops, marine supply stores, repair facilities, and food-processing plants spread out from the hiring halls on Fisherman's Wharf. "You could always find a card game, dice game or bookie," wrote Mills. "You could always find a new political tract and someone ready to discuss it, a place to drop a crab pot or a place to simply watch the passing parade and the waters of the Bay in solitude."

This was the setting for the union, built on "a relatively tight, self-conscious community, knit together by work, a turf, a commitment to unionism and labor solidarity and a wide range of social activity." In the 1960s, however, the simultaneous development of the waterfront area and the automation of much of the work process of loading and unloading largely shattered the bonds that existed. "Pier after pier on the old Embarcadero was abandoned . . . successive portions of our world were thereafter buried beneath concrete and glass, steel and potted redwoods. . . ." A "deskilling" of the work took place. "The need for initiative, ingenuity and innovation is all but eliminated" in the new technologies, Mills argued, and the informal work groups that had produced camaraderie and mutual aid were atomized: "Most of the work associated with a modern operation is performed by individuals who can only communicate by radio from the cab of their machines. It's even hard to know who's on the job with you."[10]

For the labor-union leaders and activists attracted to SFOP, a strong sense of the need to reconnect with other elements in the community proved a central motivation.

Walter Johnson, a devout layman in his church, is also a union crusader. "Spend six months with me and I'll make you an evangelist for the union movement," he says as we sit down for an interview. His dedication grows out of a lifetime's involvement with unions. And it comes out vividly in the stories he constantly tells of people standing up for themselves in a new way, or of workers confounding all predictions. "I put out a leaflet once when it looked like we were going to lose an election," recounts Walter. Department-store workers, notoriously difficult to unionize, had been told by management that the company would look out for their interests. "Our leaflet said, 'Please vote no because there's nothing the union can do for you unless you believe in yourself.'" The union won by a large majority.

For Walter, involvement in SFOP was a natural and direct expression of what he believes to be the key to labor's vitality. "I've always had the feeling that an organization succeeds on the inside by what it does on the outside," he explains. "So we also adopted the feeling for our union that we look at the whole person. We were the first union in the United States to establish a counseling program, and one of the first to have an alchohol program. And from the beginning, I felt that we should be involved in the community. It means you have support when you need it."

His longtime involvement in his church was a very useful bridge between religious congregations and labor unions. Walter Johnson communicated the common ground he saw: "I'm afraid there's a selfishness in American culture that's going to destroy us. My philosophy is that the church should be with the carpenters, the plumbers, and the truck drivers. So should the unions. 'Insofar as you've done it to the least of these, you've done it unto me,' said Jesus. Maybe if we put the two social consciences together, it will wake both of them up."

At the founding convention, Walter Johnson was elected vice-president of SFOP. Diane Doe, an elementary-school teacher active in the San Francisco Federation of Teachers Local 61, was elected recording secretary.

Diane Doe described herself as the "party girl" for the union.

She presided over a hilarious drawing for lottery prizes at the convention, and in person she has a wry humor and a kind of earthy quality. But her title in the Teachers Federation strikes one at first acquaintance as more to the point: She holds the position of "sergeant at arms." She is large, tough, and forceful —one can imagine her organizing parties or anything else.

We talked for a while about SFOP and her own history. (Much to her delight, few in SFOP knew of her religious background. She had once been to seminary, "to meet a Lutheran minister," she says, and had first come to San Francisco for a meeting of Lutheran youth in the 1960s.) The conversation regularly returns to stories from her classrooms. Finally I remark, "You like teaching, don't you?" Diane replies, "I love it." And she launches into a zealous disquisition about public education.

In the elementary school where Diane Doe teaches, there are a myriad of nationalities. "This year I have one white kid, one black kid. Maybe four altogether who speak good English." She also has Latinos, Filipinos, children from the Fiji Islands, Samoans, Chinese, Hindu kids from India, Vietnamese. "The first year at the school, we had a Chinese kid who spoke Mandarin who couldn't speak to the other Chinese, because they spoke Cantonese." Diane laughs. Cutbacks in programs to help the immigrant children learn English complicate her work, but somehow she also exults in the difficulties.

In San Francisco, city buses charge only five cents for children during school hours. She took advantage of the cheap fares during the school year to take twenty-five field trips. "We went hiking in the mountains. We went behind the scenes at the aquarium." To study geological formations, she took her children to the park to examine the ground. To study the economy, they went to the shipyards along the waterfronts. Art programs were illustrated with trips to the art museums. She is convinced that such experiences make up an invaluable introduction to America. "A lot of these kids don't even leave their neighborhoods except to go to school," she explains. "What exposure I give them to the city is what they get."

Thus Diane's motivation for becoming active in SFOP

quickly clarified. "I like what I do, but I'd like to see some changes." After working as a teacher for many years, she is nearing the maximum salary. "But it hasn't kept up with other occupations," she adds. Money for equipment in the school is almost nonexistent. "This year we worked with microscopes. I had to buy one for the kids."

In Diane's view, SFOP will broaden community support for education and in a personal way let people get to know teachers "who love teaching." She tells a story to make the point. During the controversy about the dumpsters (which the tenants eventually won, with SFOP help), she brought one of the other teachers from her school to a meeting with Housing Authority officials. Later, the woman was having extreme disciplinary problems with a child from the housing projects. His mother came in, accusing the school of picking on the child. Then she saw the teacher. " 'Why, you're the woman who was at the meeting!' exclaimed the parent. Her whole attitude turned around," concluded Diane. "The other staff were just amazed."

Leaders like Diane Doe and Walter Johnson were eager to see their unions become involved in an alliance with diverse community groups and religious congregations. Yet resistance on both sides made coalition-building difficult. For the trade unionists, the thought of getting involved with groups that might hold demonstrations aimed at public officials seemed anathema. "If there's one thing that turns the labor unions off, it's the Alinsky approach, the idea of confrontation," explained Walter. For many involved in churches and synagogues, on the other hand, the image of "labor unions" conjured up visions of "politics as usual" and narrow self-interest that seemed foreign to the values of their faiths.

Ramona Michaels, a red-haired woman in her fifties, wore a windbreaker with an American flag stitched to the sleeve when we met. A single mother, her four children are now grown. After many years in a white-collar job with the telephone company, she has recently begun working for Saint Theresa's parish. Ramona radiates an energy and enthusiasm about her new job, as she does about SFOP. One can well understand the leadership role she takes in her own church, Saint Elizabeth's, a largely white ethnic Catholic congregation in the southeast section of San Francisco.

Ramona had seen community organizations come and go in her neighborhood and had been willing in the past "to do a bit." But the value base of SFOP, and the direct involvement of her congregation, made it seem immediately different. "In other organizations, it seemed people wanted to get things done," she explained. "But there's something else that happens when you come together in the Lord's name." The workshops on values in Saint Elizabeth's gave people in her congregation a unique chance to talk about things that had been troubling them. "One day I remember we had fifty people show up for a brainstorming session that lasted five hours. We talked about what we believe in—our families, neighborhoods, respect, being tolerant. And we talked about what threatened those values, and how much of society today is being run by media hype. Calvin Klein jeans. The Jordache look. How can you bombard children with all of this and not have them buy into it?"

SFOP offered Saint Elizabeth's a chance to begin to act on its values. The parish also went through a renewal process as a part of the organizing. Lay leaders interviewed a large number of community residents, many of whom the church had lost contact with. And the church held two large parish conventions, both of which Ramona Michaels chaired. "The first time I was nervous. I'd never chaired a big meeting like that. The second one I felt like an old pro," she describes. Different parts of the parish were recognized, with people explaining why they were involved in each—the Marriage Preparation Team, the Divorce/Separated/Widowed Club, the Spanish Group, the Women's Club, the St. Vincent de Paul Society, the Youth Choir, the Legion of Mary, and a host of others. Finally, the group discussed a number of proposals for action in the parish, on issues ranging from crime to use of an old school building in the community. Through it all, Ramona felt a strong spirit of celebration. "I began the day by saying, 'We're here today because we love Saint Elizabeth's,' " she recounts. "I made them repeat it." Both conventions ended on such a note. People seemed enthusiastic. "During the intermissions, people came up and said, 'You know, Ramona, you're right. We don't always say we love Saint Elizabeth's, but I really do.' "

Ramona and other leaders from Saint Elizabeth's found interacting with people from different churches a new experience. It was sometimes awkward, with people being overly polite at first, wary of saying things that might offend each other. But Ramona found the experience very exciting as well, and a great education. "We're getting a better understanding about what poor people go through, for instance. My mentality before had always been, as I worked for the phone company, 'If I can do that, raise four children by myself, why can't these people? They should get out and work.' " But in various meetings of delegates from member churches and synagogues involved in SFOP, she had come to know people from housing projects and on welfare personally. "It gives me a totally different perspective," she explained. "We work together and find common values. It makes all the difference."

For Ramona, however, the issue of whether unions should be invited to join the new organizing effort was far more difficult. "My attitude was, 'I don't quite trust unions. It was well and good when they first started out, but I'm afraid they may have sold us out.' " She was willing to talk about it in the hope that "maybe we can bring this country and this city back to a few of the old-fashioned values." But Ramona remained skeptical, as did many of her friends.

Such fears were common through much of the religious community that had come together in SFOP's original group of congregations. The founding statement had defined the group as "an organization of San Francisco congregations that is based on and guided by Judeo-Christian and democratic values. Our purpose is to develop our congregations so that we and all who are powerless in San Francisco have an effective voice in making the decisions that determine the quality of our communities and our lives." The document had spoken of "seeking other allies beyond the religious community who share our concerns and values." But it was unclear to many that trade unions fit such a description. Naomi Lauter, for instance, who came from a strong labor-union background herself, discovered that many people in synagogues voiced strong antiunion sentiment and even younger Jews were skeptical. "Labor is not part of their experience. Their grandparents were members, but their memory is very short." Sister Kathleen Healey, a member of the order of Presentation Sisters, explained that though her father had been a fireman and union member, "I was afraid of unions. I was really nervous that they had a different language and were into their own issues."[11]

A few who knew the language of both the religious community and the labor movement helped make ties. Walter Johnson, whose talk is rich with biblical stories and allusions, "knew how to speak both languages," for instance. So did Father Peter Sammon at Saint Theresa's parish; his own father had been a strong union man. But tensions around the question of whether unions should be involved in SFOP remained high. It was unclear that the gap could be bridged.

An important breakthrough came with help from an unexpected source. Mike Miller, who regularly attends organizational development seminars and knows a number of people in the corporate world, remembered a friend who headed a training unit for a large corporation. The man had developed ways for different divisions of the bureaucracy to overcome histories of antagonism. "You put all the people in the same room and ask everyone to brainstorm about the larger purpose for working together and the obstacles to that. Then you put each group in separate rooms and have them think about each one's images of the other, and what the *other* might think of them."

SFOP tried out the technique. Religious representatives and people from the unions talked together about the city, and about why an organization such as SFOP might be valuable. Then they split up into two groups to list answers to a series of questions: What are the values which guide you in your work? What are the values which you think guide the other (labor, religious) groups? What are *your* problems with the other? On what concerns and problems would you like support from them? Finally, what do you think the other group will say about us?

Responses to the final question were self-revelatory: "Fat cats," "Only concerned about money," "Too narrow," "Don't care about the community," "Don't feel like we really represent our constituency," "Discriminate against minority people" —the fearful notions that labor had about their own image made up an extended list. But it turned out that religious people also felt that they were liable to draw harsh judgment: "Pie-in-the-sky otherworldliness," "Do-gooders," "Not enough minorities and women in leadership," "Conservative," "Management-oriented" were a few of the negative statements that the religious group listed about itself.

Discussing the lists brought laughter—and a recognition of important overlap. Both unions and religious congregations, for instance, put a high priority on the "dignity of the person," on principles of fairness and justice, on a spirit of community variously defined (labor people called it "brotherhood and sisterhood"), on security, on the elimination of powerlessness. Both felt the need for more knowledge about the other and were concerned with many similar issues: housing, crime prevention, unemployment, quality services.[12]

The experience, in many peoples' memories, was an important step in building some connections across a gap grown large over the years, and the congregations issued a formal invitation to unions to join the coalition. At least as important in building ties, moreover, has been the meeting process that subsequently occurred around many issues and the underlying values involved in them. Indeed, the creation of a new public forum— what COPS would term a "public life" connected with people's specific communities but with an integrity and life of its own as well—allowed dialogues and education to take place in a number of directions, across not only labor-religious lines but also other historic antagonisms.

Joe Landry, a leader in SFOP from its earliest days, has observed the process at work with an expert eye. Landry combines friendliness with a judicious toughness ("Kids have it too easy these days," he tells me. "Nobody challenges them to *be* anything in school or the community"). Landry is a black Vietnam veteran who earned a reputation in the air force as an astute mediator in conflicts. ("What you have to do is learn from the men," he explains, recounting his experiences as an officer. "You let the one who knows the most do the job.") His great enthusiasm for SFOP, based on his perception that it gives people a new kind of "meeting ground where they can talk, work together on specific problems, and develop some respect," commands attention.

Before SFOP, according to Landry, "everybody was in their own kingdom." But in the organization, "a job has to be done, so you just start doing it." The week before we talked, he had seen two members of different churches, a black man and a white woman, work through some planning for the convention. "When she got ready to leave, she said, 'It was really nice working with you.' That's something people haven't experienced before. Now when you see somebody on the street, it's not 'she' or 'he,' it's names with faces."

I asked Joe what allowed the communication in the first place. He said he thought the stress on values reinforces the process a good deal, bringing people "back into line about what's really important." He continued, with a wave toward the neighborhood: "It's easy to lose your direction out there. It might be materialistic values, it might be a job structure or a type of power, but you lose sight of why we're really here." He thinks SFOP reconnects people with the essentials: "a decent neighborhood, a place where your kids can grow up and play, a decent school, a job. You don't want all the riches, really, all you want is comfortability."

Arelious Walker, the new president of SFOP, says much the same thing. Walker's black Pentecostal church includes many former drug addicts and criminals. He radiates a seriousness of purpose that reminds me of Bertha Gilkey in Cochran Gardens, recounting instance after instance of people's transformation after they came to "accept themselves as a person, as a human being regardless of what's happened."

True Hope was the center of his work, but he had often tried to get other congregations involved with the problems of the poor. He had also, frustratingly, worked in a number of citywide interracial coalitions in the past. "In my experience," he explains, "there wasn't a really deep commitment. The interracial coalitions were somewhat passive. People would say they were working together, but it was shallow." Walker says indignantly, "With all the adverse things happening in people's lives, why would you get involved in situations where you say you're giving people hope, when you're not? It's just a fantasy."

He perceived SFOP as different. Like COPS and other value-based organizing efforts, a good deal of the early work in the organization was training sessions—teaching people basic skills of running meetings, raising money, analyzing problems, doing research, and so forth. What impressed Walker especially was that training involved many from the congregation, not only leaders. "Leaders are overloaded and tired. This was an opportunity to get grass-roots people involved and trained. Instead of having someone tell them what their problem is, it lets them define their own problems. This was something different." He also appreciated the diversity: "We had black and Hispanic and whites, talking about coming together on an issue basis and a principle basis. It was very inspiring."

Walker helped bridge the suspicions between religious groups and labor unions. He remembered the South of his youth where there was little union organization. "People were taken advantage of." Though there was suspicion among blacks that unions continued exclusionary policies, there was also an overall inclination toward sympathy. For the whole organizing committee, moreover, the brainstorming session was a breakthrough: "We had negative things about each other and they had negative things, but it turned out we have values in common. Family, hope, a good community."

Other controversies have arisen. At one point, for instance, a gay member of Saint John's Episcopal Church questioned Archbishop Quinn's being a keynote speaker at the convention because of his stand on homosexuality. Walker played a bridging role again, pointing to the respect with which Quinn was viewed in the community and the fact that the organization had not previously discussed homosexuality. The trust that had developed among diverse groups allowed people to talk about the issue. Archbishop Quinn remained a keynote, and Donneter

Lane of the Council of Churches was also added. Jim Borrazas, the man who brought up the issue in the planning meeting for the convention, expressed great enthusiasm about what had occurred. "I thought the willingness to listen and the response I got was very, very heartening," he told me.

Others anticipate that further controversies will arise in the future, perhaps frequently. Diana Samuelson, a dynamic young woman who is SFOP treasurer, was elected to that office because she had declined the nomination for another. "I wasn't going to be a secretary. In an organization which has black, white, Latino, Protestant, Catholic, and Jewish and labor leaders, you can't have men in the role of president, vice-president, and treasurer." She believes women's leadership will continue to be an issue, but like others she believes the organization has developed ways of working through controversies. "The only way you can deal with anything is if you can sit down and talk about it," concluded Walker. I commented that such controversies are better talked about in SFOP meetings than in the news media. "Oh, my goodness, right on!" He smiled.

If there is ultimately a key to the sort of community-renewing organization represented by COPS and SFOP that creates a positive framework for resolving past antagonisms, it seems to me to lie in the seriousness and commitment with which these groups address basic questions of values, different cultures and traditions. Like Bertha Gilkey in Cochran Gardens or COPS, the organizers and leaders in SFOP do not give lip service to principles. A continuing discussion of basic values and how they should shape the organization forms the centerpiece of organizational life.

The process is illustrated sometimes in individual stories. For instance, Ramona Michaels, who had worked for months on preparations for the founding convention and was running for corresponding secretary of the organization, had her granddaughter's first communion the same afternoon.

"Any other community group I'd ever worked with would have put tremendous pressure on her to come to the meeting," remarked Larry Gordon. "If she hadn't been there, she couldn't have been elected." But in SFOP, other leaders insisted that she go to her granddaughter's Communion, a major event in the Catholic faith. Her absence was explained—and applauded from stage as the nominations were read.

Josie Mooney used the story to illustrate the meaning of a "value base" to an organization like SFOP. "If you take the values seriously," she explained, "you have to separate your public and personal life and honor your personal life. That's how we view the work." Mooney continued with a story of a True Hope training session she had once conducted that seemed to me to suggest the ways values begin to shape organizational vision as well.

Mooney, like Miller and Gordon, is a veteran organizer. But she had been nervous about holding any sort of "value discussion" at True Hope, a congregation deeply versed in biblical stories and theology ("One time I asked about an issue and fifteen people quoted me chapter and verse from Deuteronomy!" she remembers). But Walker had insisted that his congregation, like others, needed such a process of discussing their values and the ways they could be advanced through the San Francisco Organizing Project.

Over time, Josie Mooney built strong ties with congregation members. With such a foundation, she tried an experiment one day. Instead of a scheduled session on what makes for accountability in leaders, she decided to let imagination go. "We did a session on visions. What kind of world would you like to see?"

She continued: "It was incredible. People talked about a world in which everybody could be friends, where the races would be treated the same. 'I envision a neighborhood in which I can go out at night and take a walk and not be afraid.' 'A community where my children will be as well educated as the white children.' By the end we had a picture of the city painted that was so wonderful. Then I said, "Who here thinks we can't do this?"

No hands went up. So Mooney paused, took a breath, and challenged the group. "You're all lying," she said with her organizer's toughness. "Every one of us thinks we can't accomplish this list."

Gradually people raised their hands, agreeing. "Then we talked about how we could make our work in SFOP part of achieving that vision for our children and grandchildren. It was very powerful."

Mooney looked at me. "Unless we operate out of this vision, what's the point? So what if we get a streetlight or whatever? Is that honestly going to make a difference? I could be organizing from now until the day I die and the real power is not going to change if it's one issue at a time." To her, however, what suggested the possibilities for broader change "are the incredible changes I see in people's lives. I'm astounded." And she is heartened by what may be possible.

7

Visions of the Commonwealth

During the latter years of the nineteenth century, dark forebodings grew among American intellectuals. Ignatius Donnelly's dystopian novel *Caesar's Column* expressed such anxieties, for instance, in its portrayal of a future America in which humans had become slaves to machines; Christian ideals of communal love and justice had been obliterated; and an oppressive, hedonistic elite ruled without challenge. Yet there were other voices. In his work *A Traveler from Altruria*, William Dean Howells suggested a different possibility.

Contemporaries of Howells held him in high regard. He was sometimes called "the dean of American letters," and his writings appeared in the leading publications of the day. His column in *Harper's Monthly* was a regular feature.

Howells was given to social criticism. He defended the anarchists charged with the Haymarket bombing in Chicago. He remained fascinated with cooperative experiments, and often lent his support. But he was not unaware of the irony in his situation, far removed as it was from the modest circumstances of his childhood in Ohio. "After fifty years of optimistic content with 'civilization' . . . I now abhor it," he wrote to his friend Henry James. "Meanwhile, I wear a fur-lined overcoat, and live in all the luxury my money can buy."

In Howells's novel, a traveler, Mr. Homos, comes from the far-off land of Altruria to a New Hampshire resort frequented by the well-to-do. Purporting ignorance of American ways, he describes himself as an eager student and asks the guests to describe their lives. Their initial roseate portrayals of America gradually give way to stark self-revelations. Under surface imagery, American business is run according to principles far different from the common good: "The good of Number One first, last and all the time." Despite their wealth, the men he talks with are desperate, scrambling after illusory goals. Their wives, similarly, experience "a most hideous slavery" to social expectation under their veneers of cultured sociability. "Going to lunches and teas, and dinners, and concerns, and theaters and art exhibitions and charity meetings," says the representative Mrs. Makely, "you don't have a moment to yourself; your life isn't your own."

The resort guests at last ask to hear Mr. Homos's story. He describes Altruria's transformation from a society much like late-nineteenth-century America. After its initial revolution many years before, changing monarchy into republic, Altrurians had become all too enraptured with "progress." Uncontrolled technology and unbridled greed had ensued, destroying Altruria's initial ideals: "We did not see that the machines for saving labor were monsters that devoured women and children, and wasted men at the bidding of the power which no man must touch." Yet Altrurians had at last awakened from their nightmare. Mounting another revolution—this one nonviolent and electoral—they determined to become a "commonwealth" bearing resemblance to American visions of agriculturally based, egalitarian society. Decentralized and democratic communities of the commonwealth were linked together through rapid electrical transportation systems. Networks of regional capitals served as centers of commerce and deliberation. But most lived in villages and the countryside. All machines destructive of the natural or human environment had been tamed, abandoned, or transformed. Men and women had come to focus on their lives in common, instead of on material acquisition. As a result they had struck a healthy balance between individuality, allowing private space and diversity, and the common good. Accompanying such values, a new appreciation for beauty and craft had also grown: "not a furrow driven or a swarth mown, not a hammer struck on house or on ship, not a stitch sewn or a stone laid, not a line written or a sheet printed, not a temple raised or an engine built, but it was done with an eye to beauty as well as to use."

As *A Traveler from Altruria* suggested, the commonwealth vision had not entirely disappeared from mainstream American thought in the 1890s. But it retained only a thin echo of its former power. In the novel's conclusion, Mr. Homos's host, Mr. Twelvemough, remarks that the man seems "no more definite or tangible than a bad conscience." Such a designation could easily enough be applied to Howells himself. Between the aspirations of such writers and their notions of how ideals might be realized "yawned an immense gulf," as historian John Kasson has described in his book *Civilizing the Machine,* which rendered their views largely "ethical tonic, . . . sweetened with Christian molasses and laced with a reproving sulphur." As the new century dawned, forces of centralization were reshaping the nation apace.[1]

The story recurs again and again: Conscience of the commonwealth, no matter how serious and creative, is no antidote to the lure of affluence, the momentum of technology, or the dynamic of the marketplace. By the 1980s in America, the commonwealth utopia of William Dean Howells had been all but forgotten by any except the most specialized of scholars, and the word *commonwealth* itself was rarely heard. Yet the themes that it suggests continued to move citizens and shape communities. Nowhere could such a process be seen more vividly and poignantly than in Lowell, Massachusetts, often called "the city that led America into the Industrial Age, birthplace of the American Industrial Revolution."

In recent years, Lowell has again become a model. As the *Boston Phoenix* put a common perception not long ago, "The gritty, aging factory town on the Merrimac River is experiencing a spectacular rebirth." Massachusetts governor Michael Dukakis, who enjoys claiming partial credit for renovation of downtown areas—he supported the city's new historic park, and encouraged Wang laboratories to move its headquarters to Lowell—describes the city as "one of the great urban success stories in this country."[2]

Changes in the last decade have indeed been striking. But up close, the story is more complicated. Progress, to the extent it has occurred, has entailed pain and dislocation. And it has not come without a struggle.

During the years 1810 and 1811, Francis Cabot Lowell, of the old Massachusetts family, toured the ironworks in Edinburgh, Scotland. Like many of his peers among the affluent and powerful in America, Lowell was anxious that the new nation not reproduce the "disgusting and loathsome forms of destitution, and utter vice and profligacy" that observers like Henry Colman reported as products of the Industrial Revolution across the ocean.

When he toured the factories, he was thrilled by the new technology and memorized its design—thus circumventing the strictures against taking plans from the country abroad. But he and his partners, infused with American faith in "republican virtue" and the ideals of community, influenced greatly by utopian experiments conducted by Robert Owen, were convinced they could create an alternative to the social misery and degradation he saw overseas.

Like other "total institutions" through which early-nineteenth-century reformers set out to rehabilitate the marginal—insane asylums, for instance, and reformatories—Lowell was intended to "stand as a model of enlightened republican community in a restless and dynamic nation," as John Kasson described their mission. The founders organized company boardinghouses, schools, and compulsory religious services, all with the professed aim of instilling "habits of order, regularity and industry" in the new work force. Owners like Nathan Appleton strenuously disavowed profit-making as their chief aim: "My mind has always been devoted to many other things." To avoid the development of a permanent working class, they planned to hire mainly young single women from nearby areas who would stay in the mills only a brief period, "an honorable stage in a young woman's maturation."

The mill owners and factory builders had a knack for organization and finance, and they joined such talents to the new technologies and favorable geography; they were able to build miles of canals along the Merrimac River. Lowell became famous throughout the nation for its mass-produced cotton and other products. Other New England towns rapidly sought to emulate its achievements.

From the vantage point of the growing work force, however, the situation looked rather different. Many young women did indeed initially welcome the mills and their diverse institutions as exciting new opportunities. But over time, the mood turned radically. Machinery—noisy, dangerous, ruthless in its inexorable pacing—took an exacting toll on the lives and health of young women accustomed to natural rhythms of farming. The affluence of the owners' families, contrasted with the poverty of the work force, seemed to mock professions of common interest and republican virtue.

In response, workers began to create early, fabled chapters in American social and labor history. In 1834, as many as 2,000 turned out to protest a 15-percent cut in wages. But workers saw themselves as concerned with far more than material interest: The very definitions of liberty and virtue were at stake. "We do not estimate our liberty by dollars and cents," one explained. "It was not the reduction of wages alone which caused the excitement, but that haughty, overbearing disposition, that purse-proud insolence, which was becoming more and more apparent." Two years later, Lowell women again demonstrated against a wage cut, turning the mill owners' rhetoric on its head as they drew on the Revolutionary heritage: "As our fathers resisted unto blood the lordly avarice of the British ministry, so we, their daughters, never will wear the yoke which has been prepared for us."[3]

In the 1850s, immigrants replaced the "Yankee mill girls" in Lowell factories. Irish, French Canadians, Greeks, Poles, Portuguese, eventually Puerto Ricans and Columbians arrived in wave after wave—more than forty nationalities settled in the area. Tenements rose in place of the old boardinghouses. But the mills and factories simultaneously began to suffer a steady, slow decline.

After the Civil War, owners of factories like the Lowell Machine Shop, which had previously done a booming business in

locomotive boilers, began to lose money. They moved operations to other areas of New England, sold off equipment, and
finally closed down completely in the 1930s. Factory after factory followed suit. In 1957, the last of the old mills shut its door
forever. Unemployment in the city steadily rose, to over 16
percent by the mid-Seventies. Many wrote the area off as a
casualty of a rapidly changing economy that was said to be
making such older industrial regions increasingly obsolete. Pat
Mogan, however, superintendent of Lowell's public school system, had other ideas.[4]

Mogan is a slightly portly, slightly disheveled man, now
retired from the school system. He speaks with zeal and enthusiasm about the changes that have come to Lowell in the last
decade. And he is a man who bristles with ideas. George Duncan, president of First Bank, who organized other bankers to
help with the revitalization of the downtown area, tells me a
story about Pat that makes the point, and also reflects both the
affection and humor with which he is viewed. At the annual
party of Duncan's business group, Mogan was portrayed in a
skit, wearing hunting clothes, roaming in some distant marsh.
"He was looking for a duck in the wilderness to tell his latest
idea to," Duncan laughs.

I meet Pat Mogan in the Lowell Tourist Center, a refurbished
old mill building in the center of the Lowell Historic Park,
which was established in 1976. In the background I can hear the
tape that accompanies the continuous slide show downstairs,
reciting the story of Lowell's recent transformation: "In the
1960s . . . some citizens recognized that the city's heritage could
be the key to its revitalization. Lowell has rediscovered its past
and renewed its faith in the future."

That the park has had effect is obvious. Old mill buildings are
sandblasted, renovated, turned into museums like the Tourist
Center and apartments. Across the street, a row of new shops
and stores reminds me of the changes I had seen in Brooklyn,
New York. State and federal government has channeled over
$40 million into the city as part of the historical park restora-
tion. Wang Laboratories made Lowell its headquarters, creat-

ing thousands of jobs and leading to new programs in technology, computers, and science at the high school and the state university.

In a concept paper Mogan coauthored with two University of Massachusetts professors, he expanded on the theme of the tape downstairs: "The National Park is dedicated to the interpretation of this rich social and cultural heritage . . . how the various ethnic groups coped with this process of industrialization . . . and the nationally important technological and architectural resources. . . . Lowell is a living exhibit of the process and consequences of the American Industrial Revolution. Around this theme is being orchestrated the historical, cultural, economic, and educational rebirth of the city." When Mogan tells me how the idea came about, he begins with his own history.[5]

Pat grew up in a town not far from Lowell, part of an Irish community desperately eager to be accepted by the dominant Yankee population that lived up on "Christian Hill." "We lived in an area called 'the Flats,' " he tells me. "We were looked down on. And we believed we were different."

For his community, the mark of difference was seen as disastrous. "There was a whole denial process going on. We thought to become something better, you had to become something else. You take my name, Patrick Joseph, for instance. Patrick was the name for the firstborn. Joseph was the saint's name nearest my birthday. But the guys I went to school with never named their kids this way. They believed they were running into barriers because they were Irish. So they tried to hide. They looked for ways to accommodate. They believed anything the institutions said."

Mogan, however, rebelled from an early age. "We Irish were seen as a problem by the school. When we were given the story of what was acceptable in society, we were mute. But I felt this was a hoax. I could have given them terrific stories of my family, and it would have created bonds between school and the home."

When he became an educator, he sought to change the system by developing ways that different nationalities could find pride and identity in who they are. "Schools were saying that in order to get ahead, you had to dissociate." Children were embarrassed about their backgrounds. Parents refused to teach them their native language. "I was bucking the tide. History didn't treat the industrial or ethnic setting very well."

In the 1960s, he became a leader in a Model Cities program for Lowell. It created new opportunities to talk about different cultural heritages. "When I got people together, it was like the United Nations," he remembers. "We had forty different cultural groups coming together. Indian, Greek, French, Irish . . . I said, 'If you found out you could *help* your kids by teaching your background rather than adapting, would you do it?' They said yes. So then I brought in educational experts who pointed out that learning occurs through diversity. People began to feel, 'We don't have to deny ourselves.'

"Then we talked about Lowell's history. People had lost the history. They didn't even know what the canals were. I said, 'Imagine having a kid and not giving him a name.' People had been brainwashed into believing Lowell's past was negative, nothing. But we looked into the past and found we had a terrifically interesting story: how America came to be what it is, the transition from agrarianism to industrialism." Such discussions laid the basis for beginning work to get Lowell declared a national historic park, the first such park, designating a city as a historical site, in the country.

I ask Pat if he has any association with the word *commonwealth,* aside from its use in the Massachusetts State Constitution. He nods vigorously. "The commonwealth is really just what we've been talking about. It's not what people think it is —the melting pot."

We continue. What, I wonder, does his notion of the commonwealth have to say about the way industrialism and the pursuit of wealth can destroy people's history? He tells stories of affluent men who have been the worst offenders in abandoning their heritage—"people who say, 'You can be inwardly a Greek, but outwardly try to be "a good American." ' " From the beginning, he continues, he had wanted the park to tell the story of common people and different ethnic groups, as well as the rich in Lowell.

Then I ask about a current controversy that has exploded in the city. An ethnic neighborhood not far from downtown called the "Acre," originally settled by Irish and then by Greeks, has most recently experienced an influx of the city's newest immigrants, Puerto Ricans. Not long before, the city manager, George Tully, had backed a developers' plan to destroy existing housing stock and replace it with new apartments. He had called the area "a decrepit, desolate place" that could not be rehabilitated because "it's too far gone." But the local newspaper had been far more venomous, using the issue to launch into a remarkable peroration about the entire Hispanic population: "It's not far from the truth to say that almost everything the Hispanics have touched in Central and South America, they have ruined," read the lead editorial. "That part of the world is a mess and, probably, always will be because the people from Spain who settled there and their descendants were incompetent then and still are today." It called for "rats to leave the ship" of Lowell, completing the invitation with a graphic cartoon.[6]

Pat Mogan was quiet for a moment. When he spoke, his voice was lowered. Several months before, he had sent the paper an article in response. "I said, 'We stand at the crossroads. How much potential we achieve depends on how we deal with bigotry against Hispanics.' My article has never been printed."

The Lowell story was obviously more complicated than it appeared from a distance. I wanted to hear other perspectives as well.

Entering the Acre, a five-minute walk from the sandblasted brick buildings downtown, is like entering another world. Successive waves of immigrants have left legacies that remain. Across the Merrimac Canal down along Market Street, George the Tailor's stands near Anthony Oriental Pastry, Giavis Market, Panagiotopoulos Real Estate, and the Zorba Room. Down the way is Saint Patrick's Church, a large, Gothic structure built by Irish immigrants in 1854 out of stone painstakingly carved from the canal beds. Nearby is Holy Trinity Greek Orthodox Church, whose gold-leaf dome and Byzantine architecture one can see from far away. Holy Trinity, too, was created through the sacrifice of its parishioners, in 1908, who donated their watches, crucifixes, and other valuables for the monument to their religion and their native homeland.

Greek clubs like the Acropolis continue to be meeting places. In midday, old men are in the windows, playing games and watching the passersby. But there are new additions next door: Puerto Rican residents, talking sociably outside. Across the way, in the large public housing project spreading around the churches, Puerto Ricans now make up most of the tenants.

A community coalition of organizations, called the Coalition for a Better Acre, has joined together a number of church groups, the Puerto Rican Festival Committee, and Lowell Fair Share to oppose the destruction of the Acre and seek instead its renovation. In the CBA office I meet leaders and staff. It is a diverse group.

Frank Melendez, a well-dressed, precise, friendly man who is pastor at a Puerto Rican Pentecostal church, describes what he sees as the "rootlessness" of many new immigrants who have come recently to the city. Arva Clark, director of the YWCA, idealistic and articulate, describes the consternation her "respectable" organization's support for Acre residents has stirred up in polite Lowell society. Two CBA staff members are there. Jerry Rubin, an earnest and hardworking former staff member of Massachusetts Fair Share, brings skill as a researcher and financial analyst to the problems of neighborhood rehabilitation. In coming months, he will play a key role in putting together needed financing for building rehabilitation. Angel Bermudez, the "community organizer" for CBA, is an intelligent, self-conscious young man. He is from one of the first Puerto Rican families to settle in Lowell, and he grew up in the city. Through a special program for gifted students, Angel later attended Groton, a private school. For a time, "hating Lowell," he was determined to leave. But like George Ozuna in San Antonio, he finally decided to come back to do something about the problems of discrimination and hardship he remembered.

Finally, there is Charlie Gargiulo, slender, intense, blond. He had brought the group together in the first place, and is president of CBA. Gargiulo, too, has a vision for Lowell's future. But it complements, challenges, and opposes, in various turns, the understanding of the city voiced by Lowell's more prominent spokesmen. Gargiulo's aspirations grow out of the underside of city history and are grounded in a fierce loyalty to its "ordinary citizens." They are also born of personal, traumatic experience.

Charlie grew up in a section of Lowell on the edge of the Acre. His father was of Italian ancestry; his mother came from the French-Canadian immigrants who settled in the area around the turn of the century. He remembers his childhood neighborhood as "an old area, where people had a strong sense of community." But when he was thirteen, in the mid-1960s, urban renewal began to destroy the houses. "When it started to sink in, it was too late. People didn't know what to do. This is the thing that shaped my life."

When Charlie talks about this experience, he develops a riveting intensity and his normally loud voice softens. "I had an aunt, Aunt Rose," he continues. "She had lived there all her life." Charlie's mother, raising him alone, worked when she could and as a child he spent most of his time with Aunt Rose. She was very religious, he says, and she was crippled. He remembers her in the window overlooking Ostridge Street where kids played, doing her rosary beads and saying prayers and watching out for the children. "She did this every day. This was her life. She hardly ever left the house."

When notice came that she was to be moved out, she called Charlie inside. "She told me, 'If they move me out, I'll die. I don't want to live anymore.' I said, 'Oh, come on, Aunt Rose.' They moved her across the river to a little apartment. A week later I came back from school. My mother was in the kitchen. I knew something was wrong. Aunt Rose had died. No physical reason. Just died.

"It's like the whole world is being ripped away from you," Charlie explains. "One day you come home, one friend has been moved. The next week, someone else. I'll never forget that sense of powerlessness. Who are these people? What right do they have? I didn't even know them. I remember one night I was so angry I just went over and punched the Urban Renewal Office."

As a teen-ager, Charlie went through what he calls "rough times," often in trouble, confused and aimless. He joined the service and worked with the Special Forces, where he found an inspirational role model in a black staff officer who showed him how one could battle injustice more effectively.

When he was discharged, he returned to the city and went to the university. Then he heard of Massachusetts Fair Share. "I saw this average-looking guy on television taking on the governor on auto insurance rates. He looked like my uncle. And I said, 'He's taking on the governor and getting the best of him.'" None of the other groups he knew about in the city seemed to speak for all the different groups that he felt were left out of decision-making. "I thought, this Fair Share is the kind of thing we need here. So I called them and told them I'd work my ass off if they would come down."

Mary Ochs, a remarkably talented organizer who now is employed by Organize Training Center in San Francisco, was at that time working with Massachusetts Fair Share. She came to Lowell. "She was the best organizer I ever saw," says Charlie. "She showed me how to take anger and mold it to create change, instead of just letting it go off blindly and self-destructively." For two years Charlie served as president of the Lowell Fair Share chapter. He spearheaded the campaign to clean up the Silresim dump site. ("My God, I thought when we heard about it, can this be real? We checked it out. It was real. Then we got attacked because we were using scare tactics.") The group began to hear rumors that the Triangle—a jumble of old houses, shops, and storefronts at the heart of the Acre neighborhood—was to be torn down. Charlie talked to people in the community. They didn't want to move. He helped form the Coalition for a Better Acre (CBA) to do something about it.

"Tully Plan Would Raze Acre 'Triangle' Buildings," read the headline in the January 29, 1982, issue of the *Lowell Sun*. The article went on to describe the city's plan to replace low-income housing with "moderately priced apartments/condominiums."[7]

To the Coalition for a Better Acre, however, the plan was displacement and "gentrification"—removal of poor residents to make way for more affluent renters, more in keeping with the downtown's refurbished image. There was no small irony as well. The city's revitalization theme was its industrial and ethnic heritage, and the Acre was Lowell's oldest ethnic neighborhood, port of entry for immigrants since the 1840s. "It's like the only way to talk about working-class people is to talk about them in the past," Angel Bermudez observed with some bitterness. For Charlie, the plan struck home. It recalled all too vividly his own childhood and the obliteration of his neighborhood.[8]

This time, however, the neighborhood had resources and allies. "When they announced the plan to raze the Triangle, it catalyzed the opposition," Charlie explains. People started coming to meetings in large numbers. Small businesses, worried that their own survival would be jeopardized by a new and sanitized version of the Acre, lent their support. To top it off, Aetna Life Insurance—which the city had counted on for backing in its own development plan—chose to support the coalition, through a program designed in cooperation with the National People's Action, an alliance of neighborhood groups around the country. It offered $2 million in mortgage financing, directed through the coalition, for renovation of buildings. I came not long after the Aetna announcement, and CBA was jubilant. In subsequent months, others also joined in. A Boston bank agreed to put up loan money as part of the plan. George Duncan's First Bank agreed to help, and the coalition was able to work with the city planning department in applying for an Urban Development Action grant to build scattered-site housing. "I think we're beginning to see real hope for development," concluded Jerry Rubin. "The community could really be renewed."

Whatever the outcome, Charlie Gargiulo sees the Acre struggle as part of a never-ending pattern. His philosophy recalls that of the famous nineteenth-century abolitionist Frederick Douglass: Ordinary people never get anything without challenge and effort. Common people in Lowell will enjoy new opportunities when they win them.

Charlie cites not only Silresim and the Acre but the historic park itself. He did not disagree with the beginning approach, which stressed the role of the owners and the importance of technology. But he thought it was a dramatically incomplete portrayal of "the Lowell story." The Tourist Center now has recordings of oral histories, with old-timers from the mills recalling their lives and what it was like. Wall murals depict ordinary workers as well as notables. Information tells about the injuries and deaths caused by the machinery, as well as the growth.

"There have been changes for the better," says Charlie, "partly because of the criticisms we helped generate. At the beginning, you'd have guides showing you the machines but not even mentioning the people who had been hurt or killed. There was a list of contributors to Lowell, but no working people were being honored. Only later did I learn that there were people like Sara Bagley, one of the first women labor organizers in the country. I want the positive aspects of Lowell history told. But the full story." Charlie believes in ethnic pride, as does Pat Mogan. "But I also want people to be able to work together, to stress what we have in common, to learn to fight."

I ask Gargiulo what he understands "organizing" to be about. He begins with negative examples: "It doesn't mean going in and telling people what the problem is. Mary Ochs was a good organizer because she didn't try to put things there. She helped draw things out that were within me." Such a view shapes his understanding of the positive alternative, which recalls the faith of a Bertha Gilkey, or an Ernie Cortes. "There's a lot of beauty and a lot of power within people that needs to come out. And that can be built upon when people start believing that they do matter," Charlie says. "Organizing means trying to pull out the visions that have been submerged, trying to break down the barriers that hold people back." I ask him what he thinks of the word *commonwealth*. "I love the word," he tells me.

"The problem is, it's gotten all turned around, like the Commonwealth of Massachusetts."

Charlie Gargiulo, like Pat Mogan from a different vantage point, seeks to rebuild an authentic commonwealth. It is a word that is nearly forgotten, but others can be found who similarly rekindle memories of that oldest of American communal visions. At times, their work impacts on their fellow citizens and their areas in ways that would be hard to ever forget.

Crossing the country to Seattle, I thought about the trails of settlers who had trekked to "the end of the railroad line": Swedes, Norwegians, Irish, blacks, Chinese; prospectors on their way to the Alaska gold rush; foundry workers and sailors and fisher families and itinerant loggers. For many in the past, the commonwealth was their hope. Indeed, American radicals in the latter years of the nineteenth century, sometimes despairing of changing the rest of the country, looked to Washington State as the area in which to establish "a commonwealth" that could serve as a model of cooperative, egalitarian society. The grand, elaborate plans were waylaid, but many smaller settlements formed, declared themselves to be "cooperating commonwealths," and left a legacy that shaped the region during later decades of explosive growth and change.

Seattle on first impression seems overwhelmingly oriented to the future, not the past. The airport reflects the most advanced designs and technology, with its massive spaces and automated trains. The drive into town on an intricate highway system curves like spaghetti past the "space needle," left from the World's Fair, and takes one into the middle of glass and steel mazes created by the downtown businesses.

But there remains an older heritage under the modern gloss. On a clear spring day, the natural beauty of the setting is stunning. Cherry trees and apple blossoms, cultivated magnolias and rhododendrons are in bloom, and everywhere a cascade of flowers and shrubs: Scotch broom, purple heather, foxglove, daffodils, forsythia. To the east, down from the hills that the city straddles, Lake Washington spreads like a large piece of sky, catching reflections of the jagged, white-tipped mountains of the Cascades beyond. Mount Rainier rises like some mighty piling to the south. And back across Puget Sound to the west, the distant mountains of the Olympic Peninsula form a giant, majestic wall, partially shrouded in mists.

Similarly, the human environment, richly textured, mingles old-fashioned scenes with the landmarks of what is called "progress." Seattle is obviously a city of neighborhoods. Many, I later learn, still bear the names of the original ethnic villages, such as Greenwood, Belltown, Ballard, and Fremont, which linked together in the early years of the century to form a larger whole. Rapid growth and rolling hills dictated building patterns, as in San Francisco. Seattle was laid out in twenty-five-foot lots and remains a town of small, neat, colorful houses.

Shaping the city is the waterfront. Sailboats are everywhere, alongside trawlers, ferries, tugboats, overflown by Mallard ducks, an occasional pelican or cormorant, and, everywhere, sea gulls. In the city's central district, the Pike Place Market has retained the sort of jumbled, crazy-quilt diversity and informality that downtown San Francisco has largely lost. Merchants from dozens of nationalities display their foods: Alex's Phillippine Cuisine; Hassan Brothers; the Athenian, where old retired sailors from the low-income housing across the street gather and sip coffee, still 14 cents a cup. There are fruit and vegetable and fish stalls everywhere, selling hundreds of different goods, from garlic to crabs in from Alaska. Out in front of the market is an expression of entrepreneurial spirit, forever untrammeled: A young woman whose cart did not conform to some kind of city regulations looks out the window of her trailer. She has been there for days, sleeping on the premises to keep officials from hauling it all away. On her window is a sign expressing her judgment: "Free enterprise died here, February 7, 1983."

I came to Seattle to interview Terry Pettus, a man often held partly responsible for the salvage of the natural and human heritage of the area. The city council had declared March 7

"Terry Pettus Day" the year before. A local television commentator had noted what he called "the irony, the bittersweet irony" of the event. "Thirty-five years ago, the city establishment would not have minded at all if somebody had shot Terry Pettus and dumped him in his beloved Lake Union." But disreputable history or not, here were hundreds of people gathered to honor the man. Pete Seeger had come to sing songs on the occasion—recalling, perhaps, the concerts that Pettus had once organized with Seeger in the Northwest, models for later "hootenannies." And the mayor's proclamation, praising Pettus as a figure with "the courage to speak out, whenever the quality of life in our city has been threatened," called him "a link to our city's past, a vision of our city's future."[9]

Terry Pettus is to be found, as he normally is, on his houseboat amid several hundred others, forming a close-knit community in Lake Union, not far from downtown. As I get to know him, I realize the connection with the houseboats and the lake is far more than geographic. He reflects the spirit of the community —its color, its richness, its vitality and iconoclasm, as Helen Turner somehow reflected the old West Side of St. Paul. The starting point for Pettus's story thus turned out to be the history of the houseboat neighborhood itself. Like Pettus, it has since its beginning combined a feisty exuberance with a continuing struggle for survival.

From the beginning of settlement—at least of Europeans, arguably of Indians as well—Lake Union was a "working lake." In the 1870s, barges carrying coal and lumber crossed the water, heading from the interior to the rail lines on the western shore, which carried the resources over to Puget Sound. In those years, much of the shore was still wilderness; a hunter killed a cougar there in 1870. The south shore, now bordering on downtown, was not cleared until the 1880s.

During that decade—the first years of the great boom, which increased the city's size from 3,533 in 1880 to 237,194 in 1910 —streetcars and rail lines made the lake accessible from all the surrounding villages. In the twentieth century, boat works and dry docks appeared along the shore, servicing water vessels of all kinds. Along with the expanding commercial activity came the first houseboaters, spilling over from Lake Washington to the east.

From the beginning, the houseboaters' existence was precarious. The city health department declared the whole idea of houseboats a health hazard in 1908. In 1922, a city health commission labeled the boats "a virtual cesspool." From the affluent hill neighborhoods overlooking the lake, the sprawling, floating village—1,100 houseboats in Lake Union by the 1930s—proved a constant reminder of "the other Seattle" they would rather forget. Boatyard workers, sailors, students, and bohemians mingled with retired radicals from the Industrial Workers of the World and simply the city's poor, who could scarcely afford to live anywhere else. Along the shores, speakeasies and brothels were scattered through the small shacks and apartments. "It was a breeding ground for nonconformity," wrote Howard Droker, who authored a history of the houseboats. Through the 1940s, the houseboats were "occupied by society's outcasts."[10]

The reputation was entirely beside the point to Berta and Terry Pettus, who moved to the lake in 1933. They got what they thought was a marvelous deal on a boat—for which they paid $1,000 cash (other residents told them they had been taken). Moorage rents, paid to the owners of the docks along which the boats were tied, were dirt cheap—on the order of $6 a month. It all seemed made to order. If anything, the life-styles of the houseboat community matched their own.

The program prepared by the houseboaters' organization for the day honoring Terry Pettus described him as "the life spirit and guiding force of the Floating Homes Association for two decades." Current president Bill Keasler added that "Terry is one of those rare people whose effect on you is similar to that of a great work of art. Once you've met him, you're never quite the same again." Talking with Pettus over the course of many hours, I understood the point.

Terry waves his arms expansively when he talks, lowers and raises his voice to make points, gestures, moves back and forth in his seat, his long, lanky frame conveying perpetual energy. His stories somehow combine the colorful vernacular of a waterfront sailor with the literary insight and allusions of a literary critic and the passions of an old labor radical. Indeed, his life has included all these roles and more.

Over the years, Terry has made his living mainly from writing, everything under the sun—mystery novels, art and theater reviews, historical works, newspaper articles. His speech spills over with topics that span the world. One day he tells me in detail about the history courses he took in Oxford, England, and the "best summer of my life," when he went on an archaeological dig at Middleton-Storey, site of an ancient Celtic, Roman, and medieval town. Another day, he is full of lore and stories of the native Indian tribes he has known, like the Skokomish and Quinault, who hunted for whales off the coast and, he believes, made contact a millennium ago with Chinese junks sailing out across the ocean on merchant expeditions. He tells ribald tales of the old mansion down on Cherry Street in which he and Berta lived in the early 1930s, owned by the painter Kenneth Callahan, whose portrait of Berta, Terry's late wife, hangs on the wall of the houseboat. Under the name of Burrus Thornly, Terry wrote theater reviews for the *Seattle Town Crier,* a literary magazine whose patrons were the city's "sawdust aristocracy." The mansion was meeting ground for artists and writers of the Northwest, a place where the nouveau riche could be counted on to "bring the booze."

Pettus in these years also covered stories of the Great Depression, like Hooverville, populated by the down-and-out, "a republic of the penniless whom society had rejected, but a place where people depended on each other and built a community" with their own mail system, police, and bartering; and the battles in Tacoma, Washington, between loggers and giant timber interests, where Pettus "always got on the wrong side of the tear gas."

Born in 1904, Terry Pettus had grown up in Terre Haute, Indiana. The town was home to the famous American socialist leader Eugene Debs ("Even the Boy Scouts campaigned for him," says Terry). Terry's father was a minister whose church in the heart of the business district attracted the city's elite—bankers, mine owners, and so forth. But his father never flinched from an ardent championing of the rights of workers and the poor. Terry remembers thunderous arguments on their front porch on summer evenings, when his father would challenge some injustice perpetrated by a parishioner.

In such a milieu, Terry became what he calls "a knee-jerk socialist." But his understanding of the term resembled that of Debs himself. It drew far more from what he calls "native American radicalism" than from European importations.

In 1927, Terry and Berta moved to Seattle, where Terry had a job on the *Seattle Star.* In Seattle, he found, the commonwealth vision threaded through popular movements—the fight for public power and rural electrification; the effort to win popular initiative and referendum; the battle for industrial-accident insurance, old-age pensions. At the heart of each, in his view, was the notion of the whole, "the people versus the special interests, the common good." In later years, Terry, fascinated with the etymology of the word *commonwealth,* traced it to seventeenth-century English radicals, who used the word to mean the sovereignty of the common people.

In 1934, when representatives of labor unions, farmers, neighborhood associations, and other groups came together in a new political movement to press their interests, they drew on such rich history, calling their organization the Washington Commonwealth Federation. The Commonwealth Federation saw itself as the embodiment of America's finest and most enduring ideals. ("I used to argue with the activists in the sixties," Terry recounts. "Why give away symbols like the flag? The Fourth of July was originally the holiday of working people, celebrating the Revolution. When is the American Left going to take out its naturalization papers?") The movement featured histories of ordinary people not normally taught in schools, with a special history column in the federation's newspaper and history features on the movement's radio program. "We would describe the cooperative commonwealths that were established here, the Knights of Labor," says Terry. "One woman, Mrs. Johnson, had a large American flag that had been handed down in her family. Someone had sewn it together from red, white, and blue silk dresses. It had thirteen stars. It was quite obvious that the flag was made soon after Betsy Ross. Every event, we would take it out and raise it."

Organizing on the basis of precincts, the Commonwealth Federation in the 1930s and 1940s became the dominant force in the state Democratic party, sending a number of congressmen to Washington, at various times controlling the state legislature. Pettus himself, perhaps more than anyone else, came to symbolize the radical movement in Seattle. He was the first member of the Newspaper Guild in the Northwest. He helped lead the successful strike against William Randolph Hearst's *Seattle Post-Intelligencer.* He edited various federation newspapers. And he was constantly present on picket lines, at protests against racial discrimination—wherever a group of powerless people were fighting for their rights.

But as the mood of the country changed in the early 1950s, Terry became the target of FBI investigations. In 1952 he was indicted under the Smith Act, a product of the anti-Communist crusade of that time. He served six months in jail before his conviction was finally overturned. Those years, especially, Terry and Berta came to value the unique, tight-knit world of the houseboat community on Lake Union.

What Terry calls his "basic theory" is simple. "We are a social animal," he explains. "When disaster strikes, people work together. How come humans survived, when our infants are the most helpless, miserable things you've ever seen? Because we banded together. People do it instinctively." On Lake Union, the setting reinforced the instinct.

Terry waves out the window of his houseboat. "When you move here, you start to know what a real neighbor is. Your Main Street is the dock. Last night it was raining pretty hard. I went out on my front porch and talked to the fellow next door, who was leaning out the window." Houseboats are only a few feet apart, separated by several feet, where sailboats or dinghies are tied up. "I remember years ago," Terry continues, "detectives asked me why there were no robberies on the houseboats. There's hardly any crime—molestation, peeping toms, whatever. Women talk about how safe they feel when they hit the dock." The narrow, wooden walkway is raised slightly above the floors of each boat; it is impossible to walk down the dock without being seen by everyone. "If anyone is up to any mischief, or just has a problem, it is noticeable. You say, 'Can I help you?' In the suburbs, you drive into your carport and close the door."

Water life-styles reinforce the neighborliness. Each houseboat has a personality all its own—and despite the close ties on the docks, privacy is also carefully respected. One houseboat several down from Terry has a blacksmith emblem in the window. The man, a Spanish Civil War veteran, works outside, sculpting in wood. Another has a vegetable garden. Most have flowers. People are constantly outside, working, talking, looking at the lake and the boats going by.

Like the West Side of St. Paul, moreover, the neighborhood has its larger gathering places. The Bowtie, a former tavern owned by a retired French chef named André Bouillard, was where residents would "solve the problems of the world." "He always encouraged you to argue and discuss," Terry remembers. "He wouldn't say anything, just listen. Then, after the arguments had gone on for a while, he would go into his back room, pull out his encyclopedia, and settle the thing."

Bouillard had a large black dog named Bootleg, for the legendary activity common in the area some years earlier. When a stool in the bar was empty, Bootleg would climb up and listen. Bouillard and Bootleg could be seen sailing down the lake every afternoon in their little boat, like clockwork. Finally, Bouillard died of cancer. "The dog just lay there. He wouldn't eat. He died, too."

Terry pauses. "It was good that we lived in this community during the Smith Act trial," he explains. When he went to jail, neighbors offered their support. "The old sailor across the way came by and told Berta, 'If I'm not home, there will always be someone else there, keeping an eye out. Don't worry, you'll be safe.' She never had any problems."

After his release, Berta and Terry settled into a quiet life, thinking they had retired from politics. Terry made some money writing mysteries, and Berta wrote as well. In 1961, however, their quiet was interrupted abruptly. Controversy over the houseboats themselves propelled Terry Pettus into what Seattleans call his "second political career."

The city had long looked with disfavor on the floating homes. And developers, long desirous of the land along the shoreline, began making specific plans to acquire property and evict the residents. In 1961, the boaters formed an association to try to do something about the impending threat. Terry at first declined to become very active. In April of the following year, however, the Pettuses got an eviction notice themselves. They decided to do something.

Terry smiles. "In those years, even our so-called friends were saying, 'It's too bad, but houseboats are not a good use of the property.' We hired one lawyer to represent us before the city council. He went and told them, 'Well, let them stay for ten more years.' The director of the planning department called me in and told me that a few boats could be left on Portage Bay, but that's it. Everything else has to go. There are going to be apartments around the lake. I said, 'John, you might think that's what you're going to do. We'll see.'"

Terry drew on his years of experience in labor and political organizing. Many said the iconoclastic individualists on the houseboats could not be organized. "But I knew they could. People will fight for their existence, if not for abstractions." He helped develop a strategy that began with politicizing the issue in broad terms, and pulling the community together. "We had dock meetings, organizing each dock, where people could drop in. They were not only about business—they brought a sense of community." Out of such meetings grew some new traditions. "The first one down the way, people sat around trying to think of a reason for a party. Then they said, 'Jesus, you know, nobody observes the Fall of the Bastille in France on July 14.' Ever since —for fifteen years now—they have a Bastille Day party over on that dock, combined with a Hawaiian luau. They decorate the dock with French flags and pigs. They have contests like diving and swimming. Everyone who ever lived there comes back. It is quite an event."

The Floating Homes Association also developed a strategy for redefining the issue, away from simply the "survival of the houseboats" to a broader vision of Lake Union as the common wealth of the people of Seattle—as Terry puts it, "a gift to us from the Ice Age" that carved out the lake.

One accusation long made against the houseboats, for instance, was that their sewage polluted the lake. What critics in the city neglected to mention was that the city of Seattle itself had thirteen sewer lines dumping raw sewage there—and the houseboaters' contribution to pollution was something like one-half of 1 percent. But Terry knew they could never win by debating percentages. So they turned the issue on its head. Houseboaters, to the amazement of the community, began demanding that they be able to pay for sewer lines to their boats. They held workshops on how to weld pipes and hook up sewer lines. And they found new allies, like the city's health department.

Pettus argued, "If we fight just to save the houseboats, we're licked. Who gives a goddamn about the houseboats? Our first concern has to be with Lake Union as a whole." The Floating Homes Association made sure their arguments were constantly before the public, and that the public learned about the lake. "We began history tours of the lake and placed articles in local magazines. People over the hill began to say, 'Jesus Christ, we have a lake over there! The simple fact is that we were organized. We could focus attention."

Their concern for the broader lake environment won them quick support from small dry-dock businesses and other enterprises around the lake. Other neighborhood groups in the city —involved in battles against an everexpanding highway system that threatened to pave over vast areas of central Seattle— joined as well. So did environmental groups like the Washington Environmental Council, a statewide coalition in which the Floating Homes Association was an early member.

As a result of the Floating Homes Association's prodding, the city issued a Lake Union study in 1963, calling for protection of the lake. It accepted the basic premise of their argument: that the lake should be seen as a resource of the whole city, what Pettus calls "a diversified marine environment" with multiple uses like recreation, commerce, and residential living.

With these precedents, the association was able to block industrial use of a large area at the north end of the lake. The city acquired twenty-three acres instead, turning it into a graceful, hilly green park, called Gas Works, that has become a favorite public spot. Through the Washington Environmental Council, Terry and other houseboaters won landmark protection for all of Washington State's coastal areas. Under the State Shorelines Management Act, which community groups like the association and environmentalists lobbied for, local communities are given a certain length of time in which to draft master plans in conformance with state laws. Allowance is made for particular local zoning changes, but the overall character of the law sets strict limitations on private development.

Mayor Uhlman appointed Pettus to help draft the Shorelines Management Program for the Seattle area itself, which protected not only Lake Union—directly incorporating much of the language from the Floating Homes Association position— but also hundreds of miles of shoreline.

When the shoreline plan for Lake Union put a lid on the number of homes allowed on the Lake, residents found themselves caught in a new, ironic trap: Moorage owners now had a monopoly on the number of spaces available and began to rapidly escalate rates charged, leaping 100 percent, 200 percent, or more. The Floating Homes Association quickly petitioned the city to pass what was called an "equity ordinance," guaranteeing certain rates of profit but controlling the rental charges at the same time.[11]

By the early 1970s, the activities of the Floating Homes Association fed into other fights. For instance, Victor Steinbrueck— a leading architect in town, one of the designers of the Space Needle, but a man with old populist roots whose father had named him for Eugene Victor Debs—led a fiercely contested campaign to save the Pike Place Market from private developers who planned to demolish the maze of small stores and farmers' stalls. Steinbrueck, like Pettus, cast the issue in broad terms, talking about how the Pike Place Market, founded in the early years of the century, was a rich, total community and a vital part of the city's heritage. Despite a development consortium that included many of the city's largest banks and builders and major media owners, the campaign to save the market won a city initiative with almost 60 percent of the vote. The neighborhood groups, blocking highway-expansion plans, also raised similar themes: What would Seattle's future look like? What is the meaning and price of "progress"?[12]

Such campaigns transformed for a time the character of public life in Seattle. Even establishment figures who battled community activists acknowledged benefits. "Seattle had a major era of citizen participation," said James Ellis of the prestigious law firm Preston, Thorgrimson, Ellis & Holman, the man sometimes called the informal leader of the city's elite. As a result, he believes, "there was an incredible flowering of the city."[13] Other city leaders—such as City Councilman John Miller, now a television commentator—found themselves taking surprising positions and initiatives. "I don't think of myself as a populist," Miller explains, "but along with neighborhood groups, I started a very populist initiative called Seattle 2000, a goal-setting project for the city in which any citizen could participate. We turned the normal idea of appointed commissions on its head." The Seattle 2000 document proved to be strikingly oriented toward the concerns of small businesses, neighborhoods, and diverse cultural groups. Rarely have such goals been officially adopted by a major metropolitan area.

The reputation that Seattle achieved in the middle and late Seventies as a pioneer in neighborhood-based programs, citizen environment, alternative energy efforts, and environmental concerns thus grew directly out of the commonwealth vision, which had been renewed and reinvigorated by Terry Pettus and others who remembered. Pettus sees such a constant process of revitalization as the heart of America—indeed, the only hope for America. But he is not optimistic about the current state of things. "With affluence," he argues, "people have had their roots severed. They've thought they had it made, that they owned their homes, that they had a job they could count on. Now every illusion is being destroyed." Terry welcomes the gains made in Seattle and elsewhere, but believes they will be only temporary without the development of a major new force in the society. "We created a society that is contrary to our basic needs for sociability. That atomizes people. We may have to go through some blood and sweat to remember our traditions." In Seattle, the convergence of concerns in the early 1970s was one revitalizing moment, in his view. "Now we need something to carry the ball for another ten yards. We're in one of those periods where something is gestating, incubating—something that needs encouragement and definition."

Others as well fear that the gains Seattle has made in recent years might be jeopardized by a new wave of development. Unemployment in the city continues to be higher than the national average, and the struggle of the houseboaters themselves is yet to be finally settled. In the summer of 1983, the state supreme court struck down the city council's Equity Ordinance controlling moorage fees. Hoping to reap much higher profits—which already often run at several hundred percent—some owners issued eviction notices to the residents tied up at their docks. "The idea of inordinate profit is ridiculous," argues Bill Fritz, lobbyist for the moorage owners. "The market means what a willing buyer will pay a willing seller. That's the free market and that's the way it should be."

For houseboat residents like Barbara Nelson, however, who lives with her retired husband, Elmer, on a boat that has been their home for twenty-one years, other values are involved beyond those of the market. "All the people that live here are not only our neighbors," she explained, "they are our friends. We have a feeling of closeness that's very important to us."[14]

The controversy between moorage owners and houseboat residents may ultimately be resolved in a way that allows the houseboaters to stay. After all the years of organizing, the city council quickly responded to the court decision by redrafting the Equity Ordinance in a way that met constitutional objections. But the underlying question remains. It is the key to America's future.

Afterword:
American Populism

> What has made this land of ours a source of wealth is a
> social element vast and precious as the blood and lives of
> men. . . . We owe all that we value to the Community in
> whose life we live and move and have our being.
> —Joseph Wood, in *Commonwealth* magazine,
> January 1893

> Our whole mode of thinking must be turned upside
> down. . . .
> A political being is not to be defined as the citizen has
> been, as an abstract, disconnected bearer of rights, privi-
> leges, and immunities, but as a person whose existence is
> located in a particular place and draws its sustenance from
> circumscribed relationships: family, friends, church, neigh-
> borhood, workplace, community, town, city."
> —Sheldon Wolin, in *Democracy* magazine, Fall, 1982

In recent years, the call for a "new populism" has emerged
from all parts of the political spectrum. Democrats like Jim
Hightower, Texas secretary of agriculture; Barbara Mikulski,
congresswoman from Baltimore; Raymond Flynn of Boston,
and the Reverend Jesse Jackson all are called "populist" or use
the word in self-description. In the fall of 1983, seven Harvard
Law School professors explained their support for George
McGovern's new presidential bid in the *New York Times* on the
grounds that "he alone is speaking for a fundamental reorienta-
tion of our politics toward a democratic populism at home and

justice and restraint abroad." Yet conservatives have similarly claimed the label, especially those with ties to the New Right, such as Congressman Jack Kemp. Ronald Reagan came to power as rhetorical champion of "the people." His convention speech invoked the spirit of American rebels like Thomas Paine. Again and again as president he decried "abstract economic theories" that ignore "concrete human pain" and slight "simple values" such as religious conviction, neighborliness, hard work, and family loyalty.

For the volatile "middle American" constituencies at the center of the American electorate—the family farmers and small business people, the skilled workers, the lower-middle-class Jewish neighborhoods of New York or the Polish-American communities of Chicago—economic dislocations of the last decade are emblematic of deep and traumatic disruptions in values and ways of living themselves. Appeal to impersonal institutions or abstractions like "the federal government" or "the marketplace," or reliance on criticism of the state of things, in the vein of customary liberal attacks on racism, sexism, militarism, and various other ills, have little evocative power for a public whose focus is on those pressing concerns they know only too well: Their children may get into trouble; their closest relationships may end; they may be robbed or assaulted in their own neighborhoods; they may never find work that is meaningful, satisfying, and dignified.

In such an environment, the call for a return of power to ordinary people—the defining project of populism—gains tremendous force. If experts, distant problem-solvers, and the rich and powerful seem perplexed, impotent, and avaricious, the appropriate solution is to devolve authority to those closer to home and to institutions grounded in the life of actual, textured communities. Indeed, such proposals, in different form, also strike a responsive chord among much of the upper middle class. Thus Gary Hart, declaring himself the candidate free of "the demands and pleadings of special interest warlords," gained the enthusiastic backing of young professionals with his call "to put power in the hands of the people, not put the people in the hands of the powerful."[1]

Yet it is also not surprising that present-day populist expressions seem ambiguous. In the first instance, the call for a return of "power to the people" is subject to very different interpretations. Whom "the people" includes; whether the conception of the people's destiny is open and evolving or static, defensive, and unchanging; what structures are responsible for "usurping" power and must be transformed in order to achieve popular rule—all such questions can be answered in dramatically different ways, or used by public-relations-wise spokespersons for wealthy and powerful interests themselves.

A further complication grows out of popular amnesia about what *populism* means concretely in America, for the word is not only a generic concept; it acquired specific content in the late 1880s and 1890s in the farmers' movements of the South and Midwest.

Across the agricultural belt in those years, millions of people found themselves sinking ever deeper into debt as a result of a national monetary system that operated in the obvious self-interest of bankers. Though the heart of the exploitative system was located in the New York banking establishment, its arterial network of usurious credit pulsed into every agricultural district in the nation. Desperate to retain their land and escape tenantry, the nation's farmers devised a new method of cooperatively marketing their crops and purchasing their supplies. They formed organizations called Farmers Alliances to spread the solution.

The gospel of "large-scale cooperation" swept the South and West in a huge social movement. Supported by their own system of over 1,000 insurgent newspapers, an enormous internal lecture circuit, and revivallike encampments, the farmers constructed a phalanx of cooperatives. They created the People's party to advance their program when banks refused to extend credit to the cooperatives and their very existence was threatened. And they discussed another kind of society, a "cooperative commonwealth" envisioned in magazines like *Commonwealth,* which would "restore the government of the Republic to the hands of the 'plain people,' the class where it originated."[2]

Never making significant inroads into ethnic working-class populations of urban areas, ambivalent and uncertain themselves about doctrines of technological progress, the farmers' revolt in the end fell short of its aspirations. Yet it left what historian Alan Brinkley called "a vivid legacy from which later protest movements could draw," well into the twentieth century. To rebels like Huey Long and Father Coughlin whom he depicted in his book *Voices of Protest,* like those who had gone before, "Large, faceless institutions; wealthy, insulated men; vast networks of national and international influence: all were exercising power and controlling wealth that more properly belonged in the hands of ordinary citizens." From such an analysis came "the central element of the message of both men: an affirmation of the ideal of community. Power, they argued, should not reside in distant, obscure places; the individual should not have to live in a world in which he could not govern or even know the forces determining his destiny." The nation should instead embark upon an alternative approach: breaking up concentrated wealth, decentralizing power, dispersing ownership and grounding it in community life.

Yet as Brinkley points out, by the 1930s broad public confidence that any substantive return to "local control" and integral community life was possible had sharply declined. The consolidation of bureaucratic and corporate structures on enormous scales, the growth of modern communications systems, the consumer culture, and other developments bred what he calls a "thinly veiled sense of resignation" at the heart of movements like Coughlin's and Long's.[3]

By the 1980s, moreover, such processes have developed much further still. Even the vocabulary of populism—like the central word *commonwealth,* which in the 1930s wove through a variety of popular movements—has by and large disappeared (though a few seek to resurrect it: Coretta Scott King, for instance, and Ralph Nader, who wonders why "wealth held in common," such as air, water, government land and resources, airways, pension funds, and other assets, "aren't managed as common wealth but corporate wealth"). As Lawrence Goodwyn, historian of the first populist revolt, described it, "We live in an age of sophisticated despair" about the very possibility of any democracy in which ordinary men and women actually participate in substantive, serious fashion in basic decisions about their lives.[4]

The populist idea in America has a final element of ambiguity. Appeal to the heritage of the American people can take on very different meanings, depending on the social position and nature of the group making the appeal. The notion of a people is associated with a specific space. It is to be understood symbolically rather than abstractly or quantitatively. A people have a point of origin, a moment of birth. This is the case with the Muslim Hegira, with the mythic origin of Athens or Rome, and with our own Declaration of Independence. Such a founding moment allows for celebration and for ritual commemoration sustaining memory, connecting the present to the past. A people are also defined by a common space, settled by ancestors, claimed, defended, and "filled in" by subsequent generations.

The sense of constituted peoplehood is the essence of what Simone Weil meant when she defined *roots* by saying "a human being has roots by virtue of his real, active, and natural participation in the life of a community which preserves in living shape certain particular treasures of the past and certain particular expectations for the future." It is also the insight developed by John Schaar when he described the psychological bases of patriotism as "a whole way of being in the world captured best by the word 'reverence,' which defines life by its debts: one is what one owes, what one acknowledges as a rightful debt or obligation. The gift of the land, people, language, gods, memories and customs . . . the very tone and rhythm of a life, the shapes of perception, the texture of its dreams and fears come from membership in a territorially rooted group."[5]

Consciousness of national peoplehood thus coexists with, is nourished, and also is fragmented by the discrete communities that make up "the people." In turn, each community itself forms a "people of its own." A sense of dual peoplehood, for instance, forms a striking theme throughout American black history, as Manning Marable has shown.[6]

In the main populist tradition, calls to return power to local communities were powerful indeed. But they suffered from the restrictive understandings of "the people" widespread in America, presuming a white, Christian, middle-class, and male model of true citizenship as the norm. Thus the tradition, as conventionally understood, all too often slighted divisions—along racial, class, gender, and other lines—*within* communities. And it neglected, too frequently, the bitter antagonisms that arise among them.

Thus, when Martin Luther King, Jr., described the civil-rights movement in populist terms, as representing "the best in the American dream and the most sacred values in our Judeo-Christian heritage," as "carrying our whole nation back to the wells of democracy dug deep by the founding fathers," he did more than revitalize the old idiom; he simultaneously broadened and democratized its meaning. In black theology, America has always been portrayed, simultaneously, as Egypt, the land of bondage, and as Canaan (at least in potential), the promised land of milk and honey. For him to suggest that we must return to "the wells of democracy" contains both the insight that we have forgotten most of the original meaning of the term, and the ironic challenge that in original terms the meaning was far from adequate. This sort of dualism is constitutive of any authentically democratic populism.[7]

Finally, for King the civil-rights movement was not only directed at transformation of unjust structures; it was also a "school for citizenship" through which ordinary men and women would acquire a "new sense of somebodyness." According to King, the most important result of the Montgomery bus boycott was "not so much the desegregation of the buses as it is a new sense of dignity and destiny." Through such arguments, King began to adapt the commonwealth vision to the problems and circumstances of advanced industrial society, a world removed from that of the pilgrims. He not only called for an active, continuing sense of citizenship on the part of ordinary men and women, but also posed as problematic the moral ground of such activity, suggesting the need to learn again the skills of democracy and the values of public discourse.[8]

The lines of connection between King's insights and the community ferment of recent years are often obvious. Bertha Gilkey's comment that the renewal of Cochran Gardens—beginning with the building they named Martin Luther King, Jr. —meant at the heart of it "self-respect and giving people the right to have a say-so over their lives" was powerful testimony both to King's democratic vision and to the creativity and commitment of Cochran tenants who brought it to life. Even where the connections are not overt, they are strong. Organizing of the sort pioneered by COPS in San Antonio and taken up by groups like the San Francisco Organizing Project build on King's sense that we have forgotten the democratic heritage. And they give such insight new and deeper meaning as well, understanding that revitalization of democratic community and the creation of instruments for empowering its values on a continuing basis are essential to any significant change. The invocation at the founding convention of SFOP, given by the Reverend Jim Brown of Saint John's Episcopal Church, bore an unmistakable resemblance to the spirit of the civil-rights movement two decades before, and also represented a further elaboration: "May we bring together the scattered fragments of our lives and our town to a new integrity," said Brown. "Make San Francisco shine as the New Jerusalem." The SFOP choir followed, singing "Glory, Glory, Hallelujah."

Such values begin to renew public life, where people "learn to do for themselves" and "politicians' work is to do your work," as Sonia Hernandez put it. Indeed, this sort of perspective is frequently voiced by the most insightful leaders of the community movement. Thus, John Kromkowski, president of the National Center for Urban Ethnic Affairs, pointed out that any approach to securing justice that ignores communal bonds ignores the very foundations: "Civility and civil rights are not merely the products of inspired speech and law," said Kromkowski. "They spring from the best and most generous impulses in human society and culture and are created, experienced and learned by most through and in living communities." From such a perspective, then, "to rebuild community in America on an understanding of its complexity, its pluralism, and the importance of small-scale community based institutions is the agenda for the renewal and recovery of solidarity in the pursuit of justice."

Just as the all too common myopia about the depth, vitality, and importance of community ferment in America represents a kind of foolhardiness, however, it would equally be a mistake to take such signs of renewal for more than what they are. Community action represents simply the stirrings of a different way—a "commonwealth" way—of looking at things in a society "whose spiritual muscles have atrophied through generations of disuse," in the words of Indian educator Robert Powless. The most talented organizers are well enough aware that only a start has been made. Ernesto Cortes, for example, sees little prospect for major challenge to the centers of corporate power behind the Reagan presidency, "at least through this decade." In his view, what organizations like COPS and others begin to do is to create the framework for serious discussion of "neopopulism": "What is democracy? How does it operate in a technological culture? There has to come out a vision which is relevant to this culture, this situation, that is decentralist and pluralist. These organizations don't have the answers. What we have is the beginnings of a process. There has to be a recreation of an agenda for the United States. What will be exciting will be to see that agenda put together, with everybody participating."[9]

Indeed, like the Oneida community near Green Bay, Wisconsin, what can be said at this point about the communitarian, populist spirit that has begun to appear once again is that it charts another direction, away from conventional notions of "progress," "success," and unbridled individualism. Where it might take us, how fully it might prevail in the face of the enormous forces that move against it in the modern world, is an open question. We will all be involved, however, in the answer.

Notes

Prelude

1. The Dekanawidah legend is described briefly in Gary Nash, *Red, White and Black: The Peoples of Early America* (Engelwood Cliffs, N.J.: Prentice-Hall, 1974), 18–20; also in Bruce Johansen, *Forgotten Founders: Benjamin Franklin, the Iroquois and the Rationale for the American Revolution* (Ipswich, Mass.: Gambit, 1982). Internal conflicts, as well as conflicts with outside authorities, are described in some detail for the Iroquois in the Wisconsin Iroquois official history, *History of the Oneida Indians* (Oneida: 1973). Dutch and Jesuit missionaries quoted from Nash, *Red*, 20. Franklin quoted from Johansen, *Forgotten Founders*, 85, 88, 104–5; Jefferson in Ibid., 102, 112, 114.
2. Riggs quoted in John Bodley, *Victims of Progress* (Menlo Park, Calif.: Benjamin Cummings, 1982), 115.
3. The internal history of the tribe is drawn from *History of the Oneida Indians*. Figures on tribal holdings from internal memo from the Tribal Sovereignty Project to the Youth Project, in Youth Project files, Washington, D.C., dated 24 June 1980. U.S. legal policies toward the Oneida and other tribes are described in John Niemisto, "The Legal Powers of Indian Governments," *Wisconsin Academy Review* 28, no. 2 (Mar. 1982): 7–11. Martin quoted from tribal *History*, 25.
4. Parker J. Palmer, *The Company of Strangers: Christians and the Renewal of America's Public Life* (New York: Crossroad, 1982), 19–20.

1. A Tradition Without a Name

1. William Hoffman, *Neighborhood House: A Brief History of the First 75 Years, 1897–1972* (St. Paul: Neighborhood House, booklet, 1972), 10. Hoffman, *Those Were the Days* (Minneapolis: T.S. Denison, 1957), 253. Bill Kuehn, "West Side Flats Revisited," *West Side Voice*, 10 Sept. 1982.
2. John Winthrop in Richard Lingeman, *Small Town America* (Boston: Houghton-Mifflin, 1980), 24. Recent immigration research on these themes

is summarized in Rowland Berthoff, "Peasants and Artisans, Puritans and Republicans: Personal Liberty and Communal Equality in American History," *Journal of American History* 69, no. 3 (Dec. 1982): 579–598. Peter Laslett, *The World We Have Lost* (London: Methuen, 1965), 64. Lingeman, *Small Town America*, 30.

3. Everett quoted from John Kasson, *Civilizing the Machine: Technology and Republican Values in America, 1776–1900* (New York: Penguin, 1976), 45. Franklin quoted in Ibid., 38. The quote from the advice manual is taken from Herbert Gutman, *Work, Culture and Society in Industrializing America* (New York: Vintage, 1977), 69.

4. Scott Greer and David Minar, *The Concept of Community* (Chicago: Aldine Publishers, 1969), 47. This sort of view has characterized political and social thought not only in the mainstream, it should be noted, but also in the dominant theories of social change, such as Marxism. Close-knit, organic communities where people live in richly textured, multidimensional relations with one another—what is called "Gemeinschaft" in social theory—are thought to inexorably disappear in the face of progress toward "Gesellschaft"—larger-scale institutional relationships, characterized by rationality, voluntary association, and functional identities. As Arthur Schlesinger put it in *The Vital Center:* "Modern technology created free society, but created it at the expense of the protective tissues which had bound together feudal society. . . . New social structures must succeed where the ancient jurisdictions of the family, the clan and the guild and nation-state have failed." (Cambridge: Houghton-Mifflin, 1949), 4, 51. Or as Marx and Engels put it in *The Communist Manifesto:* "All fixed, fast-frozen relations with their train of ancient and venerable prejudices are swept away, all newly formed ones become antiquated before they can ossify." In Lewis Feuer, ed., *Marx and Engels: Basic Writings on Politics and Philosophy* (Garden City, N.J.: Doubleday, 1969), 10.

The problem with such views is their hidden (and often not so hidden) prescriptive dimensions—assuming the end of strong communal ties is the only possible road to social justice and enlightened consciousness. There are two major flaws in such prescriptions: They take the experiences of the emergent new middle class as universal experiences, to be imposed on all of society; and they rest upon a static and one-dimensional understanding of communal life. Liberal perspectives and more radical Left positions are analyzed in some detail on these issues in *The Backyard Revolution: Understanding the New Citizen Movement* (Philadelphia: Temple University Press, 1980); "Populism and the Left," *Democracy,* Apr. 1981, 53–66; and in my forthcoming work, coauthored with Sara Evans, *All for One: The Seeds of Democracy* (New York: Harper & Row, forthcoming).

5. *Newsweek,* 7 Mar. 1983, 16. The report is by J.F. Coburn et al., "Hazardous Waste Cleanup: Silresim Site in Lowell Massachusetts" (Bedford: Mitre Corporation, 1979); conditions described pp. 2–4. Law described in chapter 407, "Acts and Resolves," Massachusetts State Legislature, p. 1.

6. "Hazardous Waste Cleanup," 4, 7.
7. Letter from Dr. Michael Gilchrist of Lowell Medical Associates to Mr. and Mrs. Pinard, dated 1 Mar. 1982; copy in author's possession.
8. Figures on public alienation from *USA Today,* 17 Mar. 1983; also Gallup poll, 11 Sept. 1983, *Minneapolis Tribune.* Naisbitt, quoted from B.G. Yovovich, "The New Localism," *Advertising Age,* 5 Apr. 1982. Naisbitt expands this argument considerably as one of his "ten trends" in *Megatrends: Ten New Directions Transforming Our Lives* (New York: Warner, 1982).
9. John Herbers, "Citizen Activism Gaining in Nation," 16 May 1982; and "Grass Roots Groups Go National," *New York Times* magazine, 4 Sept. 1983. Larry Green and Joanna Brown, "Grass Roots Politics," reprinted in *Seattle Times,* 20 Mar. 1983.
10. Arlook quoted in Green and Brown, "Grass Roots."
11. Figures on voluntarism are given, for example, in Bruce Stokes, "Self Help in the Eighties," *Citizen Participation,* Jan.–Feb. 1982, 5, which also shows how the new forms of community activism represent the area of increase. The *Christian Science Monitor* poll was reported 9 Sept. 1977. Figures on New York block clubs cited in Neal Pierce; "Self Help in New York," *Minneapolis Tribune,* 16 Apr. 1978. A sketch of numbers of community organizations in Janice Perlman, "Grass Roots Empowerment and Governmental Response," *Social Policy,* Sept.–Oct. 1979. A wealth of material on voluntary action can also be found in the new book by Brian O'Conn ll, *America's Voluntary Spirit* (Washington: Independent Sector, 1983). Role of citizen groups in fighting crime described in William Robbins, "Anticrime Patrols Grow in Number and Effect," *New York Times,* 30 Aug. 1982; and "Crime Down 4% in '82: Citizens Get Credit," *USA Today,* 20 Apr. 1983.
12. Quotes from Susan Chira, "Atomic Freeze Backed at NY Meetings," *New York Times,* 27 May 1982. Willens quoted from Judith Miller, "Effort to 'Freeze' Nuclear Arsenal Spreads in U.S.," *New York Times,* 15 Mar. 1982.
13. Terkel, "Across America There's a Flowing of Life Juices," *Parade,* 12 Oct. 1980.
14. Republican party platform quoted from Neighborhood Action, *Social Policy,* Nov.–Dec. 1980, 29. Reagan from Leonard Inskip, "Grants Aim to Bolster Neighborhoods," *Minneapolis Tribune,* 3 Oct. 1982.
15. Kundera, *The Book of Laughter and Forgetting* (New York: Penguin, 1981).
16. Barbara Myerhoff, *Number Our Days: A Triumph of Continuity and Culture Among Jewish Old People in an Urban Ghetto* (New York: Simon & Schuster, 1978), 96–7.
17. Figures on moving from *USA Today,* 13 Apr. 1983; see also John Herbers, "Study Indicates People Change Home More Often in Some Parts of the Nation," *New York Times,* 2 Mar. 1983.
18. Baker Brownell, *The Human Community* (New York: Harper & Bros., 1953), 77.

19. Throughout *Community Is Possible,* "community" is intended as a concept suggesting density and texture of relationship. Thus, though community in this sense most normally has a spatial dimension—a "neighborhood" implication—such a dimension is not part of the definition; rather, communal ties depend upon a complex set of social relationships that overlap and reinforce each other. Craig Calhoun has characterized community in these terms as meaning a "greater 'closeness' of relations" than is true for society as a whole. "This closeness seems to imply, though not rigidly, face-to-face contact, commonality of purpose, familiarity and dependability."

John Pfeiffer, *The Emergence of Man* (New York: Harper & Row, 1978), 313. Craig Calhoun, "Community: Toward a Variable Conceptualization for Comparative Research," *Social History* 5 no. 1 (Jan. 1980): 111.

20. Southern merchant quoted in Alan Brinkley, *Voices of Protest: Huey Long, Father Coughlin and the Great Depression* (New York: Knopf, 1982), 147.

21. Robert Park et al., *The City* (Chicago: Univ. of Chicago, 1925), 16.

22. Loren Halvorson, *Primary Enterprise: A Study of Basic Communities* (St. Paul: Luther Northwestern Seminary, 1983), 8, 163–4.

23. East Brooklyn Churches described in Jim Sleeper, "East Brooklyn's Second Rising," *City Limits,* Dec. 1982, 12–17. Youngblood quoted pp. 13–14.

2. Those Were the Days

1. William Kuehn, "West Side Revisited," *West Wide Voice,* 10 Sept. 1982.

2. Rev. Edward D. Neill, *History of Ramsey County and the City of St. Paul* (Minneapolis: North Star Publishing, 1881), 330.

3. Description of Lake Agassiz and the creation of the flats in Anne Cowie, "Explorers, Traders, Farmers: The Early History of St. Paul," *Ramsey County History* 11, no. 1 (Spring 1974): 18–19; and in Stephen W. Tanner, *An History Survey of Pig's Eye Island and Environs,* report with state Planning Agency, Nov. 1980, which also describes in some detail the history of Indians in the area. Carver quoted in Cowie, "Explorers," 19. Pig's Eye description in Tanner, *History Survey,* 56.

4. Early years of European settlement are described in Neill, *History of Ramsey,* 331–4; the *West Side Voice* special issue, July 1976; and also the funding proposal written by the West Side Citizens Organization, "Youth Helping Neighborhoods: Proposal for a Local History Program, 1982."

5. Neill, *History of Ramsey,* 333.

6. Lafayette (originally River) school ledgers, in possession of Helen Turner.

7. William Hoffman, *Those Were the Days,* 119.

8. Myerhoff, *Number Our Days* (New York: Simon & Schuster, 1978), 3, 27, 59, 60–61, 67.

9. Bill Kuehn makes similar estimates.

10. From the interview with Ralph Stacker, part of the "Oral History of the St. Paul Jewish Community Project, 1978," deposited with the St. Paul United Jewish Fund and Council.

11. Stacker interview.
12. Winthrop in Robert Bellah, *The Broken Covenant: American Civil Religion in a Time of Trial* (New York: Seabury, 1975), 15. Adams quoted in John Kasson, *Civilizing the Machine*, 36.
13. An extensive historiographic discussion and debate has emerged in the last decade on the American republican tradition and its continuing role through American history. See for example Joyce Appleby, "Ideology and Theory: The Tension Between Political and Economic Liberalism in Seventeenth-Century England," *American Historical Review* 81, no. 5 (June 1976): 499–515; and "Jefferson: A Political Reappraisal," *Democracy* 3, no. 4 (Fall 1983): 139–145; and, exponent of quite a different perspective, J. G. A. Pocock, *The Machiavellian Moment: Florentine Political Thought and the Atlantic Republican Tradition* (Princeton: Princeton University Press, 1975); and "The Machiavellian Moment Revisited: A Study in History and Ideology," *Journal of Modern History* 50 (March 1981): 49–72. Much of the discussion is summarized in Rowland Berthoff, "Peasants and Artisans, Puritans and Republicans," *Journal of American History* 69, no. 3 (1982): 579–598.

   In the views of the nation's founders, the vitality of the Republic depended upon a balance between power, liberty, and virtue of the citizens. Public virtue, in turn, as John Kasson has put it, "flowed from men's private virtues, so that each individual vice represented a potential threat to the republican order. Republicanism, like puritanism before it, preached the importance of social service, industry, frugality, and restraint. Their opposing vices—selfishness, idleness, luxury, and licentiousness—were inimical to the public good and, if left unchecked, would lead to disorder, corruption, and ultimately tyranny. The foundation of a just republic consisted of a virtuous and harmonious society, whose members were bound together by mutual responsibility." *Civilizing the Machine*, p. 4.
14. Stacker interview.
15. Werner Solors, "Theory of American Ethnicity," *American Quarterly* 33, no. 3 (Bibliography 1981): 271. Colin Greer, *The Great School Legend* (New York: Penguin, 1972).
16. Jackson Lears, "Ghetto of Illusion," *Democracy* 3, no. 1 (Winter 1983): 115.
17. Gale Cincotta, testimony, Subcommittee on Housing and Commercial Development of the Committee on Banking, Currency and Housing, Hearings on the National Commission on the Neighborhoods, HR 14756, 14361, 15388, 9 Sept. 1976, 185.
18. Gallup poll, in *Minneapolis Tribune*, 14 Jan. 1982; Minnesota poll, in *Minneapolis Tribune*, 27 Mar. 1983; Gallup polls on church attendance, 31 Dec. 1978 and 23 Jan. 1983.
19. Kathy Vadnais interviewed in "People Power: Neighborhood Group Action," a videotape by the Urban Concerns Workshop in St. Paul, 1975.
20. *West Side Voice*, Dec. 1973.

21. Ron Shiffman, quoted in Neal Pierce, "Islands of Hope in the Slums," *Minneapolis Tribune,* 13 Mar. 1977.

3. Alternatives

1. Emerson quoted in Sydney E. Ahlstrom, *A Religious History of the American People,* vol. 1 (Garden City, N.Y.: Doubleday, 1975), 593. Amana refrigerators, it is fascinating to note, are the continuing legacy of Amana.
   Quotes from Oceana in William M. Kephapt, *Extraordinary Groups: The Sociology of Unconventional Life Styles* (New York: St. Martin's Press, 1976), 284, 286.
2. Crèvecoeur, quoted in John Tracy Ellis, *American Catholicism* (Chicago: University of Chicago Press, 1969), 52. Sheriff in Dallas Lee, *The Cotton Patch Evidence* (New York: Harper & Row, 1977), 126.
3. Lee, *Evidence,* p. 1; Jordan quoted pp. 73–4, 185, 227. Jordan's perspectives on metanoia from "Metamorphosis," a record produced by Koinonia Records, Americus, Georgia.
4. Michael Nelson, "Jubilee Partners: How a Christian Community Was Born —Again," *Orientation '81,* publication of the United Methodist Board of Higher Education, Fall 1981, 5. Smith quoted p. 5.
5. *Ibid.* Also described in interviews.
6. Gov. Bradford is quoted from Gary Nash, *Red, White and Black* (Englewood Cliffs, N.J.: Prentice-Hall, 1974), 83.
7. Loren Halvorson, *Primary Enterprises* (St. Paul: Luther Northwestern, 1982), 12–13.

4. Bakesales, Barn Raisings, and Bootstraps: Helping Ourselves

1. Republican platform, Neighborhood Action, *Social Policy,* Nov.–Dec. 1980, 29. The study of the Campaign for Human Development is described in the memorandum by Kathy Desmond, associate director for allocations, "Preliminary Results of Survey of Impact of Budget Cuts on CHD Funded Organizations," 3 Apr. 1981.
2. Alexis de Tocqueville, *Democracy in America* (New York: Washington Square Press, 1964), 193. Corporate concentration in Richard J. Barnet and Ronald E. Muller, *Global Reach: The Power of the Multinational Corporations* (New York: Simon & Schuster, 1974), 230. Concentration by industry, *Just Economics,* Mar. 1975. Polk quoted from People's Bicentennial Poster, 1976.
3. The growth of big government described in Peter Clecak, *Crooked Paths: Reflections on Socialism, Conservatism and the Welfare State* (New York: Harper & Row, 1977), 72–73.
4. Thomas R. Dewar, "The Professionalization of the Client," *Social Policy,* Jan.–Feb. 1978, 4–9. McKnight quoted from "Are the Helping Systems

Doing More Harm than Good?" Speech to the 1976 membership retreat of the Community Planning Organization of Minnesota, held in Brainerd, Minn., in author's possession.

5. Riessman, "A New Politics via the Neighborhoods," *Social Policy*, Sept.–Oct. 1979, 2. Figures on self-help from Bruce Stokes, "Self Help in the '80s," *Citizen Participation*, Jan.–Feb. 1982, 5.

6. Carl Holman, testimony before the House Committee on Banking, Currency and Housing, Hearings on "Rebirth of the American City," 20–24 Sept. 1976, part 1, 554.

7. There has been little written about Cochran Gardens in national publications, though many accounts of tenants' efforts there can be found in the *St. Louis Post-Dispatch* and the *Globe Democrat*. The most striking evidence of Cochran Gardens' transformation, however, can come only from visual observation: The neighborhood's stunning renovation in buildings and spirit stands in remarkable contrast to the old building left "as it was."

8. Steven Roberts, "The Handicapped Are Emerging as a Vocal Political Action Group," *New York Times*, 19 June 1978.

9. John Gliedman and William Roth, from reprinted chapters in *Law Reform in Disability Rights*, vol. 2 (Berkeley: Disability Rights Education and Defense Fund, 1981), p. F-12. Ugly law quoted in Sonny Kleinfield, *The Hidden Minority: America's Handicapped Americans*, excerpted in *The New Republic*, 2 Feb. 1980, 31. Description of institutions from Robert Funk, "Disability Rights: From Caste to Class—the Humanization of Disabled People," in *Law Reform in Disability Rights*, vol. 1, p. A-4. Adrienne Asch and Lawrence H. Sacks, "Lives Within, Lives Without: Autobiographies of Blind Women and Men," *Journal of Visual Impairment and Blindness*, June 1983, 242, 246.

10. Facts from the Center for Independent Living pamphlet "History." Also Kleinfield, *The Hidden Minority: A Profile of Handicapped Americans* (Boston: Atlantic *Monthly*, 1979), gives a good summary history of CIL.

5. Empowerment

1. Paul Burka, "The Second Battle of the Alamo," *Texas Monthly*, Dec. 1977, 139–150; and Calvin Trillin, "U.S. Journal: San Antonio," *New Yorker*, 2 May 1977, 92–95, describe the early years of COPS and the original battle over drainage.

2. G. Richard Fowler, "Communities Organized for Public Service," *People, Building Neighborhoods*, National Commission on Neighborhoods Report, vol. 1, Case Study Appendix (Washington: 1979), 474.

3. *San Antonio Light*, 4 July 1983.

4. Interview with Saul Alinsky, *Playboy*, March 1972, 59–78, 150, 169–178. Robert Bailey, Jr., *Radicals in Urban Politics: The Alinsky Approach* (Chicago: University of Chicago, 1972), 1.

5. *Playboy* interview.

6. "Organizing for Family and Congregation," excerpted in "Neighborhood Action," *Social Policy,* Jan.–Feb. 1981, 30.

7. Saul Alinsky, *Reveille for Radicals* (Vintage: 1946), 13–14; Alinsky, "Is There Life After Birth?" speech to the Centennial Meeting of the Episcopal Theological School, Cambridge, Mass., 7 June 1967, 12–13.

8. Rodriguez quoted from Burka, "Second Battle," 144.

9. Cortes workshop was held as part of the Industrial Areas Foundation two-week training session, 9 Oct. 1980, Chicago. Described also in the Neighborhood Action section for *Social Policy,* Jan.–Feb. 1981, 30. "Don Politico," *San Antonio Light,* 24 Nov. 1974.

10. For a contemporary description of the impact of COPS and allied groups on the new Texas governor and Texas politics more generally, see Geoffrey Rips, "New Politics in Texas: COPS Comes to Austin," *Texas Observer,* 14 Jan. 1983. Frost and Dement quoted from Burka, "Second Battle," 146, 148.

11. *San Antonio Light,* 22 Nov. 1976. *San Antonio News,* 16 Nov. 1976.

12. Leader quoted in "Don Politico," *Light,* 24 Nov. 1974.

13. COPS funding base is described in detail in Fowler, "COPS," 455–480.

14. Sarabia quoted in "Don Politico," *Light.* 24 Nov. 1974.

15. Rev. Albert J. Benavides, "The Catechumenate as Experienced in a Large Urban Mexican-American Parish," mimeographed article in author's possession, pp. 12, 13.

16. *San Antonio Light,* 21 Nov. 1977; *Light* editorial, 23 Feb. 1978. *Commercial Reporter,* 28 Mar. 1978. "Don Politico," *Light,* 27 Nov. 1977. See for example James Flanigan, "A Story for Our Times," *Forbes,* 15 May 1978, 58–60. *The Fantus Report: Economic Development Program Industrial Relocation Appraisal,* quoted pp. 48, 50.

17. Most Reverend Patricio F. Flores, "A New Pentecost: A Vision for the Archdiocese of San Antonio," 7 June 1981.

18. *Light,* 15 Nov. 1981; 5 Nov. 1982; 24 June 1983.

6. "God's Laboratory"

1. William Shakespeare, *The Life of Henry the Fifth* (New Haven: Yale University Press, 1918), 94–95.

2. Press release of San Francisco Organizing Project, 10 May 1983.

3. Lane quoted from "San Francisco Organizing Project Gets Going," *The Monitor,* 26 May 1983.

4. *Ibid.*

5. Douglas Henry Daniels, *Pioneer Urbanites: A Social and Cultural History of Black San Francisco* (Philadelphia: Temple Univ. Press, 1980), 144.

6. Urban-renewal report and agency director quoted from Joe Feagin, *The Urban Real Estate Game* (Englewood Cliffs, N.J.: Prentice-Hall, 1983), 174–75. Neighborhood leaflet quoted in *Ibid.,* 64. Figures on housing from SFOP research.

7. DuBois's findings in Daniels, *Urbanites*, 34. Description of Bridges from Estolv E. Ward, *Harry Bridges on Trial: How Union Labor Won Its Biggest Case* (New York: New Modern Age, 1940), 3–4.

8. David Broder, "The Issues Facing U.S. Workers," reprinted in *Minneapolis Tribune*, 31 Aug. 1983; AFL Study described in Broder's column.

9. For a description of labor's efforts to respond to its plight, see for example, the special issue of *Progressive*, "Labor's Uphill Struggle," Aug. 1983. In that collection, David Moberg's "Hard Organizing in Sunbelt City," pp. 34–36, describes the labor campaign in Houston, and Richard Moore and Elizabeth Marsis's "Will Unions Work for Women?" pp. 28–30, describes labor's efforts among female office workers. Figures on declining membership from *USA Today* cover story, "Splintered Future Looms for Unions," 15 May 1983. Gallup polls have regularly documented the unpopularity of labor leadership over the past ten years. See for instance *Minneapolis Tribune*, 30 Aug. 1977. Decertification figures from the *USA Today* article.

10. Herb Mills, *Labor, Technology and Culture: The San Francisco Waterfront* (Berkeley: Institute for the Study of Social Change, 1982), 10, 13, 14, 15, 16, 18.

11. "Interim Statement of Purpose," San Francisco Organizing Project, Nov. 1980. The full text reads:

> We are an organization of San Francisco congregations that is based on and guided by Judeo-Christian and democratic values.
>
> Our purpose is to develop our congregations so that we and all who are powerless in San Francisco have an effective voice in making the decisions that determine the quality of our communities and our lives.
>
> We are a multi-ethnic, cross cultural, interreligious group acting to bring about quality education, decent and affordable housing, safe and wholesome neighborhoods, civil and equal rights, health care and rehabilitation, employment opportunities and training.
>
> Our participation in this organization will have two phases: the development of our congregations and our participating in the planning and work of the larger city wide organization that links our communities.
>
> We pledge ourselves to seek other allies, beyond the religious community, who share our concerns and values.

12. Notes from Labor and Religious Organization Leaders Meeting, in author's possession.

7. Visions of the Commonwealth

1. Letter to James, quoted from John Kasson, *Civilizing the Machine* (New York: Penguin, 1976), 224; Howells's characters quoted from Ibid., 225–28; Kasson, *Machine*, 234.

2. Dukakis interviewed in *USA Today*, 12 Sept. 1983.

3. The story of Lowell's founding is told in Kasson, *Civilizing the Machine,* Chap. 2. The vision of republican community described p. 65; Colman quoted p. 61; Appleton quoted p. 71; workers quoted p. 93.
4. Lowell's decline and economic revitalization is described in detail in Patrick Mogan, Arthur Eve, and Michael Greensbaum, "The Lowell Leadership Program: A Concept Paper," in author's possession, N.D. See also, for instance, "Lowell: A Town Is Reborn," *Newsweek,* 28 Sept. 1981.
5. Quoted from "Leadership Program," 26.
6. Tully quoted in *Holyoke Transcript,* 17 Nov. 1982. "The Acre," *Lowell Sun,* 25 Oct. 1981.
7. *Lowell Sun,* 29 Jan. 1982.
8. See for instance Terrence Williams, "Conflicting Forces Batt [*sic*] Philosophies in the Acre," *Lowell Sun,* 21 Mar. 1982; and Williams, "Aetna Kicks Off Acre Project," *Lowell Sun,* 9, July 1982.
9. Mayor's proclamation quoted from "Subversive?," a Documentary Special on Terry Pettus, by John de Graaf, KCTS, Seattle, Sept. 5, 1983.
10. Howard Droker, *Seattle's Unsinkable Houseboats* (Seattle: Watermark Press, 1977), 75.
11. The campaign for the equity ordinance was described in the KCTS "Evening Edition Report," Seattle, 4 Oct. 1983.
12. Steinbrueck's battle is described in detail in Alice Shorett and Murray Morgan, *The Pike Place Market: People, Politics and Produce* (Seattle: Pacific Search Press, 1982).
13. Ellis quoted from Leonard Silk, "Seattle Looks for its Future," *New York Times,* 22 Apr. 1983.
14. Fritz and Nelson quoted from KCTS "Evening Edition Report," 4 Oct. 1983.

Afterword: American Populism

1. *New York Times,* 16 Oct. 1983; *NYT,* 23 February, 1984.
2. The first large-scale populist movement is detailed in Lawrence Goodwyn, *Democratic Promise* (New York: Oxford, 1977) and *Populist Moment* (New York: Oxford, 1978). The "hands of the plain people" quote is from the preamble to the Populist party platform of 1892, reprinted in Richard Hofstadter, ed., *Great Issues in American History* (New York: Vintage, 1969), 147–152.
3. Alan Brinkley, *Voices of Protest* (New York: Knopf, 1982), 144, 162, 166.
4. Lawrence Goodwyn, "A Democratic Awakening," *New Republic,* 14 Mar. 1981, 36.
5. John Schaar, "The Case for Patriotism," *New American Review,* May 1973, 63–64. Simone Weil, *The Need for Roots* (Boston: Beacon Press, 1955), 43.
6. Marable points out that the black elite has tended historically toward an integrationist stance, "while the majority of working class and rural blacks have more often been mobilized to support national ideas and move-

ments," based on black cultural experiences. "Black Nationalism in the 1970s," *Socialist Review,* nos. 50–51 (1980): 76.

7. Description of the civil-rights movement in "Letter from a Birmingham Jail," in Martin Luther King, Jr., *Why We Can't Wait* (New York: Harper & Row, 1963), 99.

8. King's depiction of the most important achievement of Montgomery is in William Robert Miller, "The Broadening Horizons," in C. Eric Lincoln, ed., *Martin Luther King, Jr.: A Profile* (New York: Holt & Wang, 1970), 58.

9. John Kromkowski, "Look to Our Nation's Neighborhoods," *Building Blocks* (Summer 1983): 5. Robert Powless, "Modern American Indian Values," *Wisconsin Academy Review* 28, no. 2 (March 1983), 33.

List of Interviews

ADRIENNE ASCH, New York, N.Y., Feb. 17, Feb. 20, 1983.
HELEN AYALA, San Antonio, Tex., July 6, 1983.
NORMA JEAN BELL, St. Louis, Mo., Aug. 20, 1983.
REV. ALBERT BENAVIDES, San Antonio, Tex., Feb. 1, 1980.
ANGEL BERMUDEZ, Lowell, Mass., Feb. 24, 1983.
HEATHER BOOTH, Chicago, Ill., Feb. 27, 1983.
JIM BORRAZAS, San Francisco, Calif., May 14, 1983.
MARY LOU BRESLIN, Berkeley, Calif., May 18, 1983.
RALPH BROWN, St. Paul, Minn., Feb. 4, 1983.
GARY BRUEGGERMAN, St. Paul, Minn., June 13, 1983.
PETER CERNADA, East Boston, Mass., Feb. 23, 1983.
ISOBA CERNICEROS, St. Paul, Minn., May 6, 1983.
ED CHAMBERS, Chicago, Ill., Oct. 9, 1980; New York, N.Y., Feb. 22, 1983.
ARVA CLARK, Lowell, Mass., Feb. 24, Feb. 25, 1983.
SUSAN COBIN, St. Paul, Minn., Mar. 11, 1983.
PRESTIN COOK, San Francisco, Calif., May 17, 1983.
RANDY CORNELIUS, Oneida, Wis., Sept. 11, 1983.
VICKI CORNELIUS, Oneida, Wis., Sept. 11, 1983.
ERNESTO CORTES, Los Angeles, Calif., May 17, 1977, July 23, 1977; San Antonio, Tex., July 4, 1983.
BEATRICE CORTEZ, San Antonio, Tex., July 8, 1983.
MARY CROSSEN, St. Paul, Minn., Nov. 30, 1977.
AL DANLEY, Lowell, Mass., Feb. 26, 1983.
NORINE DANLEY, Lowell, Mass., Feb. 26, 1983.
ANNA DE FRONZO, East Boston, Mass., Feb. 23, 1983.
KATHY DESMOND, Washington, D.C., Mar. 16, 1982, Feb. 15, 1983.
DIANE DOE, San Francisco, Calif., May 17, 1983.
MELINDA DOXTATOR, Oneida, Wis., Sept. 12, 1983.

PHIL DRAPER, Berkeley, Calif., May 18, 1983.

GEORGE DUNCAN, Lowell, Mass., Feb. 25, 1983.

REV. JOHN EGAN, South Bend, Ind., Sept. 14, 1979, Aug. 2, 1980.

PABLO EISENBERG, Washington, D.C., Feb. 16, 1983.

RUDY ENRIGUEZ, San Antonio, Tex., July 7, 1983.

TIM FULLER, Washington, D.C., Feb. 14, 1983.

BOB FUNK, Berkeley, Calif., May 18, 1983.

CHARLIE GARGIULO, Lowell, Mass., Feb. 24, 1983.

TOM GAUDETTE, Chicago, Ill., Jan. 5, 1980, Feb. 27, 1983.

BERTHA GILKEY, St. Louis, Mo., Aug. 20, 1983.

CAROL GILLIES, Boston, Mass., Feb. 23, 1983.

NAOMI GLESSING, St. Paul, Minn., May 7, 1983.

JANIE GONZALEZ, San Antonio, Tex., July 7, 1983.

TINO GONZALEZ, San Antonio, Tex., July 6, 1983.

LARRY GORDON, San Francisco, Calif., May 18, 1983.

DAREL GROTHAUS, Seattle, Wash., Mar. 17, 1983.

STAN HALLET, Chicago, Ill., Feb. 27, 1983.

LOREN HALVORSON, St. Paul, Minn., Apr. 20, 1983; Grandee, Minn., Sept. 23, 1983.

RUTH HALVORSON, Grandee, Minn., Mar. 28, 1983, Sept. 23, 1983.

MARY HANSEN, Little Falls, Minn., Feb. 11, 1983.

KAREN HANSMANN, Little Falls, Mn., Feb. 11, 1983.

GARY HATTEM, New York, N.Y., Mar. 6, 1982.

SISTER KATHLEEN HEALEY, San Francisco, Calif., May 14, 1983.

SONIA HERNANDEZ, San Antonio, Tex., July 5, 1983.

JUDY HEUMANN, Berkeley, Calif., May 16, 1983.

RICK HILL, Oneida, Wis., Sept. 12, 1983.

RON HILL, Oneida, Wis., Sept. 11, 1983.

WILLIAM HOFFMAN, St. Paul, Minn., Mar. 24, 1983.

JARLATH HUME, Seattle, Wash., Mar. 18, 1983.

REV. RICH JAECH, San Francisco, Calif., May 19, 1983.

JAMES JENNINGS, Washington, D.C., Feb. 15, 1983.

NELLIE STONE JOHNSON, Minneapolis, Minn., Mar. 29, 1983.

WALTER JOHNSON, San Francisco, Calif., May 17, 1983.

REV. JOHN KING, Lowell, Mass., Feb. 25, 1983.

LaVAUGHN KING, San Francisco, Calif., May 14, 1983.

RON KRIETEMEYER, Washington, D.C., Feb. 15, 1983.

WILLIAM KUEHN, St. Paul, Minn., Feb. 7, Apr. 12, Apr. 20, 1983.

JOE LANDRY, San Francisco, Calif., May 14, 1983.

NAOMI LAUTER, San Francisco, Calif., May 15, 1983.

TRANG LE, St. Paul, Minn., May 7, 1983.

LILLIE LOPEZ, San Antonio, Tex., July 6, 1983.
STEVE MAX, Minneapolis, Minn., Dec. 5, 1982.
BETH MEANS, Seattle, Wash., Mar. 14, 1983.
FRANK MELENDEZ, Lowell, Mass., Feb. 24, 1983.
RICHARD METCALF, St. Paul, Minn., Jan. 26, 1983.
RAMONA MICHAELS, San Francisco, Calif., May 14, 1983.
JOHN MILLER, Seattle, Wash., Mar. 15, 1983.
MIKE MILLER, San Francisco, Calif., May 19, May 20, 1983.
PAT MOGAN, Lowell, Mass., Feb. 25, Feb. 26, 1983.
JOSIE MOONEY, San Francisco, Calif., May 17, 1983.
MAT MORENO, St. Paul, Minn., Apr. 27, 1983.
CAROLYN MOSLEY, Comer, Ga., Aug. 8, 1983.
DON MOSLEY, Comer, Ga., Aug. 8, Aug. 9, 1983.
REV. PHILIP MURNION, New York, N.Y., Feb. 22, 1983.
REBECCA NINHAM, Oneida, Wis., Sept. 12, 1983.
GEORGE OZUNA, San Antonio, Tex., July 6, July 7, 1983.
KAREN PAGET, Washington, D.C., Feb. 14, Feb. 16, 1983.
TERRY PETTUS, Seattle, Wash., Mar. 14, Mar. 17, Mar. 18, 1983.
JEAN PINARD, Lowell, Mass., Feb. 25, 1983.
RITA PINARD, Lowell, Mass., Feb. 25, 1983
REV. GARY POMETTA, San Francisco, Calif., May 14, 1983.
WALLACE ROBERTS, Boston, Mass., Feb. 23, 1983.
PHYLLIS ROBEY, Lowell, Mass., Feb. 25, 1983.
JEROME RUBIN, New York, N.Y, Feb. 20, 1983; Lowell, Mass., Feb. 24,
    Oct. 1, 1983.
JOE RUST, San Antonio, Tex., July 8, 1983.
REV. PETER SAMMON, San Francisco, Calif., May 19, 1983.
DIANA SAMUELSON, San Francisco, Calif., May 16, 1983.
STEVE SANDALL, St. Paul, Minn., Dec. 20, 1982
ANDRES SARABIA, San Antonio, Tex., July 5, 1983.
JIM SCHEIBEL, St. Paul, Minn., Apr. 8, 1977, Jan. 26, 1983.
MARI JO SHANNON, Washington, D.C., Feb. 15, 1983.
NANCY SISLEY, St. Louis, Mo., Aug. 20, 1983.
ARTLEY SKENANDORE, JR., Oneida, Wis., Sept. 11, Sept. 12, 1983.
SISTER CHRISTINE STEPHENS, San Antonio, Tex., July 4, July 6, 1983.
PETER STEINFELS, New York, N.Y., Feb. 18, 1983.
VICTOR STEINBRUECK, Seattle, Wash., Mar. 16, 1983.
SISTER JUDITH STOUGHTON, Grandee, Minn., Mar. 28, 1983.
HELEN GRANSBERG TURNER, St. Paul, Minn., Mar. 23, Mar. 31, Apr.
    20, May 6, 1983.
ENRIQUE VELASCO, San Antonio, Tex., July 6, 1983.

REV. ARELIOUS WALKER, San Francisco, Calif., May 20, 1983.
KENDELL WALLACE, Lowell, Mass., Feb. 26, 1983.
ED WEIR, Comer, Ga., Aug. 8, 1983.
MARY RUTH WEIR, Comer, Ga., Aug. 8, 1983.
CHAS (CHARLES) WHEELOCK, Oneida, Wis., Sept. 11, Sept. 12, 1983.
MICHAEL WINTER, Berkeley, Calif., May 18, 1983.
RUTH WITUCKI, Little Falls, Minn., Feb. 11, 1983.

Index